Our Unitar
By Mino

UNITARIANISM.

THROUGH the lack of having made themselves familiar with the matter, there is a common and, I think, a widespread impression among people generally that Unitarianism is a new-fangled notion, a modern fad, a belief held only by a few, who are on one side of the main currents of religious life and advance.

Even if it were new, even if it were confined to the modern world, this would not necessarily be anything against it. The Copernican theory of the universe is new, is modern. So are most of the great discoveries that characterize and glorify the present age.

But in the case of Unitarianism this cannot be said. It is not new: it is very old. And, before I come to discuss and outline a few of its great principles, it seems to me well that we should get in our minds a background of historic thought, that we may see a little what are the sources and origins of this Unitarianism, and may understand why it is that there is a new and modern birth of it in the modern world.

All races start very far away from any Monotheistic or Unitarian belief. The Hebrews are no exception to that rule. The early part of the Bible shows very plain traces of the fact that the Jews were polytheists and nature-worshippers. If I should translate literally the first verse of the Bible, it would read in this way: In the beginning the Strong Ones created the heavens and the earth. "The word that we have translated God is in the plural; and I have already given you its meaning. This is only a survival, a trace, of that primeval belief which the Jews shared with all the rest of the world."

From this polytheistic position the people took a step forward to a state of mind which Professor Max Muller calls henotheism; that is, they believed in the real existence of many gods, but that they were under allegiance to only one, their national Deity, and that him only they must serve.

I suppose this state of thought was maintained throughout the larger part of the history of the Hebrew nation. You will find traces constantly, in the early part of the Old Testament, at any rate, of the belief of the people in the other gods, and their constant tendency to fall away to the worship of these other gods. But by and by all this was outgrown, and left behind; and the Hebrew people came to occupy a position of monotheism, spiritual monotheism, that is, they were passionate Unitarians, so far as the meaning of that word is concerned. Though, of course, I would not have you understand that many, perhaps most, of the principles which are held today under the name of Unitarian were known to them at that time, or would have been accepted, had they been known.

In the sense, however, of believing in the oneness of God, they were Unitarians.

Now, when Christianity comes into the world, what shall we say? It is the assumption on the part of most of the old- time churches that Jesus made it perfectly plain to his disciples that he was a divine being, that he claimed to be one himself, and that the claim was recognized.

So far, however, as any authentic record with which we are familiar goes, Jesus himself was a Unitarian. All the disciples were Unitarians. Paul was a Unitarian. The New Testament is a Unitarian book from beginning to end. The finest critics of the world will tell you that there is no trace of any other teaching there. And so, for the first three hundred years of the history of the Church, Unitarianism was its prevailing doctrine.

I have no very good memory for names. So I have brought here a little leaflet which contains some that I wish to speak of. Among the Church Fathers, Clement, Polycarp, Irenaeus, Tertullian, Origen, and Lactantius, all of them in their writings make it perfectly clear and unquestioned that the belief of the Church, the majority belief for the first three centuries, was Unitarian. Of course, the process of thought here and there was going on which finally culminated in the doctrine of the Trinity. That is, people were beginning more and more to exalt, as they supposed, the character, the office, the mission of Jesus; coming more and more to believe that he was something other than a man, that he was above and beyond humanity.

But one other among the Fathers, Justin Martyr, one of the best known of all, takes care to point out explicitly his belief. I will read you just two or three words from it. He says: "There is a Lord of the Lord Jesus, being his Father and God, and the Cause of his existence."

This belief, then, was universal, practically universal, throughout the first three centuries. But the process of growth was going on which finally culminated in the controversy which was settled by the Council of Nicaea, held in the early part of the fourth century; that is, the year 325. The leaders of this controversy, as you know, were Arius, on the Unitarian side, and Athanasius, fighting hard for the doctrine then new in the Church, of the Trinity.

The majority of the bishops and leading men of the Church at that time were on the side of Arius; but at last the Emperor Constantine settled the dispute. Now you know that the sceptre of a despotic emperor may not reason, may not think; but it is weightier than either reason or thought in the settlement of a controversy like this at such a period in the history of the world. So Constantine settled the controversy in favor of the Trinitarians; and henceforth you need not wonder that Unitarianism did not grow, for it was mercilessly repressed and crushed out for the next thousand years.

Unitarianism, however, is not alone in this. Let me call your attention to a fact of immense significance in this matter. All this time the study of science and philosophy, that dared to think beyond the limits of the Church's doctrine, were crushed out. There was no free philosophy, there was no free study of science, there was no free anything for a thousand years. The secular armed forces of Europe, with penalties of imprisonment, of the rack, of the fagot, of torture of every kind, were enlisted against anything like liberty of thinking.

So you need not wonder, then, that there was neither any science nor any Unitarianism to be heard of until the Renaissance. What was the Renaissance? It was the rising again of human liberty, the possibility once more of man's freedom to think and study. Though the armed forces of Europe were for a long time against it, the rising tide could not be entirely rolled back, and so it gained on human thought and human life more and more. And out of this the Renaissance came, the new birth of science, on the one hand, and on the other, issuing in the Reformation's assertion of the right of thought and of private judgment in matters of religion; and along with this latter the rebirth of Unitarianism, its reappearance again as a force in the history of the world.

During this Reformation period there are many names of light and power, among them being Servetus, whom Calvin burned because he was a Unitarian; Laelius and Faustus Socinus, Bernardino Ochino, Blandrata, and Francis David; and, more noted in some ways than any of them, Giordano Bruno, the man who represents the dawn of the modern world more significantly than any other man of his age, not entirely a Unitarian, but fighting a battle out of which Unitarianism sprung, freedom of thought, the right of private judgment, the scientific study of the universe, the attempt, unhampered by the Church's dogma or power, to understand the world in which we live.

As a result of this Renaissance, what happened? Let me run over very rapidly the condition of things in Europe at the present time, with some glances back, that you may see that Unitarianism has played just as large a part as you could expect it to play, larger and grander than you could expect it, considering the conditions.

In Hungary, one of the few countries where freedom of thought in religion has been permitted, there has been a grand organization of the Unitarian Church for more than three hundred years, not only churches, but a Unitarianism that has controlled colleges and universities and directed the growth of learning.

Let us look to the North. In Sweden and Norway it is still a crime to organize a church that teaches that Jesus is not God. So we may expect to find no Unitarian churches there; though there are many and noble Unitarian men, thinkers and teachers. Come to Germany. There are no organized Unitarian churches under that name here; but there is a condition of things that is encouraging for us to note. There is a union of the Protestant organizations, in which the liberals, or Unitarians, are free, and have their part without any question as to their doctrine.

There are hundreds and thousands of Unitarians in South Germany. In the city of Bremen I called on a clergyman who had translated one of my books, and found out from him the condition of things there. The cathedral of Bremen has half a dozen different preachers attached to it. Some of them are orthodox, and some are Unitarian, all perfectly free; living happily together in this way, and the people at liberty to come and listen to which one of them they choose. This is not an uncommon thing in Germany. That is the condition of things, then, there.

In Holland there are no Unitarian churches, no churches going by that name; but there are thousands of Unitarians particularly among the educated and leading men, and one university, that of Leyden, entirely in control of the liberal religious leaders of the country.

When you come to France, which you know is dominantly Catholic, you still find a large body of Protestants; but one wing of their great organization is virtually if not out and out Unitarian. And a few of the most noted preachers of the modern time in France have been Unitarians. I have had correspondence with men there which showed that they were perfectly in sympathy with our aims, our purposes, our work.

In Transylvania and Poland there were large numbers of Unitarian churches which were afterwards crushed out.

You find, then, all over Europe, all over civilization, just as much Unitarianism as you would expect to find, when you consider the questions as to whether the law permits it and as to whether the people are educated and free.

I should like, not for the sake of boasting, but simply that you may see that you are in good company, to mention the names of some of those who are foremost in our thought. Take Mazzini, the great leader of Italy; take Castelar, one of the greatest men in modern Spain; take Kossuth, the flaming patriot of Hungary, all Unitarian men.

Now let us come a step nearer home: let us consider England, and note that just the moment free thought was allowed, you find Unitarianism springing into existence. Milton was a Unitarian; Locke, one of the greatest of English philosophers, a Unitarian; Dr. Lardner, one of its most famous theological scholars, a Unitarian; Sir Isaac Newton, one of the few names that belong to the highest order of those which have made the earth glorious, a Unitarian.

And, then, when we come to later England, we find another great scientist, comparatively modern, Dr. Priestley, who, coming to this country after he had made the discovery of oxygen which made him famous for all time, established the first Unitarian church in our neighbor city of Philadelphia.

The first Unitarian church which took that name in the modern world was organized in London by Dr. Theophilus Lindsey in 1774; and its establishment coincides with the great outburst of freedom that distinguished the close of the eighteenth century.

You must not look for Unitarians where there is no liberty; for it is a cardinal principle of their thought and their life.

2

Soon after the London movement, the first Unitarian church in this country was organized, or rather the first Unitarian church came into existence. It was the old King's Chapel of Boston, an Anglican church, which came out and took the name Unitarian.

There is a very bright saying in connection with this old church, which I will pause long enough to repeat, because there is a principle in it as well as a great deal of wit. They kept there the old English church service, except that it was purged, according to their point of view, from all Trinitarian belief. It is said that Dr. Bellows, who was attending a service there some years ago, had with him an English gentleman as a visitor. This man picked up the service, looked it over, and, turning to Dr. Bellows, with a sarcastic look on his face, said, "Ah I see that you have here the Church of England service watered." Whereupon Dr. Bellows, with his power of ready wit, replied, No, my dear sir, not watered, washed. King's Chapel, then, was the first Unitarian church in this country. But the number grew rapidly, and in a few years perhaps half, or more than half, of the old historic Puritan and Pilgrim churches in New England had become Unitarian, including in that number the old First Church of Plymouth.

Now, before I go on to discuss the principles underlying our movement, I wish to call your attention to a few more names; and I trust you will pardon me for this. There is no desire for vain-glory in the enumeration. I simply wish that people should know, what only a few do know, who have been Unitarians in the past, and what great names, leading authoritative names in the world's literature and science and art, find here their place.

Among the Fathers of the Revolution, all the Adamses, Dr. Franklin, Thomas Jefferson, and many another were avowed Unitarians. And, when we come to modern times, it is worth your noting that all our great poets in this country, Bryant, Longfellow, Whittier, Holmes, Lowell, and in this city Stedman, are Unitarian names.

Then the leading historians, Bancroft, Motley, Prescott, Sparks, Palfrey, Parkman, and John Fiske, are Unitarians. Educators, like Horace Mann, like the last seven presidents of Harvard University, Unitarians. Great scientists, like Agassiz, Peirce, Bowditch, Professor Draper, Unitarians. Statesmen and public men, like Webster, Calhoun, the Adamses, the Hoars, Curtis. Two of our great chief justices, Marshall and Parsons. Supreme Court Judges, Story and Miller. Literary men, like Whipple, Hawthorne, Ripley, and Bayard Taylor; and eminent women, such as Margaret Fuller, Lydia Maria Child, Lucretia Mott, Helen Hunt Jackson, Mrs. Mary A. Livermore, and Mrs. Julia Ward Howe.

I mention these, that you may know the kind of men, ethical, scientific, judicial, political, literary, who have been distinguished, as we think from our point of view, by being followers of this grand faith of ours.

And now I wish you to note again, what I hinted at a moment ago, that it is not an accident that Unitarianism should spring into being in the modern world coincidently with the great movements of liberty in France and England, and the outburst that culminated in our own Revolution and the establishment here of a State without a king as well as of a church without a bishop.

Wherever you have liberty and education, there you have the raw materials out of which to make the free, forward looker in religious thought and life.

Now what are the three principles out of which Unitarianism is born? First, I have already intimated it, but I wish to emphasize it again for a moment with an addition, Liberty. Humanity at last had come to a time in its history when it had asserted its right to be free; not only to cast off fetters that hampered the body, not only to dethrone the despots that made liberty impossible in the State, but to think in the realm of religion, to believe it more honorable to God to think than to cringe and be afraid in his presence.

Second, coincident with the birth of Unitarianism is an enlargement and a reassertion of the conscience of mankind. A demand for justice. Just think for a moment, and take it home to your hearts, that up to the time when this free religious life was born, according to the teaching of all the old creeds, justice and right had been one thing here among men and another thing enthroned in the heavens. The idea has always been that might made right, that God, because he was God, had a right to do anything, though it controverted and contradicted all the ideas of human righteousness; and that we still must bow in the dust, and accept it as true.

If I could be absolutely sure that God had done something which contradicted my conscience, I should say that probably my conscience was wrong. I should wait at any rate, and try to find out. But, when I find that the condition of things is simply this, that certain fallible, unjust, uneducated, barbaric people have said that God has done certain things, then it is another matter. I have no direct word from God: I have only the report of men whose authority I have no adequate reason to accept.

At any rate, the world came to the point where it demanded that goodness on earth should be goodness up in heaven, too; that God should at least be as just and fair as we expect men to be. And that, if you will think it out a little carefully, is enough to revolutionize the theology of the world; for the picture of the character of God as contained in the old theologies is even horribly unjust, as judged by any human standard.

In the third place, Unitarianism sprang out of a new elevation of love and tenderness. As men became more and more civilized, they became more tender-hearted; and they found it impossible to believe that the Father in, heaven should not be as kind and loving as the best father on earth.

And here, again, if you think it out, you will find that this is enough to compel a revolution of all the old theological ideas of the world.

3

Just as soon, then, as the civilized modern world became free, there was a new expansion of the sense of the right to think; there was a new expansion of conscience, the insistent demand for justice; there was a new expansion of tenderness and love; and out of these, characterized by these, having these in one sense for its very soul and body, came Unitarianism.

Now another point. It is commonly assumed by those who have not studied the matter that, because Unitarians have no printed and published creed, they are all abroad in their thinking. They take this for granted; and so it is assumed by people who speak to me on the subject. They think that there must be just as many views of things as there are individuals.

If there are any persons here having this idea, perhaps I shall astonish them by the statement I am going to make. After more than twenty years of experience as a Unitarian minister, I have come to the conviction that there is not a body of Christians in the world to-day, not Catholic or Presbyterian or Methodist or Congregational or any other, that is so united in its purposes, not only, but in its beliefs, as these very Unitarians.

And the fact is perfectly natural. Take the scientific men of the world. They do not expect a policeman after them if they do not hold certain scientific opinions. There is no authority to try them for heresy or to turn them out of your society unless they hold certain scientific ideas. They have no sense of compulsion except to find and accept that which they discover to be true. The one aim of science is the truth. There is no motive for anything else.

And truth being one, mark you, and they being free to seek for it, and all of them caring simply for that, they naturally come together, inevitably come together. So that, without any external power or orthodox compulsion, the scientific men of the world are substantially at one as to all the great principles. They discuss minor matters; but, when they discuss, they are simply hunting for a deeper truth, not trying to conquer each other.

Now Unitarians are precisely in this position. The only thing any of us desire is the truth. We are perfectly free to seek for the truth; and, the truth being one, we naturally tend towards it, and, tending towards it, we come together. So there is, as I said, greater unanimity of opinion in regard to the great essential points among Unitarians than among any other body in Christendom.

Now, as briefly as I can, I want to analyze what I regard as the fundamental principles of Unitarianism. I am not going to give you a creed, I am not going to give you my creed: I am going to give you the great fundamental principles which characterize and distinguish Unitarians.

First, liberty, freedom of the individual to think, think as he will or think as he must; but not liberty for the sake of itself. Liberty for the sake of finding the truth; for we believe that people will be more likely to find the truth if they are free to search for it than they will if they are threatened or frightened, or if they are compelled to come to certain preordained conclusions that have been settled for them. Freedom, then, for the sake of finding the truth.

Second, God. The deep-down conviction that wisdom, power, love, that is, God, is at the heart of the universe. Third, that God is not only wisdom and power and love, but that he is the universal Father, not merely the Father of the elect, not merely the Father of Christians, not merely the Father of civilized people, but the Father of all men, equally, lovingly, tenderly the Father of all men.

In the next place, being the Father of all men, he would naturally wish to have them find the truth. So we believe in revelation. Not in revelation confined to one book or one epoch in the history of the world, though we do not deny the revelation contained in them. We believe that all truth, through whatever medium it comes to the world, is in so far a revelation of our Father; and it is infallible revelation when it is demonstrably true, and not otherwise.

The next step, then: in the words of Lucretia Mott, we believe that truth should be taken for authority, and not authority for truth. The only authority in the world is the truth. The only thing to which intellectually a free Unitarian can afford to bow is ascertained and demonstrated truth. We believe, then, in revelation.

In the next place, we believe in incarnation. Not in the complete incarnation of God in one man, in one country, in one age, in the history of the world. We believe in the incarnation of God progressively in humanity. All that is true, all that is beautiful, all that is good, is so much of God incarnate in his children, and reaching ever forth and forward to higher blossoming and grander fruitage. The difference between Jesus and other men, as we hold it, is not a difference in kind: it is a difference in degree. So he is the son of our Father, our elder brother, our friend, our leader, our helper, our inspiration.

The next principle of Unitarianism is that character is salvation. We do not even say that character is a condition of salvation. Character is salvation. A man who is right, who is in perfect accord with the law and life of God, is safe, in this world, in all worlds, in this year, in all future time.

And, then, lastly, we believe in the eternal and universal hope. We believe that God, just because he is God, is under the highest conceivable obligation, not to me only, but to himself, to see to it that every being whom he has created shall sometime, somewhere, in the long run, find that gift of life a blessing, and not a curse.

We believe in retribution, universal, quick, unescapable; for we believe that this is mercy, and that through this is to come salvation.

4

These, then, are the main principles, as I understand them, of Unitarianism.

There is one point more now that I must touch on. When I was considering the question of giving this series of sermons, one of my best friends raised the question as to whether I had better put the word Unitarian? into the title. He was afraid that it might prejudice people who did not like the name, and keep them from listening to what I had to say. This is a common feeling on the part of Unitarians. I was trained as a boy, and through all my youth and early manhood in the ministry, to look with aversion, suspicion, on Unitarianism, and to hate the name. But to-day, after more than twenty years of experience in the Unitarian ministry, I have come to the conviction, which I wish to suggest to you, that it is the most magnificent name in the religious history of the world; and I, for one, wish to hoist it as my flag, to inscribe it on my banner, not because I care for a name, but because of that which it covers and comprehends.

Now, not in the slightest degree in the way of prejudice against other names or to find fault with them, let me note a few of them, and then compare Unitarianism with them. Take the word "Anglican," for example, the name of the Church of England. What does it mean? Of course, you know it is simply a geographical name. It defines nothing as to the Church's government or belief or anything else. There is the word "Episcopal," which simply means a church that is governed by bishops; that is all. Take the word "Presbyterian," from a Greek word which means an elder, a church governed by its old men or its elders. No special significance about that. Then "Baptist," signifying that the people who wear that name believe that baptism always means immersion, indicating no other doctrine by which that body is known, or its method of government. "Congregational," no doctrine significance there. It simply means a church whose power is lodged in the congregation. It is democratic in its methods of government. "Methodist,", applied to the members of a particular church because they were considered over-exact or methodical in their ways. There is no governmental significance there. The name Catholic? or Universal? is chiefly significant from the fact that the claim implied by it is not true. Now let us look for a moment at the word Unitarian, and see whether it has a right to be placed not only on a level with these, but infinitely above and beyond them in the richness, in the wonder of its meaning. Let me lead you to a consideration of it. I want you to note that unity? is the one word of more significance than any other in the history of man; and that it is growing in its depth, its comprehensiveness. What have we discovered? We have discovered in this modern world, only a few years ago, that this which we see, the earth, the stars, and all the wonders of the heavens, is one, a universe. Not only that. We have discovered the unity of force. There are not, as primitive man supposed, a thousand different powers in the universe, antagonistic and fighting with each other. We have learned to know that there is just one force in the universe. That light, heat, electricity, magnetism, all these marvellous and diverse varieties of forces, are one force, and can be at the will and skill of man converted into each other.

Next, we have learned that there is one law in the universe. Should we not be Unitarians? Should we not believe in the unity of God, when we can see, as far as the telescope can reach on the one hand and the microscope on the other, one eternal, changeless Order?

Another point. We have learned the unity of substance. We know how Comte, the famous French scientist, advised his followers not to attempt to find out anything about the fixed stars, because, he said, such knowledge was forever beyond the reach of man. How long had Comte been dead before we discovered the spectroscope? And now we know all about the fixed stars. We know that the stuff we step on in the street this morning as we go home from church is the same stuff of which the sun is made, the same stuff as that which flamed a few years ago as a comet, the same stuff as that which shines in Sirius, in suns so many miles away that it takes millions of years for their light to reach us. One stuff, one substance, throughout the universe; and this poor old, tear-wet earth of ours is a planet shining in the heavens as much as any of them, of the same glorious material of which they are made.

Then, again, we have discovered the unity of life. From the little tiny globule of protoplasm up to the brain of Shakspere, one life throbbing and thrilling with the same divinity which is at the heart of the world.

We have discovered not only the unity of life, we have discovered the unity of man. Not a hundred different origins, different kinds of creatures, different-natured beings, but one blood to dwell in every country on the face of the earth: the unity of man.

We have discovered the unity of ethics, of righteousness, of right and wrong, one right, one wrong. A million applications, but one goal towards which all those who hunger and thirst after righteousness are striving.

One religion: for underneath all the diversity of creeds and religions, barbaric, semi-civilized, civilized, enlightened, we find man, the one child of God, hunting for the clearest light he can command, after the one Father, that is, the one eternal, universal search of the religious life of the race.

Religion then one; one unifying purpose; every step that the world takes in its progress leading it towards liberty, towards light, towards truth, towards righteousness, towards peace. One goal, then, for the progress of man.

And, then, one destiny. Some day, every soul, no matter how belated, shall arrive; some day, somewhere, every soul, however sin stained, shall arrive; every soul, however small, however distorted, however hindered, shall arrive. One destiny. Not that we are to be just alike; only that some time we are to unfold all that is possible in us, and stand, full statured, perfect, complete, in the presence of our Father.

5

Do I not well, then, to say that Unity, Unitarianism, is a magnificent name, a name to be flung out to the breeze as our banner under which we will fight for God and man; a name beside which all others pale into insignificance; a name that sums up the secret, the centre, the hope, the outcome of the universe? Greatest name in the religious history of man, it coincides with that magnificent hope so grandly uttered by Tennyson, "One God, one law, one element, And one far-off divine event, To which the whole creation moves."

"WHAT DO YOU GIVE IN PLACE OF WHAT YOU TAKE AWAY?"

MY theme is the answer to the question, What do you give in place of what you take away? For my text I have chosen two significant passages of Scripture. One is from the seventh chapter of Hebrews, the nineteenth verse; and it sets forth, as I look at it, the drift and outcome of the process of which we are a part, the bringing in of a better hope. Then from the eleventh chapter of Hebrews, the thirty- ninth and fortieth verses, expressing the relation in which we stand to those who have looked for God and his work in the past: And these all, having obtained a good report through faith, received not the promise; God having provided some better thing for us, that they without us should not be made perfect.

What do you give in place of that which you take away? This is a question which is proposed to Unitarians over and over and over again. It is looked upon as an unanswerable criticism. We are supposed to be people who tear down, but do not build; people who take away the dear hopes and traditional faiths of the past, and leave the world desolate, without God, without hope.

Not only is this urged against us, from the other side, but there are a great many Unitarians, possibly, who have not thought themselves out with enough clearness to know the relation between the present conditions of human thought and the past; and sometimes even they may look back with a regretful longing towards something which they have outgrown, and left behind.

I propose this morning to answer this question, just as simply, as frankly, as I can; to treat it with all reverence, with all seriousness, and try to make clear what it is that the world has lost as the result of the advances of modern knowledge, and what, if anything, it has gained.

But while I stand here, on the threshold of my theme, and before I enter upon its somewhat fuller discussion, I wish to urge upon you two or three considerations.

It is assumed, by the people who ask this question, that, if we do take away anything, we are under obligation straightway to put something in its place. I wish you to consider carefully as to whether this position is sound. Suppose, for example, that I should discover that some belief that has been held in the past is not well founded, not true. Must I say nothing about it because, possibly, I may not have discovered just what is true?

To illustrate what I mean: Prince Alphonso of Castile used to say, as he studied the Ptolemaic theory of the universe, that, if he had been present at creation, he could have suggested a good many very important improvements. In other words, he was keen enough to see that the Ptolemaic theory of the universe was not a good working theory. Must he keep still about that because, forsooth, he was not able to establish another theory of the universe in its place?

Do you not see that the criticism, the testing of positions which are held, are the primary steps in the direction of finding some larger and grander truth, provided these positions are not adequate and do not hold?

The Rev. Dr. George A. Gordon, of the historic Old South Church in Boston, told us, in an address which he gave in Brooklyn the other day, that Calvinism was dead; that it was even necessary to clear the face of the earth of it, in order to save our faith in God. At the same time Dr. Gordon said frankly that he had no other as complete and finished system to put in place of it. Was he justified in telling the truth about Calvinism because he has not a ready-made scheme to substitute for it?

I wish you to note that I do not concede for an instant that I must not tell the truth about anything that I perceive because I have not a ready-made theory of some kind to put in the place of that which is taken away. It is my business to tell what seems to me true in all reverence, seriousness, earnestness and love, and trust the consequences to God.

In the next place, another consideration. I have been talking as though I conceded that Unitarians, or that I myself, sometimes take away things, beliefs. Now I wish to ask you who it is that takes away beliefs. Has Unitarianism ever taken away any faith or hope or trust from the world? Has anybody ever done it?

If we pit ourselves against one of God's eternal truths, is that truth going to suffer? Rather shall we not beat ourselves to pieces against God's adamant? If a thing is true, nobody is going to take it away from the world; for nobody has the power to uproot or destroy a divine truth.

Who is it, then, that takes these beliefs away? Is it not just this? Does it not mean that men have discovered that what they supposed to be true is not true, and it is the old belief that passes away in the presence of a larger and clearer light? Is not that the process?

When Magellan, for instance, demonstrated that this planet of ours was round by circumnavigating it, the ship returning to the port from which it started, did he take away the old flat earth, fixed and anchored, immovable, around which the sun moved? Why, there was no old, flat and anchored, stationary earth to take away. There never had been. All Magellan did was to demonstrate a new, higher, grander truth. He took away a misconception from the minds of ignorant and uneducated people, and helped put one of God's grand, luminous truths in the place of it. That is all he did.

6

It is modern intelligence, increasing knowledge, larger, clearer light that takes away old beliefs. But, if these old beliefs are not true, it simply means that we are discovering what is true; that is, having a clearer view and vision of God's ways and methods of governing the world.

I wish you to note, then, in this second place, that Unitarianism does not take away anything.

One third consideration: Suppose we did. Suppose we took away belief in the existence of God. Suppose we took away belief in man as a soul, leaving him simply an animal. Suppose we took away faith in continued existence after death. Suppose we had the power to sweep all of these grand beliefs out of the human mind. Then what?

If I had my choice, I would do it gladly, with tearful gratitude, rather than keep the old beliefs of the last two thousand years.

The late Henry Ward Beecher, in a review article published not long before his death, said frankly this which I am saying now, and which I had said a good many times before Mr. Beecher's article was written, that no belief at all is infinitely, unspeakably better than those horrible beliefs which have dominated and darkened the world.

I would rather believe in no God than in a bad God, such as he has been painted. And, if I had my choice of the future, what would it be? I have, I trust, just over there, father, mother, two brothers, numberless dear ones; and I hope to see them with a hope dearer than any other which I cherish. But, if I were standing on the threshold of heaven itself, and these loved ones were beckoning me to come in, and I had the choice between an eternity of felicity in their presence and eternal sleep, I would take the sleep rather than take this endless joy at the cost of the unceasing and unrelieved torment of the meanest soul that ever lived. And I would have no great respect for any man who would not. I would not care to purchase my joy at the price of endless pangs, the ascending smoke of torment, the wail going up to the sweet heavens forever and ever and ever.

So, even if it were a choice between no belief at all and the old beliefs, the darkness would be light to me; and I would embrace it with joy rather than take the selfish felicity of those men who estimate it as a part of their future occupation to be leaning over the battlements of heaven and witnessing the torture of the damned. This, though sounding so terrible to us now, is good old Christian doctrine, which has often been avowed. Thank God we are outgrowing it.

These, then, for preliminary considerations.

Now let me raise the question as to what has been taken away. You remember I said that I have taken nothing away, Unitarianism has taken nothing away. But the advance of modern knowledge, the larger, clearer revelation of God, has taken away no end of things. What are they?

Let me make two very brief statements right here. I am in the position, this morning, of appearing to repeat myself; that is, I must go over a good many points that I have made from this platform before. But please understand that it is not on account of lapse of memory on my part. I am doing it with a distinct end in view, which can only be attained by these steps.

In the next place, my treatment has so much ground to cover that what I say will appear somewhat in the nature of a catalogue; but I see no other way in which to make the definite statement I wish to lay before you. I am going to catalogue, first, a lot of the things that modern knowledge has taken away. Then I am going to tell you some of the things that modern knowledge is putting in place of what it has removed.

In the first place, the old universe is taken away; that is, that little tiny play-house affair, not so large as our solar system, which in the first chapters of Genesis God is reported to have made as a carpenter working from outside makes a house, inside of six days. That little universe, that is, the story of creation as told in the early chapters of Genesis, is absolutely gone. I shall tell you pretty soon what has taken the place of it.

Secondly, the God of the Old Testament, the God of most of the creeds has been taken away, that God who was jealous, who was partial, who was angry; who built a little world, and called it good, and then inside of a few days saw it slip out of his control into the hands of the devil, either because he could not help it or did not wish to; who watched this world develop for a little while, and then, because it did not go as he wanted it to, had to drown it, and start over again; the God who in the Old Testament told the people that slavery was right, provided they did not enslave the members of their own nation, but only those outside of it; the God who indorsed polygamy, telling a man that he was at liberty to have just as many wives as he wanted and could obtain, and that he was free to dispose of them by simply giving them a little notice and telling them to quit; the God who indorsed hypocrisy and lying on the part of his people; the God who sent a little light on one little people along one edge of the Mediterranean, and left all the rest of the world in darkness; the God who is to damn all of these people who were left in darkness because they did not know that of which they never had any chance to hear; the God who is to cast all his enemies into the pit, trampling them down, as Edwards pictures so horribly to us, in his hate for ever and ever. This God has been taken away.

In the third place, the story of Eden, the creation of man and then immediately the fall of man and the resulting doctrine of total depravity, this has been taken away. That man was made in the image of God, and then, inside of a few days, fell into the hands of the Power of Evil, and that since that day he has been the legitimate subject here on this earth of the prince of this world, that is, the devil, and that is taught both in the Old Testament and in the New, that man is this kind of a being, this is forever gone. There is no rational, intelligent, free belief in it left.

7

Then the old theory of the Bible has been taken away, that theory which makes it a book without error or flaw, and makes us under the highest obligation to receive all its teachings as the veritable word of God, whether they seem to us hideous, blasphemous, immoral, degrading, or not. This is gone.

Professor Goldwin Smith, in an article published within a year, treats the belief, the continued holding to this old theory about the Bible, under the head of Christianity's "Millstone." He writes from the point of view of the old belief; but he says, if Christianity is going to be saved, this millstone must be taken off from about its neck, and allowed to sink into the sea.

If we hold that theory, what? Why, then, we must still believe that, in order to help on the slaughter of his enemies on the part of a barbarian general, God stopped the whole machinery of the universe for hours until he got through with his killing. We must believe the literal story of Jonah's being swallowed by the whale. We must believe no end of incredibilities; and then, if we dare to read with our eyes open, we must believe immoral things, cruel things, about men and about God, things which our civilization would not endure, were it not for the power of tradition, which hallows that which used to be believed in the past.

This conception of the Bible, then, is gone.

Then, in the next place, the blood atonement is gone. What did that mean to the world? It meant that the eternal Father either would not or could not forgive and receive back to his heart his own erring, mistaken, wandering children unless the only begotten Son of God was slaughtered, and we, as the old awful hymn has it, were plunged beneath this fountain of blood I Revolting, terrible, if you stop to think of it for one reasoning moment, that God cannot forgive unless he takes agony out of somebody equal to that from which he releases his own children! That, though embodied still in all the creeds, has been taken away. It is gone, like a long, hideous dream of darkness.

Belief in the devil has been taken away. What does that mean? It means that Christendom has held and taught for nearly two thousand years that God is not really King of the universe; that he holds only a divided power, and that here thousands on thousands of years go by, and the devil controls the destiny of this world, and ruins right and left millions on millions of human souls, and that God either cannot help it or does not wish to, one of the two. This belief is taken away.

And then, lastly, that which I have touched on by implication already, the belief in endless punishment is taken away. Are you sorry? Does anybody wish something put in the place of this? The belief that all those except the elect, church members, those who have been through a special process called conversion, these, including all the millions on millions outside of Christendom and from the beginning until to-day, have gone down to the flame that is never quenched, the worm that never dies, to linger on in useless torture forever and ever? Simply a monument of what is monstrously called the justice of God! This is gone.

Now, friends, just ask yourselves, as you go home, as you think over what I have said this morning, as to whether there is anything else lost.

Is there anything of value taken away? Let me run over now in parallel fashion another catalogue to place opposite this one, so that we may see as to what has been our loss and as to whether there has been any gain.

In the place of the little, petty universe of Hebrew dream, what have we now? This magnificent revelation of the Copernican students; a universe infinite in its reach and in its grandeur; a universe fit at last to be the home of an infinite God; a universe grand enough to clothe him and express him, to manifest and reveal him; a universe boundless; a universe that has grown through the ages and is growing still, and is to unfold more and more of the divine beauty and glory forevermore. Is there any loss in this exchange?

Now as to God. I have pictured to you, in very bald outline, some of the conceptions of God that have been held in the past. What is our God to-day? The heart, the life, the soul, of this infinite universe; justice that means justice; power that means power; love that surpasses all our imagination of love; a God who is eternal goodness; who from the beginning has folded his child man to his heart, whispering all of truth that he could understand, breathing into him all of life that he could contain, inspiring him with all love and tenderness that he could appreciate or employ, and so, in this way, leading him and guiding him through the ages, year by year and century by century, still to something better and finer and higher; a God, not off somewhere in the heavens, to whom we must send a messenger; not a God separated from us by some great gulf that we must bridge by some supposed atonement; a God nearer to us than our breath; a God who hears the whisper of our want, who understands the dawning wish or aspiration before it takes form or shape; a God who loves us better than we love ourselves or love those who are dearest to us; a God who knows better what we need than we know ourselves, and is more ready to give us than fathers are to give good gifts to their children. Is there any loss here?

In the third place, the new man that has come into modern thought. Not the broken fragments of a perfect Adam; not a man so crippled intellectually that, as they have been telling us for centuries, it was impossible for him to find the truth, or to know it when he did find it; not a being so depraved, morally, that he never desires any good, and never loves anything which is sweet and fine; a being totally depraved, a being who, as one passage in the Old Testament tells us, is so corrupt his very prayer is a sin; conceived, born, in evil, and all his thoughts tainted, and drifting towards that which is wicked. Not this kind of a man. A man who has been on the planet hundreds of thousands of years, who has been learning by experience, who has been animal, who has been cruel, but who at every step has been trying to find the light, has been becoming a little truer and better; a being who has evolved all that is sweetest and finest in the history of the world; who has made no end of mistakes, who has committed no end of crimes, but who has learned through these processes, and at last has given us some specimens of what is possible by way of development in Abraham and Moses and Elijah and David and Isaiah, and a long line of prophets and seers of the Old Testament time; not perfect, but magnificent types of actual men; who has developed in other nations such men as Gautama, the heroes and teachers of China, like Confucius; then Aristotle, Plato, Socrates; the noble men of Rome; who has given us in the modern world the great poets, the great discoverers, the great philanthropists; those devoted to the highest, sweetest things; musicians and artists; who has given us Shakspere, who has given us, crowning them all, as I believe, by the moral beauty and grandeur of his love, the Nazarene, Jesus, our elder brother, Son of God, and helper of his fellow-man; this humanity that has never fallen; that has been climbing up from the beginning, and not sinking down. Is there any loss here?

Then let us see what kind of a Bible modern science and modern discovery and modern scholarship and modern life have given us.

Our Bible is the sifted truth of the ages. There is not a passage in it or a line for which we need apologize. There is nothing incredible in it, except as it is incredibly sweet and good and true. It is the truth that has come to men in all ages, no matter spoken by whose lips, no matter written by what pen, no matter wrought out under what conditions or in whatever civilization or under whatever sky.

All that is true and sweet and fine is a part of God's revelation of himself to his children, and makes up our Bible, which is not all written yet. Every new truth that shall be discovered in the future will make a new line or a new paragraph or a new chapter. God has been writing it on the rocks, in the stars, in the hearts, on the brains of his children; and his hand does not slacken. He is not tired: he is writing still. He will write to-morrow, and next year, and throughout all the coming time. This is the Bible.

We believe, for example, that the saying of the old Egyptian, God shall wipe away all tears from their eyes, is just as divine and sweet as when said in the New Testament. We believe that the Golden Rule is just as golden when uttered by Confucius hundreds of years before Jesus as it was afterwards.

We believe that the saying about two commandments being the sum and substance of the law was just as holy when Hillel spake them as when Jesus uttered them after his time. All truth is divine, and part of God's divine revelation to his children.

Here is our Bible, then. Now let me speak about Jesus, and see if our thought is less precious than the old. In my old days, when I preached in the orthodox church, Jesus was never half so dear, so helpful to me, as he is now. If I thought of him at all, I was obliged to think of him as somehow a second God, who stood between me and the first one, and through whom I hoped deliverance from the law and the justice of the first. I had to think of him as a part of a scheme that seemed to me unjust and cruel, involving the torture of some and the loss of most of the race. You cannot pick the old-time Jesus out of that scheme of which he is a part. I could not love him then as I love him now. I could not think of him as an example to follow; for how can one take the Infinite for an example? How can one follow the absolutely Perfect except afar off?

But now I think of Jesus and his cross as the most natural and at the same time the divinest thing in the history of man. Nothing outside of the regular divine order in it. Jesus reveals to me to-day the humanness of God and the divineness of man. And he takes his place in the long line of the world's redeemers, those who have wrought atonement, how? Through faithfulness even unto death.

The way we work out the atonement of the world, that is, the reconciliation of the world to God, is by being true to the vision of the truth as it comes to us, no matter by the pathway of what suffering, true as Jesus was true, true even when he thought his Father had forsaken him.

Do you know, friends, I think that is the grandest thing in the world. He verily believed that God had forsaken him; and yet he held fast to his trust, to his truth, to his faithfulness, even when swooning away into the unconsciousness of death.

There is faith, and there is faithfulness; and he shares this with thousands of others. There are thousands of men who have suffered more than Jesus did dying for his own truth; thousands of martyrs who, with his name on their lips, have gone through greater torture than he did. All these, whoever has been faithful, whoever has suffered for the right, whoever has been true, has helped to work out the atonement, the reconciliation, of the world with God, showing the beauty of truth and bringing men into that admiration of it that helps them to come into accord with the divine life.

Then one more point. Instead of the wail of the damned that is never, through all eternity, for one moment hushed in silence, we place the song of the redeemed, an eternal hope for every child born of the race. We do not believe it is possible for a human soul ultimately to be lost. Why? Because we believe in God. God either can save all souls or he cannot. If he can and will not, then he is not God. If he would and cannot, then he is not God. Let us reverently say it: he is under an infinite obligation to his own self, to his own righteousness, to his own truth, his own power, his own love, his own character, to see to it that all souls, some time, are reconciled to him.

This does not mean a poor, cheap, an easy salvation. It means that every broken law must have its consequences so long as it remains broken. It means that in this world and through all worlds the law-breaker is to be followed by the natural and necessary results of his thoughts, of his words, of his deeds; but it means that in this punishment the pain is a part of the divine love. For the love of God makes it absolutely necessary that the object of that love shall be delivered from sin and wrong, and brought into reconciliation with himself; and the pain, the necessary results of wrongdoing, are a part of the divine tenderness, a part of the divine faithfulness, a part of the divine love. So we believe that through darkness or through light, through joy or through sorrow, some time, somewhere, every child of God shall be brought into his presence, ready to sing the song of peace and joy and reconciled love.

Now, friends, I have gone over all the main points of the theology of our question. I have told you what I think the results of modern study have taken away. I have indicated to you what I believe is to come and take the place of these things that are absolutely gone. Ask yourselves seriously, if you are not one of us, is there a single one of these things that modern investigation is threatening that you really care to keep? If you could choose between the two systems and have your choice settle the validity of them, would you not choose the second, and be grateful to bid good-by to the first?

Remember, however, at the end let me say, as I did at the beginning, that, if these things pass away and the other finer things come in their places, Unitarianism is not to be charged by its enemies with destroying the old, neither is it to take the credit on the part of its friends for having created all the new. That distinguishes us as Unitarians from any other form of faith is that we believe in the living, loving, leading God of the modern world, and are ready gladly to take the results of modern investigation, believing that they are only a part of the revelation of the divine truth and the Father's will.

We accept these things, stand for them, proclaim them; but we did not create them. If anything is gone that you did not like, we did not take it away. If anything is come that you do like, give God the glory; and let us share with you the joy and praise.

ARE THERE ANY CREEDS WHICH IT IS WICKED FOR US TO QUESTION?

ANY body of people whatsoever has, of course, an undoubted right to organize on the basis of any belief or principles which it may happen to hold. This, always, on the supposition that those principles or beliefs are not antagonistic to human welfare. They have a right to establish the conditions of membership and limit their numbers as much as they please.

For example, suppose a set of persons chanced to hold the belief that the so-called Shakspere plays were written by Bacon. They have a perfect right to organize a society, and to say that nobody shall be a member of that society unless he agrees with them in this belief. If I happen, as I do, to hold some other conviction about the matter, I have no right to blame them because they do not wish me to be a member. I can organize, if I please, another society that shall have for its cardinal doctrinal statement the belief that Shakspere was the author of these plays. There is no need that I should quarrel with people holding these other ideas.

Or, if I am a laboring man, in the technical sense of the word that is commonly used to-day, I have a right to organize a society devoted to the furtherance of the eight- hour movement, or any other specific end or aim which seems to me necessary to the welfare of society as organized in the modern world.

All this we concede at the outset. People have a perfect right to organize on the basis of their particular beliefs, and to keep out of their organization those persons who do not happen to agree with them. But, and here is a most important consideration, if these beliefs seem to us who are outside to be vital; if they appear to concern us, to touch our well-being, our future hopes, then we certainly have a right to study those beliefs, to criticise them, to put them to the test to see whether they are well founded, whether they have any adequate basis of support.

And, still further, if the people holding a certain set of beliefs tell us that they are inspired of God, that they are spokesmen for God, that they have had committed to them a certain definite deposit of faith for the benefit of the world; if they tell us that, unless we agree with them, unless we accept the conditions and come into their organization, then we are opposed to God, are endangering our own souls, and are enemies of the human race, then it becomes not merely our right to look into these matters: does it not become our most solemn duty? Are we not under the highest of all obligations to decide for ourselves one way or the other as to whether these claims are valid? For, if they are, then there is nothing so important for us as that we should accept them and live in accordance with them, join the societies that are organized on them as a basis, do our utmost to extend their acceptance throughout the world.

If they are not valid, then we ought to do our very best to prove this also, and help those who are in bondage to these false ideas to attain their liberty, in order that they may join with us in finding out that which is true, in order that together we may work for the discovery of the will of God, and that we may co-operate in helping the world to find and obey that will.

You would suppose from the ordinary assumption of those who hold the old creeds, and who have organized their churches on these creeds, as foundation stones, that there had been at the outset a clear, a definite revelation of truth, that it had been unquestioned, that it had come with credentials enough to satisfy the world that the speakers spoke by authority, and that the matter had from the beginning been well understood.

It is assumed that we who do not hold these ideas are wilfully wrong, that we are not inclined to accept the divine truth, that it is on account of the hardness and wickedness of our hearts, and that we prefer evil rather than good. We are told that we might know, if we would, that the matter is definite, and has been perfectly well settled from the beginning. This, I say, is the assumption.

Let us now, then, investigate the matter for a little while, just as calmly, just as simply, just as dispassionately as we are able.

I confess to you, at the outset, that I do not like such a task as to-day seems to be imposed upon me. I do not like to be put in the position of seeming to criticise my fellow-citizens, my friends, and neighbors; but it seems to me that it is more than a task, that it is a duty, and one that I cannot readily escape. I mean as little as possible even to seem to criticise people; but I must look into the foundations of their beliefs, and see whether they are valid, whether there is any reason why we should feel ourselves compelled to-day to accept them.

Let us take our place, then, at the outset of Christianity by the side of Jesus and the apostles. Now let us note one strange fact. For the first two or three hundred years the belief of the Church was chaotic, unconfirmed, unsettled. There was dispute and discussion of the most earnest and most bitter kind concerning what are regarded to-day as the very fundamentals of the Christian faith.

This would hardly seem possible, would it, if Jesus had made himself perfectly clear and explicit in regard to these matters? If Jesus were really God, and if he came down on to this earth for the one express purpose of telling humanity what kind of moral and spiritual condition it was in, just what it needed in order to be saved, would you not suppose that he would have been so clear that there could have been no honest question about it?

If, for example, Jesus knew he was God, ought not he to have told it so plainly that no honest man could go astray about it? If he knew that the human race fell in Adam and was in a condition of loss under the general wrath and curse of God, ought not he to have said something about Adam, something about the Garden of Eden, something about the fall? Yet it never appears anywhere that he did. If he knew it was absolutely necessary for us to hold certain ideas about the Bible, ought not he to have told us? If he knew that the great majority of the human race was going to endless and hopeless torment in the future unless they held certain beliefs, ought not he to have made it plain?

But take that which I read as a part of our Scripture lesson this morning, that magnificent picture of the judgment scene, where he divides the sheep on his right hand and the goats on his left. Who are the sheep, and who are the goats? Those who are to be admitted with glad welcome to the presence of the Father are simply those that have been morally good; and those who are told they must be shut out are simply those who have bee morally bad. There is no hint of the necessity of any belief at all. Nothing said about any Bible, about any Trinity, about any faith, about anything that is supposed to be essential as a condition of salvation, not a word. Only the good receive the welcome, and the bad are shut out. That is all.

If this is not true, ought he not to have told us something about it, and made it perfectly clear?

Now what was the condition of popular belief? Let me illustrate it by one or two points. Origen, for example, one of the most famous of the Church Fathers, believed and preached the pre-existence of the human soul and universal salvation. Now, if Jesus said anything contrary to this belief of universal salvation, either Origen did not know anything about it or he did not regard it as of any authority, one or the other. We cannot conceive of his holding a position of this sort if he had known that Jesus had pronounced explicitly to the contrary.

Take another illustration. Two weeks ago this morning I had occasion to quote to you a few words from another of the old Church Fathers, Justin Martyr, who taught explicitly that Jesus was not the equal of the Father, but a subordinate and created being. Now, if Jesus had clearly taught anything approaching the doctrine of the Trinity, is it conceivable that Justin Martyr had not heard of it, or, having heard of it, had not accepted it?

At any rate, if these things were true and important, it is inconceivable that the Church Fathers, the very founders of Christianity, should have been all at sea in regard to them, should have held divergent opinions, and should have been discussing these questions one way and the other for three hundred years.

Let us now see what we have as a basis for belief in regard to what Jesus really did say. The Gospels grew up in a time when there was no shorthand writing, no reporting. Jesus does not say one word about having any record made of his teaching, does not seem to have considered it of the slightest importance. He simply talks and converses as friend with friend, preaches to the crowds wherever they gather, but says nothing whatever about founding any system of doctrine, says nothing about the importance of having a statement of his doctrine kept.

The Gospels, as a matter of fact, did not come into their present shape for many years after his death. How long? The critics are not at one in regard to it. A book has recently been translated from the German, by a professor in the Union Theological Seminary in this State, which says that not a single one of the Gospels was known in its present shape until between the years 150 and 200 A.D. All scholars do not accept this; but they are all at one in the statement that it was a great many years after the death of Jesus before they came into the shape in which we know them to-day.

There was, then, no clear record at the first in regard to these matters of belief; and, as I said a moment ago, for the first two or three hundred years the condition of the Church was chaotic. It was a long time coming to a consciousness of itself.

Now let us note the time when a few of the creeds were formed, and what are some of their characteristics.

11

Although the Apostles' Creed would seem to take us back to the apostles, we are not to deal with that first, because it was not the first one of the creeds to come into its present shape.

The oldest creed that we have to-day is the Nicene. When was that formed? It was agreed upon at the Council of Nicaea, in the early part of the fourth century. Now note, if you please, what influences shaped and determined it.

Did those who proposed that this particular clause or that should enter into it have any proof of their belief? Did they even claim to have? Why, the idea of evidence, the thought of proof, was absolutely unknown to the mind of Christendom at that time. Nobody thought of such a thing as proposing to prove that this or that or the other was true.

The Nicene Creed came into existence very much, indeed, as does the platform of a political party at the present time. One man fought for this proposition, another man for that one; and at last it was a sort of compromise decided by a majority. And how was the majority reached? Friends, there were bribes, there were threats, there were all kinds of intimidation, there were blows, there was wrangling of every kind, there was banishment, there was murder. There has not been a political platform in the modern world evolved out of such brutal, conflicting, anti-religious conditions as those which prevailed before and in connection with the Council of Nicaea.

Anything like evidence? Not heard of or thought of. Anything like quiet brooding of those who supposed they were, under the influence of the Holy Ghost, receiving divine and sacred truth? The farthest possible from any conditions that could be suggested by such a thought.

And at the last, though undoubtedly the majority of the Church at that time was Unitarian, as I told you the other day it was the decisive influence of the Emperor Constantine which settled the controversy. Thus came into existence in the fourth century the oldest of the church Creeds which is recognized as authoritative in the Catholic, the Anglican, and the Episcopal churches of the present time.

And this Nicene Creed, if I had time to go into it and analyze it, I could show you contains elements which no intelligent man in any of these churches thinks of believing at the present time; and yet nobody dares suggest a change, or the bringing it into accord with what the intelligence of the modern world knows to be true.

Let us pass on, and consider for a moment the Apostles' Creed, so called. There was a time in the Church when people really supposed that the apostles were its author. There are persons to-day who have not discovered the contrary. I crossed the ocean a few years ago when on board were a bishop of one of the Western States and a young candidate for orders who was travelling with him as his pupil. I fell into conversation with this young man, and found that he really believed that the twelve clauses of the Apostles' Creed were manufactured by the apostles themselves. He had never discovered anything to the contrary.

A still more astonishing fact came to my knowledge last year. During that discussion over Ian McLaren's creed, in which so many people were interested last winter, Chancellor McCracken, of the University of New York, published a letter, in which he referred to the Apostles' Creed as written eighteen hundred years ago. It took my breath away when I read it. I wondered, Could the chancellor of a great University possibly be ignorant of the facts? Would he state that which he knew was not true? I could not explain it either way. I was compelled to think, if he was thoughtless and careless about it, that he had no business to be about a matter of such importance. But he said the Apostles' Creed was written eighteen hundred years ago.

Now what are the facts? The apostles had nothing whatever to do with the creed, as everybody knows to-day who chooses to look into the matter. It grew, and was four or five hundred years in growth, one phrase in one shape held in a certain part of the Church, another phrase in another shape held in another part of the Church, people holding nothing so sacred about it but that they were at perfect liberty to change it and add to it and take away from it, until, as we get it to- day, it appeared for the first time in history at about the year 500. And yet it stands in the Church to-day claiming to be the Apostles' Creed.

And this Apostles' Creed, if it were a part of the purpose I have in mind this morning, I could analyze, and find that it contains elements which nobody accepts to-day; and yet nobody dares to propose touching it, such is the reverence for that which is old. So much more reverence does the world have for that which is old than for that which is true.

If you approach a Churchman in regard to his belief in the resurrection of the body, he will say, Of course, we do not believe in the resurrection of the body: we believe in the resurrection of the soul. But he does not believe in the resurrection of the soul, either.

Let me make two statements in regard to this. In the first place, if he does not believe in the resurrection of the body, he has no right to say it, because the House of Bishops, representing the whole Church of the United states, in an authoritative pastoral letter issued within three years, declares that fixity of interpretation is of the essence of the creeds. No man, then, is at liberty to change the interpretation to suit himself.

And then, again, nobody, as I say, believes in the resurrection of the soul. Why? Because that statement, with the authority of the House of Bishops that nobody has any business to change or reinterpret, carries with it a world underneath the surface of the earth to which the dead go down; and resurrection means coming up again from that underground world. Nobody believes in any underground world to-day. You cannot be resurrected. That is, you cannot rise again unless you have first gone down. It is the ascent of the soul we believe in to-day, and not its resurrection, much less the resurrection of the body.

Now a word in regard to another of the great historic creeds.

The third one to be shaped was the Athanasian Creed. Curiously named most of these are. There was a tradition in the Church that Athanasius, who was one of the great antagonists of the Council of Nicaea, wrote this creed called after his name; but, as a matter of fact, the creed was not known in the Church in the shape in which we have it now until at least four or five hundred years after Athanasius was dead.

The Athanasian Creed dates from the eighth or ninth century; and in this for the first time there is a clear, explicit, definite formulation of the doctrine of the Trinity. It never had been shaped in perfection until the time of the Athanasian Creed; and this creed contains among other things those famous damnatory clauses? which the Episcopal Church in this country, to their credit be it said, have left out of their Prayer Book. But this Athanasian Creed is obliged to be sung thirteen times every year in the Church of England; and you can imagine with what grace and joy they must sing the statement that, unless a man believes every single word and sentence of it, he shall no doubt perish everlastingly.

The Athanasian Creed, then, takes us only to the eighth or ninth century. You see, do you not, that, instead of there having been any clear, explicit, definite statement of church beliefs on the part of Jesus and his apostles, they are long and slow growths, and not built up on the basis of proof or evidence, simply opinions which people came to hold and fight for and preach, until at last they got a majority to believe in them, and they were accepted by some council.

I wish now to ask your attention for a few moments to one or two of the modern statements of beliefs. We are face to face here in this modern world with a very strange condition of affairs. I wish I could see the outcome of it. Here are churches printing, publishing, scattering all over America and Europe, statements of belief which perhaps hardly one man in ten among their pew-holders or vestrymen believes. They will tell you they do not believe them; they are almost angry with you if you make the statement that these are church beliefs; and at the same time we are in the curious position of finding that the man who proposes himself as a candidate for the ministry in any of these churches dares not question or doubt these horrible statements. And, if it is found that he does question them after he gets into the ministry, he is in danger of a trial for heresy.

We have had a perfect storm here in New York in one of our greatest churches over Dr. Briggs. And what was Dr. Briggs tried for? Simply for raising the question as to whether every part of the Old Testament was infallible. That was all. Another professor in a theological seminary in the West was turned out of his professorship for a similar offence. An Episcopal minister, a friend of mine in Ohio, was turned out of his church for daring to entertain some of the modern ideas which are in the air, and which intelligent people believe everywhere. One of the best known Episcopal ministers in this city to-day has an indictment over his head. It has been there for eight years; and it is only by the good will of his bishop that he is tolerated. His crime is daring to think, and to believe what all the respectable text-books of the modern world teach.

And people in the pews are indignant if you say that their Church holds these ideas! It is a curious state of affairs. How long is it going to last? What is to be its outcome? I do not know.

But let us look for a moment at another. Let us note one or two points in the Presbyterian Confession of Faith.

It teaches still, with what it claims to be absolute authority, that God, before the foundation of the world, selected just the precise number of people that he was going to save; that he did this, not in view of the fact that they were going to be good people at all, but arbitrarily of his own will, not to be touched or changed by anything in their character or conduct. All the rest he is to "pass by "; and they are to go to everlasting woe. The elect are very few: those who are passed by are the many. And why does he do this? Just think for a moment. There is no such colossal egotism, such extreme of selfishness, in all the world as that attributed to God in this Confession of Faith. The one thing he lives for, cares for, thinks of, labors after, is what? His own glory. He saves a few people to illustrate the glory of his grace and mercy. He damns all the rest purely to illustrate the glory of some monstrous thing called his justice.

This kind of doctrine we are expected to believe to-day.

And worse yet, if anything can be worse. I wonder how many loving, tender mothers in all these churches know it, how many know that the little babe which they clasp to their bosoms with such infinite tenderness and love, which they think of as a gift from the good God, right out of heaven, is an enemy of God, is under the curse and wrath of God? How many of you know that your creed teaches that God hates this blessed little babe, and that, if he does not happen to be one of the elect, he must suffer torment in darkness forever and ever?

That is taught in your confession of faith, which I have right here at my hand. The only mitigation of it that I have ever heard of on the part of consistent believers is the saying of Michael Wigglesworth, a famous alleged poet of the Puritan time in New England, when he states explicitly that none of these non-elect children can be saved, but since they are infants, and not such bad sinners as the grown up ones, their punishment shall be mitigated by their having the easiest room in hell.

Friends, you smile at this. This poem of Michael Wigglesworth's was a household treasure in New England for a hundred years. No end of editions was sold. It was earnestly, verily believed; and the doctrine is still taught every time that a new edition of the Presbyterian Confession of Faith? is issued in this country or in Europe.

13

Shall we escape these things by going into other churches? Some of them, yes; but the essentials are there in all of them.

Take for one moment the Episcopal Prayer Book. I have had friends in the old churches who have become Episcopalians for no reason that I could imagine, except that it seemed to them they were escaping some of the sharpest corners of the old beliefs; and yet, if you will read carefully the form of service for the baptism of infants in the Episcopal Prayer Book as held to-day and in constant use in every Episcopal Church in this country and England and throughout Europe, you will find that it is taught there in the plainest and most forcible way that the unbaptized infant is a child of wrath, is under the dominion of the devil, is destined to everlasting death, and is regenerated only by having a little water placed on its forehead and by a priest saying over him certain wonderful words.

Can you believe, friends, for one moment that a little child this minute belongs to the devil, is under his dominion, hated of God, doomed to eternal death, then the priest puts his fingers in some water, touches its forehead, and says, "I baptize thee," etc., and the child, after this is said, five minutes later, God loves, has taken to his arms as one of his own little children, and is going to receive him to eternal felicity forever?

Can we believe such things to-day? Do people believe them? If they do not, are they sincere in saying they do, in supporting the institutions that proclaim to the world every hour of every day of every week of every month of every year that they do believe them?

I have now said all I am going to about these creeds in any special way. I wish now to discuss the general situation for a little.

I have heretofore said, I wish to say it again, to make it perfectly plain and emphasize it, that all these old Creeds are based on the supposed ruin of the race. They have come into existence for the express purpose of saving as many souls as possible from this ruin. They never would have been heard of but for the belief in this ruin. And yet to-day there is not a intelligent man in Christendom that does not know that the doctrine of man's fall and ruin is not only doubtful, but demonstrably untrue. It is not a matter of question: it is settled; and yet these churches go on just as though nothing had happened.

Is it sincere? Is it quite honest? Is this the way you use language in Wall Street, in your banks and your stores? Is this the way you maintain your credit as business men?

Oh, let us purge these statements of outgrown crudities, cruelties, falsities, blasphemies, infamies! Let us dare to believe that the light of God to-day is holier than the mistakes about Him made by those who walked in darkness.

Now let me suggest to you. Every one of these creeds sprang out of a theory of the universe that nobody any longer holds. They are Ptolemaic in their origin, not Copernican. They sprang out of a time when it was believed that this was a little tiny world, and God was outside of it, governing it by the arbitrary imposition of his law. Every one of these creeds is fitted to that theory of things; and that theory of things has passed away absolutely and forever.

Consider for just a moment. Why should we pay such extravagant deference to the opinions of men who lived in the dark ages, of the old Church Fathers, of Athanasius, of Arius, of Justin Martyr, of Origen, of Tertullian? Why, friends, just think for a moment. There was hardly a single point connected with this world that they knew anything about. How did it happen that the whole modern world should get on its knees in their presence, as though they knew everything about the Infinite, when they knew next to nothing about the finite? Is there any proof that they knew anything about it? Not one single particle.

Think for a minute. We know to-day unspeakably more about the origin of the Bible, how it grew, how it came into its present shape, than any man from the first century until a hundred years ago could by any possibility know. We know a good deal more than Paul, though he was one of the writers, unspeakably more. He had no means of knowing. We have sifted every particle of evidence, every source of knowledge that the world has to show. We know unspeakably more about this universe than any man of the olden time had any way of knowing. He had no way of knowing anything.

I said something recently about the origin and nature of man. Very little was known about this until within the present century. We know something about how religions grow. We have traced them, studied them, not only Christianity and Judaism, but all the religions of the world back to their origin, and seen them coming into shape. We can judge something about them to-day. You want the antiquity of the world? People are bowing in the presence of what they suppose to be the antiquity, that is, the hoary-headed wisdom, of the world. Why, friends, as you go back, you are not going back to the old age of the world: you are going back to its childhood. The world was never so old as it is this morning. Humanity was never so old, never had such accumulated experience, such accumulated knowledge, as it has this morning.

If you want the results of the world's hoary-headed antiquity, its wisdom, its accumulated experience, its knowledge, then get the very latest results of the very finest modern investigations; for that is where you will find them.

Then let us note in just a word some other reasons why we cannot hold these old creeds. The statements that are made about God are horrible. The statements that are made in regard to the method by which God is going to deal with his creatures are horrible; and then what they tell us in regard to the outcome of human history is pessimistic and hopeless in the extreme.

14

Where do they claim to get the authority for these old beliefs? They tell us they find them on the one hand in the Bible. What do you find in the Bible? You find almost anything you look for. Is it not perfectly natural you should? The Bible was written by ever so many different writers during a period covering nearly a thousand years. Would you expect to find the same ideas throughout it? The book of Ecclesiastes teaches that man dies like a dog. The Bible upholds polygamy, slavery, cruelty of almost every kind. You might prove almost any kind of immorality from the Bible if you wished to.

But take the highest and noblest conception of the Bible you can have. I was talking with an eminent and widely known clergyman of the Presbyterian Church during the present year; and we were speaking about the Bible. I tell you this to show how modern ideas are permeating the thoughts of men. He said: I confess that, if God had ever given the world an infallible book, I should be utterly appalled and disheartened; because it is perfectly clear that we have no such book now. And, if God ever gave us such a book, then he has lost control of his universe, and was not able to keep us in possession of it.

Here are Quakers and Methodists proving their beliefs, the Baptists proving theirs, the Episcopalians proving theirs, the Presbyterians theirs, all of them different in some particular, and each of them getting their proof from the Bible.

Let us remember that the Bible is simply a great body of national literature, and that you can prove anything out of it. Then remember that it has been proved over and over again by the facts of the handwriting of God himself to be mistaken and wrong in any number of directions.

God is writing his own book in the heavens, in the earth, in the human heart; and we are reading the story there. No creed, then, particularly if it be infamous and unjust and horrible, can prove itself to us so that we are bound to accept it to-day on the basis of an appeal to any book. But the Catholic Church claims not only that the book is infallible, but that their church tradition is infallible too. Is it? How can a church prove that its declarations are infallible? Is there any way of proving it? Think for a moment. It can make the claim: the only conceivable way of proving it is by never making a mistake. Try the Catholic Church by that test. It has committed itself over and over again to things which have been demonstrated beyond question to be mistakes. It has made grave mistakes, not only as to fact, but as to morals as well.

On what, then, shall we base any one of these "infallible" creeds? There is no basis for any such claim; and thank God there is not. For now we are free to study, here, there, everywhere; to read God's word in the stars; to read it in the rocks; to read it in the remains of old-time civilizations; to read it in the development of education, the arts, science; to read it in the light of the love we have for each other, the love for our children, and the growing philanthropy and widening benevolence of mankind.

We have thus perfect freedom to listen when God speaks, to see when he holds a leaf of his ever-growing book for our inspection, and to believe concerning him the grandest and noblest and finest things that the mind can dream or the heart can love.

WHY HAVE UNITARIANS NO CREED?

FOR a Scripture suggestion touching the principle involved in my subject, I refer you to the words found in the fifth chapter of the Gospel according to Matthew, the forty-third and the forty-fourth verses, "Ye have heard that it hath been said; but I say unto you." I take these phrases simply as containing the principle to which I wish to call your earnest attention at the outset.

Jesus here recognizes the fact that the religious beliefs of one age are not necessarily adequate to a succeeding age. So he says over and over in this chapter, Ye have heard that it hath been said by the fathers, by the teachers, the religious leaders in old times, so and so: but I say unto you something else, something in advance, something beyond.

If any one chooses to say that Jesus was infallible, inspired, and therefore had a right to modify the teachings of the fathers, still this does not change the principle at all. In any case he recognized the fact that the beliefs of the old time might not be sufficient to the new time.

And, even if any one should take the position that Jesus was the second person in the Trinity, that he was the one who revealed the old-time truth, and also revealed the new, still the principle is not changed: it is conceded, whatever way we look at it. For, even if he were God, he is represented as giving the people in the time of Moses, the time of David, certain precepts, certain things to believe, certain things to do, and then, recognizing at a later time that they were not adequate, changing those precepts, and giving them something larger, broader, deeper, to accept and to practise.

Because this principle is here involved, I have taken these words as my Scripture point of departure.

Now to come to the question as to why Unitarians have no creed. Of course, the answer, though it sounds like an Hibernicism, is to say that they do have a creed. Not a creed in the sense in which some of the older churches use the word. If by creed you mean a written or published statement of belief, one that is supposed to be fixed and final, one that is a test of religious fellowship, which is placed at the door of the church so that no one not accepting it is able to enter, why, then, we have no creed. But, in the broader sense of the word, it means belief; and Unitarians believe quite as much, and, in my judgment, things far nobler and grander, than those which have been believed in the past.

We are ready, if any one wishes it, to write out our creed. We are perfectly willing that it should be printed. We can put it into twelve clauses, like the Apostles' Creed; we can make thirty-nine clauses or articles, like the Creed of the Anglican Church; we can arrange it any way that is satisfactory to the questioner. Only we will not promise to believe all of it to-morrow; we will not say that we will never learn anything new; we will not make it a test of fellowship; we will admit not only to our meeting-house, but to our church organization, if they wish to come, people who do not believe all the articles of the creed that we shall write. Perhaps we will admit people who do not believe any of it; for our conception of a church is not the old conception.

What was that? That it was a sort of ark in which the saved were taken, to be carried over the stormy sea of this life and into the haven of eternal felicity beyond. As opposed to that, our conception of the church is that it is a school, it is a place where souls are to be trained, to be educated; and so we would as soon refuse to admit an ignorant pupil to a school as to refuse to admit a person on account of his belief to our church. We welcome all who wish to come and learn; and if, after they have studied with us for a year, they do not then accept all the points which some of us believe, and hold to be very important, we do not turn them out even on that account.

Unitarians, then, do have a creed, only it is not fixed, it is not final, and it is not the condition of religious fellowship.

Now I wish to give you some of the reasons, as they lie in my mind, for the attitude which we hold in regard to this matter.

I do not believe in having a fixed and final statement of belief which we are not at liberty to criticise or question or change. Why? Because I love the truth, because I am anxious to find the truth, because I wish to be perfectly free to seek for the truth.

Our first reason, then, is for the sake of the truth.

Now let me present this to you under three or four minor heads. The universe is infinite, God is infinite, truth is infinite. If, then, on the background of the infinite you draw a circle, no matter how large it may be, no matter how wide its diameter, do you not see that you necessarily shut out more than you shut in? Do you not see that you limit the range of thought, set bounds to investigation, and that you pledge yourselves beforehand that the larger part of, of God, of the universe, you will never study, you will never investigate?

There is another point bearing on this matter. If a man pledges himself to accept and abide by a fixed and final creed, he does it either for a reason or without a reason. If he does it without a reason, then there is, of course, no reason why we should follow his example. If he has a reason, then two things: either that reason is adequate, sound, conclusive, or it is not. If it is not adequate, then we ought to study and criticise and find that out, and be free to discover some reason that is adequate. If the reason for his holding the creed is an adequate one, then, certainly, no harm can be done by investigation of it, by asking questions.

If the men who hold these old creeds and defend them can give in the court of reason a perfectly good account of themselves, if they can bring satisfactory credentials, then all our questioning, all our criticism, all our investigation, cannot possibly do the creeds any harm. It will only mean that we shall end by being convinced ourselves, and shall accept the creeds freely and rationally.

It has always seemed to me a very strange attitude of mind for a man to feel perfectly convinced that a certain position is sound and true, and to be angry when anybody asks a question about it. If there are good reasons for holding it, instead of calling names, why not show us the reasons? He who is afraid to have his opinions questioned, he who is angry when you ask him for evidence, to give a reason for the position that he holds, shows that he is not at all certain of it. He admits by implication that it is weak. He shows an attitude of infidelity instead of an attitude of faith, of trust.

There is no position which I hold to-day that I consider so sacred that people are not at liberty to ask any questions about it they please; and, if they do not see a good reason for accepting it, I am certainly not going to be angry with them for declining to accept. The attitude of truth is that of welcome to all inquiry. It rejoices in daylight, it does not care to be protected from investigation.

Then there is another reason still, another point to be made in regard to this matter. People are not very likely to find the truth if they are frightened, if they are warned off, if they are told that this or that or another thing is too sacred to be investigated. I have known people over and over again in my past experience who long wished they might be free to accept some grander, nobler, more helpful view of truth, and yet have been trained and taught so long that it was wicked to doubt, that it was wicked to ask questions, that they did not dare to open their minds freely to the incoming of any grander hope.

If you tell people that they may study just as widely as they please, but, when they get through, they must come back and settle down within the limits of certain pre-determined opinions, what is the use of their wider excursion? And, if you tell them that, unless they accept these final conclusions, God is going to be angry with them, they are going to injure their own immortal souls, they are threatening the welfare of the people on every hand whom they influence, how can you expect them to study and come to conclusions which are entitled to the respect of thoughtful people?

I venture the truth of the statement that, if you should inquire over this country to-day, you would find that the large majority of people who have been trained in the old faith are in an attitude of fear towards modern thought. Thousands of them would come to us to-day if they were not kept back by this inherited and ingrained fear as to the danger of asking questions.

16

Do I not remember my own experience of three years' agonizing battle over the great problems that were involved in these questions, afraid that I was being tempted of the devil, afraid that I was risking the salvation of my soul, afraid that I might be endangering other people whom I might influence, never free to study the Bible, to study religious questions as I would study any other matter on the face of the earth on account of being haunted by this terrible dread?

And, then, there is one other point. I must touch on these very briefly. The acceptance of these creeds on the part of those who do hold to them does not, after all, prevent the growth of modern thought. It does hinder it, so far as they are concerned; but the point I wish to make is this, that these creeds do not answer the purpose for which they were constructed. They are supposed to be fixed and final statements of divine truth, which are not to be questioned and not to be changed.

Dr. Richard S. Storrs, of Brooklyn, the famous Congregational minister, said a few years ago that the idea of progress in theology was absurd, because the truth had once for all been given to the saints in the past, and there was no possibility of progress, because progress implied change. And yet, in spite of the effort that has been made to keep the faith of the world as it was in the past, the change is coming, the change does come every day; and it puts the people who are trying to prevent the change coming in an attitude of what shall I say I do not wish to make a charge against my brethren, it puts them in a very curious attitude indeed towards the truth. They must not accept a new idea if it conflicts with the old creed, however much they may be convinced it is true. If they do accept it, then what? They must either leave the Church or they must keep still about it, and remain in an attitude of appearing to believe what they really do not believe. Or else they must do violence to the creed, reinterpreting it in such a way as to make it to them what the framers of it had never dreamed of.

Do you not see the danger that there is here of a person's disingenuous attitude towards the truth, danger to the moral fibre, danger to the progress of man? Take as a hint of it the way the Bible has been treated. People have said that the Bible was absolutely infallible: they have taken that as a foregone conclusion; and then, when they found out beyond question that the world was not created in six days, what have they done? Frankly accepted the truth? No, they have tried to twist the Bible into meaning something different from what it plainly says. It expressly says days, bounded by morning and evening; but no, it must mean long periods of time. Why? Because science and the Bible must somehow be reconciled, no matter if the Bible is wrenched and twisted from its real meaning.

And so with regard to the creeds. The creeds say that Christ descended into hell; that is, the underworld. People come to know that there is no underworld; and, instead of frankly admitting that that statement in the creed is not correct, they must torture it out of its meaning, and make it stand for something that the framers of it had never heard of. I think it would greatly astonish the writers of the Bible and the Church Fathers if they could wake up to-day, and find out that they meant something when they wrote those things which had never occurred to them at the time.

Is this quite honest? Is it wise for us to put ourselves in this attitude?

I wish to speak a little further in this matter as to not preventing the coming in of modern thought, and to take one illustration. Look at Andover Seminary to-day. The Andover Creed was arranged for the express purpose of keeping fixed and unchangeable the belief of the Church.. Its founders declared that to be their purpose. They were going to establish the statement of belief, so that it should not be open to this modern criticism, which had resulted in the birth of Unitarianism in New England; and, in order to make perfectly certain of it, they said that the professors who came there to teach the creed must not only be sound when they were settled, but they must be re-examined every five years. This was to prevent their changing their minds during the five years and remaining on there, teaching some false doctrine while the overseers and managers were not aware of it. So every five years the professors and teachers of Andover have to reaffirm solemnly their belief in the old creed.

It is not for me to make charges against them; but it is for me to make the statement that so suspicious have the overseers and managers come to be of some of the professors in the seminary that they have been tried more than once for heresy; and everybody knows that the leading professors there to-day do not believe the creed in the sense in which it was framed.

And, to illustrate how this is looked upon by some of the students, let me tell you this. My brother was a graduate of Andover; and not long ago he said to me that when the time came around for the professors to reaffirm their allegiance to the creed, one of the other students came into his room one day, and said, "Savage, let's go up and see the professors perjure themselves."

This was the attitude of mind of one of the students. This is the way he looked at it. I am not responsible for his opinion; but is it quite wise, is it best for the truth, is it for the interests of religion, to have theological students in this state of mind towards their professor?

Modern thought does come into the minds of men: they cannot escape it. What does it mean? It means simply a new, higher, grander revelation of God. Is it wise for us to put ourselves into such a position that it shall seem criminal and evil for us to accept it? If we pledge ourselves not to learn the things we can know, then we stunt ourselves intellectually. If, after we have pledged ourselves, we accept these things and remain as we are, I leave somebody else to characterize such action, action which, in my judgment, and so far as my observation goes, is not at all uncommon.

17

We then propose to hold ourselves free so far as a fixed and final creed is concerned, because we wish to be able to study, to find and accept the truth. There is another reason. For the sake of God, because we wish to find and come into sympathy with him, and love him and serve him, we refuse to be bound by the thoughts of the past.

What do we mean by coming into a knowledge of God? Let me illustrate a moment by the relation which we may sustain to another man. You do not necessarily come close to a man because you touch his elbow on the street. The people who lived in Shakspere's London might not have been so near to Shakspere as is Mr. Furness, the great Shakspere critic to- day, or Mr. Rolfe, of Cambridge.

Physical proximity does not bring us close to a person. We may be near to a friend who is half-way round the world: there may be sympathetic heart-beats that shall make us conscious of his presence night and day. We may be close alongside of a person, but alienated from him, misunderstanding him, and really farther away from him than the diameter of the solar system. If, then, we wish to get near to God, and to know him, we must become like him. There must be love, tenderness, unselfishness. We must have the divine characteristics and qualities; and then we shall feel his presence, know and be near him.

People may find God, and still have very wrong theories about him; just as a farmer may raise a good crop without understanding much about theories of sunshine or of soil. But the man who does understand about them will be more likely to raise a good crop, because he goes about it intelligently; while the other simply blunders into it. So, if we have right thoughts about God, it is easier for us to get into sympathy with him. If we think about him as noble and sweet and grand and true and loving, we shall be more likely to respond to these qualities that call out the best and the finest feelings in ourselves.

I do not say that it is absolutely necessary to have correct theories of God. There have been good men in all ages, there have been noble women in all ages, in all religions, in all the different sects of Christendom. There are lovely characters among the agnostics. I have known sweet and true and fine people who thought themselves atheists. A man may be grand in spite of his theological opinions one way or the other. He may have a horrible picture of God set forth in his creed, and carry a loving and tender one in his heart. So he may be better than the God of his creed. All this is true; but, if we have, I say, right thoughts about him, high and fine ideals, we are more likely to come into close touch and sympathy with him.

And, then, and here is a point I wish to emphasize and make perfectly clear, this arbitrary assumption of infallibility cultivates qualities and characteristics which are un and anti-divine.

Let us see what Jesus had to say about this. The people of his time who represented more than any others this infallibility idea were the Pharisees. They felt perfectly sure that they were right. They felt perfectly certain that they were the chosen favorites of God. There was on their part, then, growing out of this conception of the infallibility of their position, the conceit of being the chosen and special favorites of the Almighty. They looked with contempt, not only upon the Gentiles, who were outside of the peculiarly chosen people, but upon the publicans, upon all of their own nation who were not Pharisees, and who were not scrupulously exact concerning the things which they held to be so important.

What did Jesus think and say about them? You remember the parable of the Pharisee and the publican. Jesus said that this poor sinning publican, who smote upon his breast, and said, "God be merciful to me a sinner," was the one that God looked upon with favor, not the Pharisee, who thanked God that he was not as the other people were. And, if there is any class in the New Testament that Jesus scathes and withers with the hot lightning of his scorn and his wrath, it is these infallible people, who are perfectly right in their ideas, and who look with contempt upon people who are outside of the pale of their own inherited infallible creeds and opinions.

We believe, then, that the people who are free to study the splendors of God in the universe, in human history, in human life, and free to accept all new and higher and finer ideas, are more likely to find God, and come into sympathetic and tender relations with him, than those who are bound to opinions by the supposed fixed and revealed truths of the past.

We reject, then, these old-time creeds for another reason, for the sake of man. A long vista of thought and illustration stretches out before me as I pronounce these words; but I can only touch upon a point here or there.

One of the most disastrous things that have happened in the history of the past and it has happened over and over again is this blocking and hindering of human advance, until by and by the tide, the growing current, becomes too strong to be held back any more; and it has swept away all barriers and devastated society, politically, socially, religiously, morally, and in every other way.

And why? Simply because the natural flow of human thought, the natural growth of human opinion, has been hindered artificially by the assumption of an infallibility on the part of those who have tried to keep the world from growth.

Suppose you teach men that certain theological opinions are identical with religion, until they believe it. The time comes when they cannot hold those opinions any more, and they break away; and they give up religion, and perhaps the sanctities of life, which they are accustomed to associate with religion.

18

Take the time of the French Revolution. People went mad. They were opposed not only to the State: they were opposed to the Church. They tried to abolish God, they tried to abolish the Ten Commandments; they tried to abolish everything that had been so long established and associated with the old regime.

Were the people really enemies of God? Were they enemies of religion? Were they enemies of truth? No: it was a caricature of God that they were fighting, it was a caricature of religion that they were opposed to. When Voltaire declared that the Church was infamous, it was not religion that he wished to overthrow: it was this tyranny that had been associated with the dominance of the Church for so many ages.

This is the result in one direction of attempting to hold back the natural growth and progress of the world. If you read the history of the Church for the last fifteen hundred years until within a century or two, and by the Church I mean that organization that has claimed to speak infallibly for God, you will find that it has been associated with almost everything that has hindered the growth of the world. I cannot go into details to illustrate it. It has interfered with the world's education. There is only one nation in Europe to-day where education has not been wrenched out of the hands of the priesthood in the interests of man, and that even by Catholics themselves; and that country is Spain. It pronounced its ban on the study of the universe under the name of science. It made it a sin for Galileo to discover the moons of Jupiter. And Catholic and Protestant infallibility alike denounced Newton, one of the noblest men and the grandest scientists that the world has ever seen, because in proclaiming the law of gravity, they said, he was taking the universe out of the hands of God and establishing practical atheism.

So almost everything that has made the education, the political, the industrial, the social growth of the world, this infallibility idea has stood square in the way of, and done its best to hinder. Take, for example, an illustration. When chloroform was discovered, the Church in Scotland opposed its use in cases of childbirth, because it said it was a wicked interference with the judgment God pronounced on Eve after the fall.

So, in almost every direction, whatever has been for the benefit of the world has been opposed in the interests of old-time ideas, until the whole thing culminated at last in this: Here is this nineteenth century of ours, which has done more for the advancement of man than the preceding fifteen centuries all put together. Political liberty, religious liberty, universal education, the enfranchisement and elevation of women, the abolition of slavery, temperance, almost everything has been achieved, until the world, the face of it, has been transformed. And yet Pope Pius IX., in an encyclical which he issued a little while before his death, pronounced, ex-cathedra and infallibly, the opinion that this whole modern society was godless. And yet, as I said, this godless modern world has done more for man and for the glory of God than the fifteen hundred years of church dominance that preceded it.

For the sake of man, then, that intellectually, politically, socially, industrially, every other way, he may be free to grow, to expand, to adopt all the new ideas that promise higher help, hope, and freedom, for the sake of man, we refuse to be bound by the inherited and fixed opinions of the past.

Now two or three points I wish to speak of briefly, as I near the close.

We are charged sometimes, because we have no creed, with having no bond of union whatever. As I said a few Sundays ago, they say that we are all at loose ends because we are not fixed and bound by a definite creed.

What is God's method of keeping a system like this solar one of ours together? Does he fence it in? Does he exert any pressure from outside? Or does he rather place at the centre a luminous and attractive body, capable of holding all the swinging and singing members of the system in their orbits, as they play around this great source of life and of light? God's method is the method of illumination and attraction. That is the method which we have adopted. Instead of fencing men in and telling them to climb over that fence at their peril, we have placed a great, luminous, attractive truth at the centre, the pursuit of truth, the love of truth, the search for God, the desire to benefit and help on mankind. And we trust to the power of these great central truths to attract and keep in their orbits all the free activities of the thousands of minds and hearts that make up our organization.

Then there is one more point. Suppose we wanted an infallible creed; suppose it was ever so important; suppose the experience of the world had proved that it was very desirable indeed that we should have one. What are we going to do about it? I suppose that men in other departments of life than the ecclesiastical would like an infallible guide. Men engaged in business would like an infallible handbook that would point them the way to success. The gold hunters would like an infallible guide to the richest ores. Navigators on the sea would like infallible methods of manning and sailing their ships. The farmer would like to know that he was following an infallible method to success. It would be very desirable in many respects; it would save us no end of trouble.

But it is admitted that in these other departments of life, whether we want infallible guides or not, we do not have them. And I think, if you will look at the matter a little deeply and carefully, you will become persuaded that it would not be the best for us if we could. Men not only wish to gain certain ends, but, if they are wise, they wish more than that, to cultivate and develop and unfold themselves, which they can only do by study, by mistakes, by correcting mistakes, by finding out through experience what is true and what is false. In this process of study and experience they find themselves, something infinitely more important than any external fact or success which they may discover or achieve.

So I believe that a similar thing is true in the religious life. It might be a great saving of trouble if we were sure we had an infallible guide. I am inclined to think that a great many persons who go into the Roman Catholic

Church, in this modern time, go there because they are tired of thinking, and wish to shift the responsibility of it on to some one else.

It is tiresome, it is hard work. Sometimes we would like to escape it: we would like infallible guides. But I have studied the world with all the care that I could; and I have never been able to find the materials out of which I could construct an infallible guide, if I wanted it ever so much.

Whether it is important or not to have infallible teaching in the theological realm, there is no such thing as infallibility that is accessible to us; and I, for one, do not believe that it would be best for us if there were. God is treating us more wisely and kindly than, if we were able, we would treat ourselves; because it is not the discovery of this or that particular fact or truth that is so important as is the development of our own intellectual and moral and spiritual natures in the search for truth.

Lessing said a very wise thing when he declared that, if God should offer him the perfect truth in one hand and the privilege of seeking for it in the other, he should accept the privilege of search as the nobler and more valuable gift, because, in this seeking, we develop ourselves, we cultivate the Divine, and work our natures over into the likeness of God.

And now at the end I wish simply to say that God has given us the better thing in letting us freely and earnestly and simply investigate and look after the truth, cultivating ourselves in the process, and being wrought over ever more and more into the likeness of the divine.

And I wish also to say, for the comfort of those who may think that this lack of infallible guides is a serious matter, it may astonish you to have me say it, that there is not a single matter of any practical importance in our moral and religious life concerning which there is any doubt whatsoever. If anybody tells you that he is not living a religious life or not living a moral life, for the lack of light and guidance, do not believe him.

What are the things that are in question? What are the things of which we are sure? Take, for example, the matter of Biblical criticism, as to who wrote the book of Chronicles, as to whether Deuteronomy was written by Moses or compiled in the time of King Josiah. Are there any great spiritual problems waiting for those questions to be settled? Do you need to have that matter made clear before you know whether you ought to be an honest man in your business, whether you ought to judge charitably of a friend who has gone astray, whether you ought to be helpful towards your neighbors, whether you ought to be kind to your wife, and whether you ought to lovingly train and cultivate your children?

Take another of the great questions, as to the authorship of the Gospel of John. I shall be immensely interested in the settlement of that if the time ever comes when it is settled; but it would be a purely critical interest that I should have. I am not going to wait until that is settled before I lead a religious life. I am not going to let that stand in the way of my helping on the progress of the world.

I tell you, friends, that these matters that are in doubt, that need an infallibility to settle them, are not the practical matters at all. We look off into the vast universe around us, and question about God. Is he personal? Can we have the old ideas about him? One thing is settled: we know we are the product of and in the presence of an Eternal Order, and that knowing and keeping the laws of the universe mean life and happiness, but the opposite means death. That is the practical part of it.

We know that the Power that is in this universe is making gradually through the ages for righteousness; and we know that the righteous and helpful life is the only manly life for us to lead, for our own sake, for the sake of those we can touch and influence.

Are we going to wait for criticism to settle metaphysical problems before we do anything about these great practical matters?

Whatever your theory about Jesus may be, you can at least be like him, and wait; and, when you see him, you will love him, and know the truth about him, if you cannot before.

Matthew Arnold, an agnostic, has put into two or three lines, which I wish to read now at the end, what might well be the creed of the person who doubts so much that he thinks nothing is settled. If you cannot say any more than this, here is all that is absolutely necessary to the very noblest life:

"Hath man no second life? Pitch this one high. Sits there no Judge in heaven our sin to see? More strictly, then, the inward judge obey. Was Christ a man like us? Ah I let us try If we, then, too, can be such men as he."

THE REAL SIGNIFICANCE OF THE PRESENT RELIGIOUS DISCUSSION.

SCIENCE tells us that the law of growth is embodied in the phrase, "the struggle for life and the survival of the fittest." As we look beneath the surface in any department of human endeavor, analyze things a little carefully, we discover that this contest is going on. We know that it is not confined to the lower forms of life or the order of the inanimate world. It is a universal law. We are not always conscious of it; but, when we do think and study, we discover it as an unescapable fact.

In the religious world, for example, between the different thoughts and theories which are held among men as solutions of the problems of life we find this contest going on. Here, again, it is not always noticed; but in the mind of any man who thinks, who reads, who reflects, this process is apparent. This view is considered, another view mentioned by somebody else is set over against it, and the claims of the two theories are brought up for judgment. And so there goes on perpetually this debate. Now and again it comes to the surface, and attracts popular attention. We have been in the midst of an experience of this kind for the last two or three weeks here in New York City.

20

But the thing I want you to note is — and that is the great lesson I have in mind this morning that all of this superficial discussion of one point or another is only an indication of a larger, deeper contest. When, for example, men are debating as to the infallibility or inerrancy of the Old Testament, as to the story of the creation as told in Genesis, as to the nature and work of Jesus, as to the future destiny of the race, when they are discussing any one of these particular problems, they are dealing with matters that are really superficial. Underneath these there is a larger problem; and to this problem and its probable issues I wish to call your attention this morning.

There are two great world theories, complete each in itself, both of them thinkable, mutually exclusive, one of which only can be true, and one of which must finally become dominant in the educated and free thought of the world. These two theories I wish to place face to face before you this morning, call your attention to some of their special features and note the claims they have on our acceptance.

Before doing this, however, I wish you to note that there are indications of a dual tendency on the part of the human mind which has not been manifested in the development of these two theories alone, but which has had illustrations in other directions and in other times.

In the early traditions of Greece and Rome you find two tendencies on the part of the mind of man. There was, first, an old-time tradition which placed the Golden Age of humanity away back in the past. The people dreamed of a time when Saturn, the father of gods and men, lived on the earth, and governed directly his children and his people. In that happy time there was no disease, no pain, no poverty. There were no class distinctions. There were no wars. The evil of the world was unknown. That was the Golden Age which a certain set of thinkers then placed far back in the past. They told how that age was succeeded by a bronze age, a poorer condition of affairs, how the gods left the earth, and ill contentions and evils of every kind began to afflict the world. This was succeeded by the age of brass, that by the age of iron; and so the poor old world was supposed to be getting worse and worse, lower and lower, from one epoch of time to another.

But also among these same people there were another set of traditions, illustrated sufficiently for our purpose by the story of Prometheus. According to this the first age of humanity was its worst and poorest and lowest age. The people lived in abject poverty and misery. They were even neglected on the part of the gods, who did not seem to care for them, but treated them with contempt. Prometheus is represented as pitying their evil estate, caring more for them than the gods did; and so he steals the celestial fire, and comes down to the world and presents it to men, and so helps them to begin civilization, a period of prosperity and progress. For this he is punished by the gods.

The point I wish you to note is that even among the Greeks and the Romans there were two types of mind, one of which placed the Golden Age in the past, and the other of which placed it in the future as the goal of man's endeavor and growth.

A precisely similar thing we find in the Old Testament, so that these two types of mind appear among the Hebrews. In one of these we find again the Golden Age, the perfect condition of things, placed at the beginning. There was a garden, and man and woman were perfect in it. There was no labor, no toil, no pain, no sorrow, no fear, no trouble of any kind. But that was followed by sin, evil, entering the world, by their being driven out; and so the world has again been going from bad to worse, as the ages have passed by.

On the other hand, among the Hebrews, as illustrated in the writings of the great prophets, the master minds of the Hebrew race, there is the opposite belief manifested. There is no fall of man, no perfect condition of things, no Golden Age at the beginning, in the prophets. There is none in the teaching of Jesus. Rather do they look forward with kindling eye and beating heart to some grander thing that is to be.

Here is this dual tradition, then, in the world, in different parts of the world, this dual way of looking at the problem of life.

Now I wish to place before you the two great contrasted theories of the universe. In presenting that which has been dominant for the last two or three thousand years, two thousand, perhaps, speaking roughly, I am quite well aware that I shall have to seem to tell you what you perfectly well know, what I have said on other occasions; but it is necessary for me to run over it, and I will do so as briefly as I can, setting it before you in outline as a whole, so that you may see it in contrast with the other theory which I shall then endeavor to set forth also as a whole.

According to that theory of the world, then, which lies at the foundation, the old-time and still generally accepted theory of Christendom, the world was created in the year 4004 B.C. It was created in a week's time. This was the general teaching until thinkers were compelled to accept another theory by the advances of modern investigation. The world was created inside of a week. God got through, pronounced it good, and rested. Then in a short period of time we do not know how long evil entered this world which God had pronounced perfect. Satan, a real being, the leader of the hosts of the fallen angels, the traditional enemy of God, who had fought him even in his own heaven and been cast out, invades this fair earth. He seduces our first parents, gets them to commit a sin against God which makes them his enemies, turns them into rebels against his just and holy government. The world, then, is fallen. Now from that day to this the one effort on the part of God, according to this theory, has been to deliver the world from this lost condition. Jonathan Edwards, for example, published a book called "The History of Redemption." He conceived the entire history of the world under that title, because the history of the world, according to this theory, has been the history of the effort of God to deliver man from the effects of the fall.

Now let us note the story as it proceeds a little further. The world exists for I think I have a date here which may interest you 1,656 years, God meantime doing everything he could, by sending angels and special messengers and teaching the people; and he had accomplished so little that the world was in such a condition that he was compelled to drown it. So came the flood. After that, he chooses one family, one little family and the descendants of that family, one little people, and bends all his energies to the education and training of that people,— a small people inhabiting a country on the eastern coast of the Mediterranean Sea just about as large as the State of Massachusetts.

For more than two thousand years he devotes himself to the training of this people. How does he succeed here? He sends his messengers again, his angels, his prophets, one after another. He inspires a certain number of men to write a book to deliver his will to the people, fallen into such condition that they are incapable of discovering the truth for themselves. But, after all his efforts, they are so far from the truth that, when the second person of the Trinity appears, they have nothing to do with him except to put him to death. After that, God sends the third person of the Trinity, the Holy Spirit, to organize his Church, spread his truth, convert men, bring them into the Church, and so fit them to be saved. And, after two thousand years of that kind of effort, what is the result? They tell us that not more than a third part of the inhabitants of the world have heard anything about it, that the majority of those who have heard about it reject it. Mr. Moody told us last year that in this country, which we love to think of as the most favored and highly civilized and intelligent country in the world, out of seventy millions of inhabitants, not more than thirty millions ever see the inside of any kind of church. I do not vouch for the accuracy of the statistics. I wish to impress upon you the result of this theory of this six thousand years of endeavor on the part of God to bring his own children to a knowledge of his own truth. The upshot of it is that the few, the minority, will be saved, and the great majority eternally lost.

Now here is one world theory, one scheme of world history which I wish you to hold clearly and as definitely as possible in your minds, while I place alongside of it another theory.

According to this other, God did not suddenly create the world in a week or in a hundred thousand years. It is a story of continuous and eternal creation. As Jesus said, with fine and noble insight, "My father worketh hitherto." He did not recognize that God was resting on any day or through any period of time.

The world, then, has always been in process of creation. The same forces at work in accordance with substantially the same laws. The world has been millions of years in this process; and the process all around us, if we choose to open our eyes and note it, is still going on with all its wonder and divinity. And we know, as we study the heavens above us, or around us rather, with our telescopes, that there are worlds and systems of worlds in process of creation on every hand. We are permitted to look into the divine workshop and observe the divine method.

The world, then, is always in process of creation. This is the first point in the new theory. It follows, of course, from this that we are to hold the story of the antiquity of the earth, the earth millions of years old, instead of six thousand or ten thousand.

And then, in the third place, it tells us the story of the antiquity of the human race.

All scholars, for example, as bearing on this I will give you just this one illustration, know that there was a civilization in Egypt, wide- spread, highly developed, with nobody knows how many ages of growth behind it, there was this civilization in Egypt before the world was created according to the popular chronology that has been generally received until within a few years.

We know that man has been on the earth hundreds of thousands of years.

This is the next point in that story.

In the next place, they tell us a wondrous tale of the origin and nature of man, tracing his natural development from lower forms of life. When I say "natural," I do not wish you to think for one moment that I leave out the divinity; for, according to this story of the world which I am hinting and outlining now, God is infinitely nearer, more wonderfully in contact with us, than he ever was in the old. Natural, then, but divine at every step, so that we are seeing God face to face, if we but think of it, and are feeling his touch every moment of our lives.

No fall of man, then, on this theory. No invasion of this world by any form of evil or any evil person from without. This story of the fall of man came into the world undoubtedly to account in some philosophical fashion for the existence of pain, of evil, and of death. We account for it on this new theory much more naturally, rationally, more honorably for God, more hopefully for man.

The history of the world, then, since man began has not been by any means a history of universal progression. Evolution, however much it may be misunderstood and misrepresented, does not mean the necessity of progress on the part of any one person or any one people, any more, for example, than the growth of the human body is inconsistent with the fact that cells and composite parts of the body are in process of decay and dissolution every hour, every moment of our lives.

Nations grow, advance, if they comply with the laws, the conditions, of growth and advance; and, if not, they die out and disappear. And so is it of individuals. But, on the other hand, in the presence of the loving, lifting, leading God, humanity in the larger sense has been advancing from the beginning of human history until to-day; and the grade, dim glimpses of which we gain as we look out toward the future, is still up and still on.

According to this theory of the universe, there does not need to be any stupendous breaking in of God into his own world after any miraculous fashion. We do not need an infallible guide in religion any more than anywhere else, unless we are in danger of eternal loss because of an intellectual mistake. We do not need any stupendous miracle to reconcile God to his own world; for he has always been reconciled. We do not need any miraculous bridging of any mythical gulf; for there never has been any gulf. And the outcome, not as we look forward are we haunted by fearful anticipations of darkness and evil; as we listen, we do not ever hear the clanking of chains; as we look, we know that the dimness that hangs over the coming time is not caused by "the smoke of the torment that ascendeth up forever and ever." It is a story of eternal hope for every race, for every child of man and child of God.

Here are these two theories, then, two schemes of the universe and of human history. Which of them shall we accept?

I wish you to note now, and to note with a little care, that you cannot rationally accept a part of one theory and a part of the other, and so make up a patchwork to suit yourselves. Take, for example, the one question, Is man lost or is he not? He is not half lost or sort of lost: he is either lost or he is not lost. Which is true? If he is not "lost," then he does not need to be "saved." He may need something else; but he does not need that, for the two correspond and match each other. Let us think, then, a little clearly in regard to this matter, and remember that the outcome of the conflict between these two theories must be the supremacy of either one or the other.

Now, before I come to any more fundamental and earnest treatment of the subject, let me call your attention to certain things that are happening to the old theory.

How much of that old theory is intact to-day? How much of it is held even by those who, being scholars and thinkers, still hold their allegiance to the old-time theology? Let us see. The story of the sudden and finite creation of the world is completely gone. Nobody holds that now who gives it any attention. They have stretched the six days of the week, even those who hold the accuracy of the Genesis account, into uncounted periods of time. So that is gone. The antiquity of man is conceded by everybody who has a right to have and express an opinion; that is, by everybody who has given it any study. Every competent and free scholar knows to-day that the story of the fall of man and the whole Eden story, is a Babylonian or a Persian legend that came into the life of the Jews about the time of their captivity, and was not known of till then among them, and did not take hold on the leading and highest minds of their own people. And there are, as you know, hundreds, if not thousands of clergymen in all the churches to- day who are ready to concede that the story of Eden is poetry or legend or tradition: they no longer treat it as serious history. And yet, as I have said a good many times, they go on as though nothing had happened, although the foundation of their house has been removed. Only theories which stand in the air can thus defy the law of gravitation.

Nobody to-day who has a right to have an opinion believes that God ever drowned the world. That is gone. As to the question as to whether we have an infallible book to guide us in religious matters, there are very few scholars in any church to-day, so far as my investigations have led, who hold any such opinion. That is gone; and the Bible, the Old Testament, at any rate is coming to be recognized, not as infallible revelation, but as ancient literature, immensely interesting, full of instruction, but not as an unquestioned guide in any department of life.

There are many among the nominally old churches who are coming to hold a very different theory concerning Jesus, his life, his death, and the effect of his death on the salvation of man. More reasonable ideas are prevailing here. In every direction also there are thousands on thousands who are becoming freed from that horrible incubus of fear as they look out towards the future.

As you note then, point after point of this old scheme of the universe is disappearing, being superseded by something else; until I am astonished, as I converse with friends in the other churches, to find how little of it is really left, how little of it men are ready, out and out, to defend. In conversation with an Episcopal clergyman a short time ago on theological questions, we agreed so well that I laughingly said I saw no reason why I should not become a clergyman in the Episcopal Church.

Now, friends, what I wish you to note is this: that there is not one single point in this old scheme of the universe that can be reasonably defended to-day. It is passing away from intelligent, cultivated human thought.

And note another thing: it is a scheme which is a discredit to the thought of God. It is unjust. It is dishonorable in its moral and religious implications. It is pessimistic and hopeless in its outlook for the race. It does not explain the problems of human nature and human experience half as well as the other theory does, even if it could be demonstrated as truth.

Now let us look at the other. The other theory is magnificent in its proportions. It is grand in its conception and in its age-long sweep and range. It is worthy of the grandest thought of God we can frame; and we cannot imagine any increase or heightening or deepening of that thought which would reach beyond the limits of this conception of the universe, magnificent in its thought of God. And, instead of being pessimistic and hopeless in its outlook for man, it is full of hope, of life, of inspiration, of cheer, something for which we well may break out into songs of gladness as we contemplate.

And, then, it is true. There is not one single feature of it, or point in it, that has not in the main been scientifically demonstrated to be God's truth. I make this statement, and challenge the contradiction of the world. Whatever breaks there may be in the evidence for this second theory that I have outlined, every single scrap and particle of evidence that there is in the universe is in its favor; and there is not one single scrap or particle of evidence in favor of the other. As I say, I challenge the contradiction of the scholarly world to that statement.

It is true then. Being true, it is God's truth, God's theory of things, the outline of human history as God has laid it down for us; and, as we trace it, like Kepler, we may say, "O God, I think over again thy thoughts after Thee."

Now I wish you to note one or two things concerning this a little further. There are a great may persons who shrink from accepting new ideas because they are haunted with the fear that in some way something precious, something sweet, something noble, something inspiring that they have associated with the past, is going to be lost. But think, friends. When the Ptolemaic theory of the universe gave way to the Copernican, not only did the Copernican have the advantage of being true, but not one single star in heaven was put out or even dimmed its light. All of them looked down upon us with an added magnificence and a fresher glow, because we felt at last we were standing face to face with the truth of things, and not with a fallible theory of man.

Do not be afraid, then, that any of the sanctities, any of the devoutness, any of the tenderness, any of the sweet sentiments, any of the loves, any of the charities, any of the worships of the past, are in danger of being lost. Why, these, friends, are the summed-up result of all the world's finest and sweetest achievement up to this hour; and our theories are only vessels in which we carry the precious treasure.

I am interested in having you see the truth of this universe, because I believe you will worship God more devoutly and love man more truly and consecrate yourselves more unreservedly to the highest and noblest ends, when you can think thoughts of God that kindle aspiration and worship, and thoughts of men as children of God that make it grandly worth your while to live and die for them.

Do you think there is going to be a poorer religion than there has been in the past? I look to the time when we shall have a church as wide as the horizon, domed by the blue, lighted by the sun, the Sun of Righteousness, the Eternal Truth of the Father; a church in which all men shall be recognized as brothers, of whatever sect or whatever religion, in which all shall kneel and chant or lisp their worship according as they are able, the worship of the one Father, cheered and inspired by the one universal and eternal hope for man.

Do not be afraid of the truth, then, for fear something precious is going to be lost out of human life. Evolution never gives up anything of the past that is worth keeping. It simply carries it on, and moulds it into ever higher and finer shapes for the service of man.

I intimated a moment ago? I wish to touch on this briefly for the sake of clearness that man, according to this new theory, does not need to be saved, in the theological sense, of course, I mean, because he is not lost. He has never been far away from the Father, never been beyond the reach of his hand, never been beyond the touch of his love and care. What does he need? He needs to be trained, he needs to be educated, he needs to be developed for man is just as naturally religious as he is musical or artistic, as he is interested in problems of government or economics, or any of the great problems that touch the welfare of the world.

Man needs churches, then, or societies of those interested in the higher life of the time, needs services, needs all these things that kindle and train and develop and lift him up out of the animal into the spiritual and divine nature which is in every one of us. So that none of the worships, none of the religious forms of the world that are of any value, are ever going to be cast aside or left behind.

But there is one very important point that I must deal with for just a little while. I will be as brief as I can.

I have been very much surprised to note certain things that have come out in the recent religious discussions. The editor of the Brooklyn Eagle, for example, has deprecated all talk in regard to matters of this sort, saying, in effect: What difference does it make? What is involved that is of any importance? Why not let everybody worship and believe as he pleases? A writer in the New York Times? I think perhaps more than one, but one specially I have in mind has said substantially the same thing. It does not make any difference. Let people worship as they please, let them believe as they please, let them go their own way. What difference does it make?

Friends, it makes no difference at all, provided there is no such thing in the world as religious truth. If there is, it makes all difference. Let us take this "Don't care" and "No matter" theory for a moment, and in the light of it consider a few of the grandest lives of the world.

If it makes no difference what a man believes in religion or how he worships or what he tries to do, how does it happen that we Unitarians, for example, glorify Theodore Parker, and count him a great moral and intellectual hero? Why should he have made himself so unpopular as to be cast out even of the Unitarian fellowship? Was he contending for nothing? Was he a fool? was he making himself uncomfortable over imaginary distinctions? Perhaps; but, then, why are we foolish enough to honor him?

Why is it that we glorify Channing, who at an earlier period was cast out of the best religious society of the world for what he believed to be a great principle? Why is it to-day that we lift John Wesley on such a lofty pedestal of admiration? He left the Church of England, or was cast out of it, went among the poor, preached a great religious reform, led a magnificent crusade, teaching a higher and grander spiritual religion, a religion of heart, of life, of character, against the mere formalism of the Church of his time. Was he contending about airy nothings without local habitation or a name? If so, why are we so foolish as to admire him?

Go back further to Martin Luther, putting himself in danger of his life, standing against banded Europe, and saying, "Here I stand: God help me, I can do no otherwise!" What is the use? What did he do it for? If it made no difference whether a man worshipped God intelligently or according to the things Luther thought all wrong, what was the difference? What was he contending about, and why does the world bow down to him with reverence and honor?

Why are we fools enough to honor the men who were burned at Oxford? Why do we honor to-day the line of saints and martyrs? Why do we look upon Savonarola with such admiration?

To go back still farther, why was it that the early Christians were ready to suffer torture, to be racked, to be persecuted, to be thrown into kettles of boiling oil, to be cast to the wild beasts in the arena? Were they contending for nothing at all? If it makes no difference, why were they casting themselves away in this Quixotic and foolish fashion and, if there was nothing involved, how is it that these names shine as stars in the religious firmament of the world's worship?

Go to the time of Jesus himself. A young Nazarene, he leaves his home in Nazareth, joins the fortunes of John the Baptist. After John the Baptist had been fool enough to get his head cut off contending for his theory, Jesus takes up his work, dares to speak against the temple, dares to challenge the righteousness of the most righteous men of their time, dares at last to stand so firmly that he is taken out one afternoon and hung upon a tree on the hill beyond the walls of the city, the one supreme piece of folly in the history of the world from the "Does not make any difference" point of view.

Is there any truth involved? Does it touch the living or the welfare of the world? If not, why, then, are these looked upon as the grandest figures since the world began? Are all men fools for admiring them, except these wiseacres who stand for the theory that it makes no difference and who ought not to admire them at all?

Suppose you apply the principle in other departments of life. We had a tremendous issue in this city and country last fall over the financial question. Would it have made any difference which side won? If it was just as well one way as the other, why not let the people who clamored for silver have silver, those who wanted greenbacks have greenbacks, and those who desired gold have gold? What was the use of troubling about it? We thought there were principles involved.

Take it in the economic world, the individualist here with his theory, the socialist here with his; theories outlined like those in Edward Bellamy's "Looking Backward"; a hundred advancers of these different schemes, each contending for mastery. And we feel that the welfare of civilization is at stake; and we stand for our great principles. Take it in politics. What difference does it make whether the theories embodied in the reign of the Czar of Russia prevail, or these here in the United States which we are so foolish as to laud and pride ourselves so much about? What did we have a Civil War for, wasting billions of money and hundreds of thousands of lives? Are these great human contests about nothing at all?

Friends, think one moment. Either man is a child of God or he is not. Man fell at the beginning of his history, and came under the wrath and curse of God, or he did not. God has sent angels, breaking into his natural order of the world, or he has not. He has created an infallible book or he has not. He has organized an infallible church that has authority to guide and teach the world or he has not. He himself came down to earth in the form of a man once and for all, and was crucified, dead and buried and ascended into heaven, or he did not.

These are questions of historic fact. Does it make no difference what we believe about them? If man is a fallen being, condemned to eternal death, and God has provided only one way for his escape and salvation, then it makes an infinite and eternal difference as to whether we know it or believe it or act on it or not. If the majority of the human race is doomed to eternal torture unless it escapes through certain prescribed conditions, does it make any difference whether we know it or not?

And, if he is not so doomed, does it make no difference to the heart and hope, the life, the cheer, the courage and inspiration of man, whether or not we lift from the brain and the heart this horrible incubus of dread and fear?

Here are all these churches with their wealth, their intelligence, their enthusiasm, their inspiration, ready to do something for humanity. Does it make any difference whether they are doing the right thing for it or not? We could revolutionize the world if we could be guided by intelligence, and find out what man really needs, and devote ourselves to the accomplishment of what that is. The waste, the waste, the waste of money and thought and energy and time and inspiration poured into wrong channels, unguided by intelligence, directed towards things that do not need to be done, and away from things that do need to be done!

These are the questions involved in discussions as to what God is and has done and is going to do with his world.

The one thing we need, then, almost more than all others just now, is to be led by the truth, and have the truth make us free from the errors and the burdens of the past, so that we may place ourselves truly at the disposal of God for the service of our fellows.

O star of truth down-shining, Through clouds of doubt and fear, I ask but 'neath your guidance My pathway may appear. However long the journey, How hard soe'er it be, Though I be lone and weary, Lead on, I'll follow thee. I know thy blessed radiance Can never lead astray, However ancient custom May tread some other way. E'en if through untrod desert Or over trackless sea, Though I be lone and weary, Lead on, I'll follow thee. The bleeding feet of martyr Thy toilsome road have trod; But fires of human passion May lead the way to God. Then, though my feet should falter, While I thy beams can see, Though I be lone and weary, Lead on, I'll follow thee. Though loving friends forsake me Or plead with me in tears, Though angry foes may threaten To shake my soul with fears, Still to my high allegiance I must not faithless be, Through life or death, forever Lead on, I'll follow thee.

DOUBT AND FAITH-BOTH HOLY.

THE object of all thinking is the discovery of truth. And truth for us, what is that? It is the reality of things as related to us. There has been a good deal of metaphysical discussion first and last as to what things are "in themselves." It seems to me that this, if it were possible to find it out, might be an interesting matter, might satisfy our curiosity, but is of absolutely no practical importance to us. I do not believe that we can find out what things are in themselves, in the first place; and I do not believe that, if we could, it would be of any service to us. What we want to know is what things are as related to us, as touching us, as bearing upon our life, upon our practical affairs.

Once more: there has been a good deal of discussion as to whether the universe is really what it appears to be to us. They tell us that it is quite another thing from the point of view of other creatures, to beings differently constituted from ourselves. Again, all this may be. It might be interesting to me, for example, to look at the world from the point of view of the fly or of the bird or some one of the animals; but, again, while it might satisfy my curiosity, it could be of no practical importance to me. It might be very interesting to me to know how the universe looks from the point of view of an angel. But, so long as I am not an angel, but a man, what I need to know is what the universe is as related to man.

So truth, I say, then, is the reality of things as related to us.

I must make another remark here, in order perfectly to clear the way. Philosophers and scientific men, a certain class of them, are perpetually warning us of the dangers of being anthropomorphic. Some one has said, "Man never knows how anthropomorphic he is." This means, as you know, that we look at things from the point of view of ourselves. We see things as men, as anthropoi. This has been erected in certain quarters into a good deal of a bugbear in the way of thinking. We are told we can never know the universe really, because we shape everything into our own likeness, we are anthropomorphic, we look at everything from the point of view of men.

I grant the charge; but, instead of being frightened by it, I accept it with content. How else should we look at things except from the point of view of men, since we are men? We cannot look at them in any other way. Let us be, then, anthropomorphic. The only thing we need to guard against is this: we must not assume that we have exhausted the universe, and that we know it all. This is the evil of a certain type of anthropomorphism. But I cannot understand why it is important for us to be anything else but anthropomorphic. I want to know how things look to a man, what things are to a man, how things affect a man, how I am to deal with things, being a man.

This is the only matter, let me repeat again, which is of any practical importance to us, until we become something other than men.

Truth, then, the truth that we desire to find, is the reality of things as related to us. Now doubt and faith are attitudes of mind, and are neither good nor bad in themselves, either of them. They are of value only as they help us in the discovery of this reality about which I have been speaking. If a certain type of doubt stands in our way in seeking for truth, then that doubt so far is evil. If a certain something, called faith, stands in the way of our seeking frankly and fearlessly for the truth, that is evil. If -doubt helps us to find truth, it is good: if faith helps us to -find truth, it is good. But the only use of either of them is to help us discover and live the truth.

The attitude of the Church and by the Church I mean the historic Church of the past towards doubt and faith is well known to us. It has condemned doubt almost universally as something evil, sinful. It has extolled faith as something almost universally good. But in my judgment and I will ask you when I get through, perhaps, to consider as to whether you do not agree with me the trouble with the human mind up to the present time has not been a too great readiness to doubt: it has been a too great inclination to believe. There has been too much of what has been called perhaps by the time I am through you will think miscalled faith; and there has been too little of honest, fearless, earnest doubt. This is perfectly natural, when you consider how the world begins, and the steps by which it advances.

Let us take as an illustration the state of mind of a child. A child at first does not doubt, does not doubt anything. It is ready to believe almost anything that father, mother, nurse, playmate, may say to it. And why? In the first place it has had no experience yet of anything but the truth being told it; and in the next place it lives in a world where there are no canons or standards of probability. In the child- world there are no laws, there are no impossibilities, there is nothing in the way of anything happening. The child mind does not say, in answer to some statement, Why, this does not seem reasonable. The child's reason is not yet developed into any practical activity. The child does not say, Why, this cannot be, because there is such a force or such a law that would be contravened by it. The child knows nothing about these forces or laws: it is a sort of a Jack- and-the-Beanstalk world. The beanstalk can grow any number of feet over night in the world in which the child lives. Anything is possible. If father and mother and nurse tell the child about Santa Claus coming down the chimney with a pack of toys on his back, it does not occur to the child to note the fact that the chimney flue is no more than six inches in diameter, and that Santa Claus and his pack could not possibly pass through such an opening. All this is beyond the range or thought of the stage of development at which the child has arrived.

So in the childhood world. As I said, anything may happen. But you will note, beautiful, sunny, lovely as this childhood world is as a phase of experience, as a stage of development, sweet as may be the memory of it, yet, if the child is ever to grow to manhood, is ever to be anything, ever to do anything, it must outgrow this Jack-and-the- Beanstalk world, this Santa Claus world, this world in which anything may happen, and must begin to doubt, begin to question, begin to test things, to prove things, find out what is real and what is unreal, what is true and what is untrue, must measure itself against the realities of things, learn to recognize the real forces and the laws according to which they operate, so as to deal with them, obey them, make them serve him, enable him to create character and to create a new type of civilization, new things on the face of the earth.

Now what is true of each individual child has been true of the race. The world started in childhood; and for thousands of years it believed very easily, it believed altogether too much for its good, it believed altogether too readily. Naturally, perhaps, necessary in that stage of its development; but so long as it remained in that stage there was no possibility of its becoming master of the earth.

Note, for example, the state of mind of the old Hebrews, I use them merely as an illustration, because you are familiar with their story as told in the Old Testament. Similar things are true of every race on the face of the earth. They knew nothing about the real nature of this universe. They knew nothing about natural forces working in accordance with what we call natural laws. Consequently, they lived in a child- world, a world of magic and miracle, a world in which anything might happen. It did not trouble one of the people of that time to be told that, in answer to the prayer of one of the prophets, an axe-head which had sunk in the water rose and floated on the surface. There were no natural laws in his mind contradicted by an asserted fact like that. It never occurred to him to be troubled about it. There was nothing very startling to him in being told that the sun stood still for an hour or two to enable a general to finish a battle in which he was engaged. He did not know enough about the universe to see what tremendous consequences would be involved in the possibility of a thing like that. He was not troubled when you told him that a man had been swallowed by a great fish, and had lived for three days and three nights in its stomach, and had come out uninjured. There was no improbability in it to him. Simply, a question as to whether God had chosen to have the fish large enough so that it could swallow him. To be told again that a human body that could eat food and digest it, a body like ours, might rise into the air and pass out of sight into some invisible heaven, not very far away, there was nothing incredible about it. He knew nothing about the atmosphere, limited in its range so that it would be impossible to breathe beyond a certain distance from the planet. He knew nothing about the intense cold that would make life impossible just a little way above the surface.

The world in which our forefathers lived until modern times was just this magic, Jack-and-the-Beanstalk world, a world without any impossibilities in it, without any improbabilities in it. All this thought of the true and the untrue, the possible and the impossible, the probable and the improbable, is the result of the fact that man has grown up, has left his childhood behind him, has begun to think, has begun to study, has begun to search for reality, to find out the nature of the world in which he lives, the forces with which he must deal, to understand the universe at least in some narrow range, measured by his so-far experience.

The world, then, until modern times has believed too readily, has accepted things too easily. Let us note, for example, what have been called by way of pre-eminence the Ages of Faith, the Middle Ages, the age, say, from the seventh or eighth century until the thirteenth or fourteenth. What was characteristic of those ages? Were they grand, noble? They were ages of ignorance, of superstition, of cruelty, of immorality, of poverty, of tyranny, of degradation. Almost everything existed that men would no longer bear to-day; and hardly any of the grand things that characterize modern civilization had then been heard of.

Where did this modern civilization of ours begin? Did it ever occur to you that it began when men began to doubt? It began, we say, with the Renaissance. What was the Renaissance? The Renaissance was the birth of doubt, the birth of question, the demand on the part of men, who began to wake up and think, for evidence. It was the beginning of the scientific age, the birth of the scientific spirit which has renovated, re- created, uplifted the world. Men began to think, to look about them, and to prove all things. And instead of holding fast all things, as they had been doing in the past, they began to hold fast only the things which they found by experience, and after testing and trial, to be good.

Here began, then, the civilization of the world; and all that is finest and highest in industry, in education, in discovery, in the whole external civilization of the world, came in with the coming of this spirit that questions and that asks for proof.

I do not wish you to understand me as supposing that all kinds of doubt are good, equally good. The Church, as I said a little while ago, has been accustomed to teach us that doubt was wrong; and there are certain kinds of doubt that are morally wrong, certain kinds of doubt that are disastrous to the highest and finest life of the world.

I wish now to analyze a little and define and make clear these distinctions, that you may see the kind of doubt which is evil and the kind of doubt which is good.

There are doubts which spring out of the fact that men, under the influence of personal interest, as they suppose, or strong desire, wish to follow certain courses, wish to walk in certain paths; and they doubt and question the laws, moral or mental, religious or what not, which stand in their way, which would prohibit their having their will. As an illustration of what I mean, suppose a man is engaged in a certain kind of business, or wishes to manage his business in a certain kind of way. He suspects, if he stops and thinks about it, that the interests of other people may be involved, that the way in which he wants to conduct his business is a selfish way, that the interests of other people may be injured, that the world as a whole may not be as well off; but it seems to be for his own advantage.

Now it is very difficult, indeed, for you to persuade a man that he ought to do right under such circumstances. He is ready to doubt and question as to whether these laws of right are imperative, whether they are divine, whether they may not be waived one side in the interest of the thing which he desires to do. So you must guard yourself very carefully, no matter what the department of life may be that you are facing, if you find yourself doubting under the impulse of your own wishes, if you are trying to argue yourself into the belief that you may be permitted to do something which you very much want to do.

Be suspicious of your doubts, then, and remember that probably they are wrong. Great moral questions may be involved, and doubt may mean wreck here.

There is another field where doubt is dangerous and presumably an evil. You will find most people, in regard to any question which they have considered or which has touched them seriously, with their minds already made up. They have some sort of a persuasion about it, they have a theory which they have accepted; and, if you bring them a truth with ever such overwhelming credentials which clashes with this preconceived idea or prejudice, the chances are that it would be met with doubt, with denial, not a clear-cut, intelligent, well-balanced doubt, but a doubt that springs out of the unwillingness that a man feels to reconstruct his theory.

Let me give you an illustration of what I mean, and this away off in another department of life from our own, so that it will not clash with any of your particular prejudices. Sir Isaac Newton won a great and world-wide renown, and magnificently deserved, by his grand discovery of the law of gravity. You will see, then, how natural it was for people to pay deference to his opinion, to be prejudiced in favor of his conclusions. It was perfectly natural and, within certain limits, perfectly right. Sir Isaac Newton not only propounded this law of gravity, but he propounded a theory of light which the world has since discovered to be wrong. But it was universally accepted because it was his. It became the accepted scientific theory of the time. By and by a man, unknown up to that time, by the name of Young, studied Newton's theory, and became convinced that it was wrong; and he propounded another theory, the one which to- day is universally accepted through the civilized world. But it was years before it could gain anything like adequate or fair consideration, because the preconception in favor of Newton's theory stood in the way of any adequate consideration of the one which was subsequently universally adopted.

So you will find scientific men, I know any quantity of them, grand in their fields, doing fine work, who are not willing to consider anything which would compel a reconstruction of their theories and ideas. This is true not only in the scientific field, but it is true everywhere: it is true in politics. How many men can you get fairly to consider the political position of his opponent? He not only doubts the rightness and the sense of it, but he is ready to deny it. How many people can you get fairly to weigh the position of one who occupies a religious home different from their own? And these religious prejudices, being bound up with the tenderest and noblest sentiments, feelings, and traditions of the human heart, become the strongest of all, and so are in more danger of standing in the way of human progress than anything else in all the world.

People identify their theories of religion with religion itself, with the honor of God, with the worship and the love of God, and feel that somehow it is impious for them to consider the question whether their intellectual theories are correct or not; and so the world stands by the ideas of the past, and opposes anything like finer and nobler ideas that offer themselves for consideration. And not only in the religious field; but these religious prejudices stand in the way of accepting truths outside the sphere of religion. For example, when Darwin published his book, "The Origin of Species," the greatest opposition it met with was from the religious world. Why? Had they considered Darwin's arguments to find out whether they were true? Nothing of the kind. But they flew to the sudden conclusion that somehow or other the religion of the world was in danger, if Darwinism should prove to be true. And it is very curious to note I wonder how long the world will keep on repeating that serio-comic blunder from the very beginning it has been the same; almost every single step that the world proposes to take in advance is opposed by the constituted religious authorities of the time because they assume at the outset that the theories which they have been holding are divinely authorized and infallible, and that it is not only untrue, this other statement, but that it is impious as well.

The doubt, then, that springs from preconceived ideas is not only unjustifiable, but may be dangerous and wrong.

Then there is another kind of doubt against which you should beware. There are certain doubts that, if accepted and acted on, stand in the way of the creation of the most magnificent facts in the world. Take as an illustration of what I mean: when Napoleon, a young man in Paris, was asked to take command of the guard of the city, suppose he had doubted, questioned, distrusted, his own ability; suppose he had been timid and afraid, the history of the world would have been changed by that one doubt. Take another illustration. At the opening of our war or in the months just preceding the beginning of active hostilities the man then occupying the presidential chair had no faith, no faith in himself, no faith in the perpetuity of our institutions, no faith in the people; and so he sat doubting, while everything crumbled in pieces around him. And then appeared a man in whom the people had little faith at first, and who had no great faith perhaps in his own ability; but he had infinite faith in God, faith in right, faith in the people, faith in the possibilities of freedom trusted in the hands of the people. And this faith created a new nation.

If there had been doubt in the heart of Abraham Lincoln, again the history of the world would have been &hanged. He believed that "Right is right, since God is God, And right the day must win: To doubt would be disloyalty, To falter would be sin."

You see, then, here is another field where you had better be wary of doubt. Do not doubt yourself, do not doubt the possibilities of noble action, noble character, of achievement. We say of a young man entering life, brimful of enthusiasm, that all this will be toned down by and by; and we speak of it as though the enthusiasm itself somehow was a fault or a folly. And yet it is just this enthusiasm of the young men that moves and lifts the world. It is this faith in themselves and in the possibility of great things, it is this faith that lies at the heart of every invention, of every great discovery, of every magnificent achievement. Read the history of invention. The world is full of stories of men who got a new idea. They were laughed at, they were told it was impracticable; and, if they had been laughed out of it, it would have been impracticable. It was their faith in the possibility of some great new thing, their faith in the resources of the universe, their faith in themselves as able to discover some new truth and make it applicable to the needs of the world, it was this faith which has been at the root of the grandest things that have ever been done.

It is this which was in the heart of Columbus as he sailed out towards the West. It is this which was in the heart of Magellan as he studied the shadow of the earth across the face of the moon, and believed in the story that shadow told him against the constituted authorities of the world.

But now let us turn sharply, and find out where doubt does come in, and where it is as honorable, as noble, as necessary as faith.

People misuse this word "faith." Doubt applies to all questions of fact that may be investigated, to all questions of history, to all questions open to the exercise of the critical faculty. For example, if I am told that Moses wrote the Pentateuch, and I say I accept that statement on faith, I am abusing the dictionary. I have no business to accept it on faith. Faith has nothing whatever to do with it. It is a pure matter of scholarship. It is a matter of study, of investigation, a matter of clear and hard intelligence and nothing more.

Suppose I am told that the Catholic Church is infallible, and I am asked to accept it as an article of faith. Here, again, the introduction of the word "faith" into a domain like that is an impertinence. Faith has nothing whatever to do with it. That is a question of fact. We can read history for the last eighteen hundred years. We can find out what the Catholic Church has said and what the Catholic Church has done, as to whether it has proved itself absolutely infallible or not. It is a matter of study and decision intellectually; and it is my duty to doubt that which does not bring authentic credentials in a field like this.

Take the question of the authorship of the Gospel of John. Was it written by the apostle John, who lay in the bosom of Jesus, and was called the beloved disciple? Have I any business to say I have faith that it was written by him, and let it rest there? Faith has nothing to do with it. We can trace the history of that book, find out when first it was referred to, follow it back as far as possible, find out whether it was in existence before the apostle John had died or not. It is a pure matter of criticism, a matter of study; and I have no business to accept it as a matter of faith, because, if I do, I am in danger not only of deceiving myself, but of misleading the world. And truth, we cannot say it too often or too emphatically, truth is the only thing that is holy in investigations of this kind. Men's beliefs and mistakes, old, venerable, reverenced though they may have been by thousands and for hundreds of years, are no less unworthy longer to delude the minds of men. Truth is divine, truth is the one object of our search.

Now let us come to consider for a moment the nature of faith. I said a little while ago that the word is very frequently misused. Nine times out of ten, when I hear people using the word "faith" and I see the connection in which they use it, I discover they do not know the meaning of the word. That which has favor generally under the name of faith is simple credulity. It is closing the eyes and accepting something on somebody's authority without any investigation. That, remember, is not faith.

Let us see now if I can give you a clear idea of what faith really is; and now I have the Bible and I am glad to say it behind me. This magnificent chapter,* a portion of which I read as our lesson this morning, gives precisely the same idea of faith as that which I am going to outline. What is faith? Faith is a purely rational faculty. It is not irrational, but it is perfectly understandable. Suppose there is a man suddenly accused of a crime, and I never saw him before, I do not even know his name; but I go into court when he is brought up for trial, and I say that I have faith in that man, and I do not believe that he committed the crime. Do you not see that I am talking nonsense? I have no business to have faith in him, there is no ground for faith, it is an entire misuse of the word. But now take another case. Here is a man that I have known for twenty years. I have seen him in business. I have seen him in his home, among his neighbors and friends, and in the street. I have met him in all sorts of relations. I have talked with him, I have tested him. I have been intimate with him. He is suddenly accused of crime, and is brought into court. I appear, and say I have faith in that man, I do not believe that he

29

committed the crime. I do not know that he did not commit it; but I have grounds here for faith. In the light of his past life, of his experience, of his temptations, of his opportunities to go wrong, and of his having gone right, in the light of all this past experience of years, I have faith in this man; and I say it, and I am talking reason and sense. In the other case I am talking folly.

Faith, you see, is a rational faculty. Let me give you another illustration. Suppose I am driving along through the country some morning when there is a very thick fog hanging over the landscape. The fog is so thick that I can see no more than ten or fifteen feet ahead of me; but I discover that I am near the bank of a river, and I come to the entrance to a bridge. I can see enough to know that here is an abutment of a bridge and an arch springing out into the fog. I drive on to that bridge with simple confidence. I do not know that there is any other end to the bridge. I have never seen it before. I have seen other bridges, however; and I know that, generally, bridges not only begin somewhere, but end somewhere. So, though I do not know for certain that the bridge ends on the other side of the river, for aught I know there may be a break in it, the bridge may not be completed, something may have happened to it, I confidently drive on; and in ninety-nine times out of a hundred my faith is justified by the result. This is a pure act of faith, but faith, do you not see, based in reality, springing out of experience, and so a purely rational act of the mind.

Let me give you one illustration of the scientific use of faith, very striking, beautiful, as it seems to me. The only time Mr. Huxley was in this country, I happened to be in New York, and heard him give the opening one of a brief course of three lectures in Chickering Hall. He was very much interested then in the ancestry of the horse. Most of you are probably aware of the fact that they have traced its ancestry to a little creature having five toes, like ordinary animals. At the time that Mr. Huxley was here, one link in this chain was missing; that is, one of the forms in the line of the horse's ancestors had not been discovered.

But here, for example, was the first one and the second one, we say, and the third one was missing, and here was the fourth one, and here was the horse itself. Now, in the light of the presumable uniformity of nature, Mr. Huxley went on to describe this missing animal. He said, if the remains of this creature are ever found, they will be so and so; and he went into an accurate detailed explanation as to what sort of creature it would be. He had not been at his home in England a year before Professor Marsh, of Yale College, discovered this missing link in Colorado, and it answered precisely to the description which Professor Huxley had beforehand given of it.

Now here is a case of scientific prophecy, scientific faith, a faith based on previous scientific observations, based on the experienced uniformity of nature. Mr. Huxley did not know, he could not have known; but he believed. He believed in the universe, he believed in the sanity of the universe, he believed in the uniformity, the order, the beauty of the universe; and the result justified his faith.

Faith, then, is a purely rational faculty. It has nothing to do with the past, but is always the evidence of things hoped for, the substance of something not yet seen. It is always looking along the lines of possible experience for something as possibly or probably to be.

Now at the end I wish to suggest a few things that are in the rightful province and field of faith, fields where we can fearlessly exercise this grand faculty, where indeed we must exercise it if we are to achieve the highest and finest results in the world.

And, in the first place, quoting the words of the old writer, let me say, "Have faith in God." I do not mean by this, accept certain intellectual statements or propositions about him, though they may be mine, and though I may thoroughly accept and believe them.

You may doubt the representation of God that is made in any one of the theologies of the world, as to whether the statements made about him are accurate. It is not this intellectual belief that I am talking about at this minute. Have faith in God! You may not even use the name. I am no such stickler for phrases as to condemn a man who cannot say "God." I have known a good many men, who have hesitated to pronounce the name, who were infinitely more divine in their life and character than those who are glibly uttering it every hour of their lives. It is not this I mean. It is something deeper, higher, grander than that. As you look along the lines of history from the far-off time when we begin to trace it until to-day, and see the magnificent march of advance, an orderly universe lightening and glorifying as it advances, becoming ever finer and higher and better; as you observe the order and truth and beauty and good dominant, and ever coming to be more and more dominant as the years advance, believe in this and trust this, trust to all possibilities of something finer and grander by way of outcome in the future. Have faith in God!

And, then, have faith in truth. I meet only a few people that seem to me to have utter faith in truth, who really believe that it is safe to tell the truth, always tell it. I talk with a great many people I wish to mention this as an illustration of what I mean who speak in the greatest commendation of the Roman Catholic Church. They say, We do not know what we should do in this country if we had not the Roman Catholic Church to keep a certain section of the people down, to keep them in order. I wonder if people ever realize just what this means. It means a lack of faith in God and faith in truth and faith in humanity, all three. If it is not safe to tell the truth, then I am not responsible for it. I propose to say it, although people tell me that there is danger of the explosion of the universe on account of it. If there is, I am not responsible for making it true. Oh, I get so tired of this kind of timidity, this playing hide-and-seek with people! I have had a minister tell me that he wished he was free to tell the truth in his pulpit, as I am; and then I have had people in his congregation tell me afterwards that they wished their minister would preach the truth plainly, as I did. Simply playing hide-and-seek with each other!

You remember the story of the man in Italy, who asked the priest if he really believed the religion of the country; and the priest said, "Oh, no! we have to go slowly on account of the people; they believe it." And when the people were asked if they believed it, they said, "Oh, no, we are not such fools; but the priests believe it." And so people play hide-and-seek with each other, not daring to tell the magnificent, clear truth of things.

Have faith in the truth. It is feared that it is not quite safe to tell people the truth, because they are not quite ready for it; and I have had no end of conversations during the religious discussion of the last two or three weeks right in this line. It seems to me very much like saying that, because a man has been shut up in a dark prison for a long time, you had better keep him there, because it would be such a shock to him suddenly to face the light. Undoubtedly, it would be a shock. Undoubtedly, it would trouble and stagger people for a little while to be told the simple truth; but how is the world ever to get ahead, if you keep on, as a matter of policy, lying to it for ages? How is it ever going to find the truth? Shall I lie for the glory of God, the supposed honor of God? I will take no such responsibility.

Let us have faith in the truth, then. Tell it fearlessly, simply, utterly; and, if God is not able to take care of his own world, why, the sooner it ends and we get into a stage of existence where it is safe to tell the truth, the better.

Have faith in men. Have faith in the people. This it is that we trust to in all our hopes of progress for the future. This it is which distinguished Lincoln among our statesmen. You remember that grand saying of his, true and humorous, so that it sticks in our memory, and we can never forget it, "You can fool all the people a part of the time; you can fool a part of the people all the time; but you can't fool all the people all of the time." Here is the basis on which we rest our republic. Our republic is fallen unless the people are really to be trusted.

Have faith, then, in the people, faith in their healthy instincts, faith in their general sanity, faith in their desire for the right and the true; and this is a genuine exercise of faith, for the past history of the world justifies it.

And, then, have faith in yourself as a child of God. I do not mean conceit now. I do not mean an overestimate of your ability, but belief that you can do great, grand, noble things, belief that you can become something great, noble, grand; belief in the possibility in this life or in some other life of unfolding all that is highest, truest, sweetest, in manhood and womanhood. It is this faith that is able to create the fact and make that which it trusts in.

Let us then believe in God, believe in truth, believe in humanity, believe in ourselves; and then we may work towards the coming of that far, grand time when the dreams of the world shall be realized and its faith shall become reality.

IS LIFE A PROBATION ENDED BY DEATH?

MY subject this morning is an attempted answer to the question, "Is Life a Probation ended by Death?" It will broaden itself naturally, if we cannot accept that theory of it, into the further question, What is the main end and purpose of our life? I take my text from the fifth chapter of the Epistle to the Ephesians, the fifteenth and the sixteenth verses. I will read them as they appear in the Old Version: "See, then, that ye walk circumspectly, not as fools, but as wise, redeeming the time."

The idea of the writer is that, as we pass through the world, we should do it with our eyes kept intelligently open, looking about us on every hand, trying to comprehend the situation, to see what things are, and what we ought to do to play our part in the midst of them. Not heedlessly, not unwisely, he says, perhaps hardly the harsh word "fools," but as wise, as persons intelligently ready to take advantage of the situation and make the most of the condition in which one finds himself; redeeming the time, or, as the Revised Version has it, "buying up the opportunity"; being ready, that is, to pay whatever price is necessary in order to make the most of the situation.

This, then, is the spirit according to our text in which we should look over the problem of life; and this is the method by which we should attempt to guide its practical affairs.

That which people regard as the matter of most importance, any particular theory or plan of life which they may hold to be for them the most desirable, this, of course, is that to which they will direct their chief attention, on which they will lavish their thought, on which they will pour out their care, to which they will consecrate their energies. If now the theory or plan of life be false, if it be inadequate, if one is looking in the wrong direction for the success that he desires, or if he expects to achieve the great end and object of living by means which are not real, which do not match the actual facts of the world and of human life, then of course his effort is so far thrown away. He wastes energies, power, time, enthusiasm on wrong ends which might be used to the attainment of things which are real and fine and high.

Is it not then of the utmost importance that our conception of life, what it is for, what we ought to attempt to reach, and how we should make this attempt, should be an accurate one? Any young man starting out in life, if he sets up for himself a goal which is unworthy, which does not match his faculties and powers, and if he proposes to reach it by means which are not adequate to the attainment of his desires, do you not see how he wrecks and wastes his life? His opportunity is gone; and by and by he wakes up to find that the years have been dissipated, and he has not attained any worthy or noble end.

If this be true of a young man as he looks forward to a scheme or plan of life here during these few short years, how much more is a similar thing true, when we are contemplating not merely the question of a business, or professional or social failure and success, but are looking at the grander and more inclusive theme of the beginning and aim and outcome of life itself We have inherited from the past the idea that this life here, under the blue sky for a few years, as we live it, is a probation, that we are put here on trial, and that death ends it, and that, when we have passed that line, gone over from that which is visible here into the invisible, we are either "lost" or "saved," and things are definitely fixed forever.

I am perfectly well aware that the most of us who are here have given up this idea, though there may remain fragments and suggestions of it in our minds still haunting the chambers of the brain, not yet outgrown, not yet cleared away. But with most people in the modern world, if they are sincere, if they are consistent, the one great question with them is whether they are to be saved or lost in another life. And, if this be the true theory of things, then not only ought men to bend all their thought, their energies, devote their enthusiasms, consecrate their time and money to it as much as they do, but a thousand times more.

We look, perhaps, with a sort of amused curiosity, some of us, from what we regard as our superior point of view, at a man like Mr. Moody; and yet Mr. Moody is one man out of a million for his consistency and consecration to the thought which underlies all the Protestant churches of the modern world, with the exception of a few here and there. Mr. Moody believes that this life is a probation ended by death. There are thousands on thousand on thousands of men who say they believe it, who still cast in all their influence with churches that are based on it, and who yet devote their energies mainly to making money, to attaining social success, to pleasures of one kind or another, to political ambitions, who live as though this great fate were not overhanging the world, who meet their neighbors for pleasure or business, believing, if they are sincere, that this neighbor is heedlessly walking on to the brink of a gulf, and yet never speaking to him about it, never saying a word to imply that they really believe it; and yet this fear hangs over them, haunts their consciousness waking or sleeping; and, if you ask them if they believe it, they will say they suppose they do. In hours of danger, when disease threatens them or they are looking death in the face, they are affrighted, and try to flee to the traditional refuge as a place of safety.

The whole great Catholic Church teaches that nobody has the slightest chance of being saved except by becoming a member of her great body of believers and partaking of her sacramental means of grace.

This, I say then, is the great underlying belief of Christendom; and, if it is true, the world ought to consecrate itself, head and brain and soul, time, money, power, prayer, enthusiasm, everything, to delivering men from the imminent danger. If it is not true, then it ought to be brushed completely one side, put out of consciousness, of thought, of fear. The world ought to be dispossessed of its haunting presence. Why? So that we may fix our attention on the true end and aim of life, and find out what it means to live, how we ought to live, and why and what for, what ought to be the goal of our human endeavor.

So long, then, as this belief does lie at the foundation of all the great churches of Christendom, so long as it is employed in all the criticisms of us who do not any longer accept it, it seems to me that it is worth our while to reconsider the question for a little while, so that we may clear our minds and thoughts, and may fix our attention definitely and earnestly on that which ought to be the goal of all our endeavor, our enthusiasm and our hope.

Let us, then, look for just a few moments at this theory, and see what it means and implies.

It is said that our first father was put on probation, was called upon to decide, not for himself only, but for all his descendants, as to what the future history of the inhabitants of this planet should be. Two famous books were published only a few years ago by Dr. Edward Beecher, the eldest son in that famous family. These were "The Conflict of Ages" and "The Concord of Ages." Dr. Beecher argued that anything like a fair probation on the part of Adam was an impossibility. This in the face of the prevailing beliefs of the time when the books were written. He said that, if a man were to choose on such a momentous question as this, choose adequately, choose fairly, he must be so circumstanced and endowed that he could comprehend the entire result of his choice. He must be able to look down the ages imaginatively, and see on one hand all the line of sin and misery, of death, finite and eternal, which should issue from his choosing in one direction. He must be able to comprehend all the good, the music, the joy, the beauty, the glory, the infinite perfectibility, in this world and the next, which should follow his choice in the other direction. And he said that Adam had no such opportunity as that, and was not endowed with the ability or the experience to make any such momentous choice; in other words, that the fundamental basis of the whole theological scheme of the world was unjust and unfair.

This was Dr. Beecher's contention. How did he get over the difficulty? He believed in the pre-existence of human souls, and that in some other life before Adam there must have been an intelligent and fair choice, and that we here and now are only fighting out one stage of the results of that far-off decision. But, if you will stop to think of it a moment, you will see that this puts the difficulty only a little further back: it does not solve it. How does this first person, if it is so, countless millions of ages ago, happen to be endowed with intelligence and experience and ability enough to make such a momentous choice?

And now just consider a moment. Is it conceivable that a sane person should intelligently choose evil, unless he had some inherited bias or tendency in that direction? For what does the choice of evil mean? It means sorrow, it means pain, it means death, it means everything horrible, everything undesirable, and means that a person deliberately and intelligently pits himself against an infinite and almighty power in what he knows must be an eternally losing battle. Can you conceive of a sane person making such a choice as that?

If one of these first ancestors in the Garden of Eden, or no matter how far back, had a right to choose for himself, I deny his right to choose for me. What right had he to choose for you? What right had he to determine that you should be born with a perverted and corrupt nature, so that you would be certain to choose evil instead of good, helpless in the hands of a fate like this?

Now you may look at this theory any way you please, place this probationary choice at the beginning of human history on this planet, or place it just as far back as you will, it is inconceivable, it is unfair, it is unjust, it is insane, it is everything that is foolish and wrong. And yet, note clearly one thing. So long as the world believes this, so long as the one end and aim of human life, as held up to people, is to be saved, think of the waste, think of the time, the anxiety, the enthusiasms, the prayers, the consecrations; think of the wealth, think of the intellectual faculties, think of the moral devotion, this whole power of the world expended on a false issue, turned into wrong channels!

Is this a dead question? Is there no reason for us to consider it here in this latter part of the nineteenth century? Why, nine-tenths of Christendom to-day is spending its time in trying to propitiate a God who is not angry and trying to "save" souls that are not "lost." Expending its energies along mistaken channels towards issues that are entirely imaginary! Think, for example, if during the last two thousand years all the time and the money, all the intelligence, all the consecration, could have been spent on those things that would have really helped men to find out the meaning of life, and to illustrate that meaning in earnest living; suppose the money that has been spent on the cathedrals, on the monasteries, spent in supporting hordes and hordes of priests, spent in all the endeavor to save men in a future life, if all this had been used in educating men and training them into a comprehension of what kind of beings they really are, what kind of a world this is in which they have found themselves, spent in training them into mastery of themselves, spent in teaching them how to understand and control the forces of nature in order to serve and develop the higher life, think what a civilization might have been developed here on this poor old planet by this time! How much of the disease, how much of the corruption, how much of the unkindness, how much of the cruelty, how much of all that still remains in us of the animal, might have been outgrown, sloughed off, put underneath our feet!

Is it not, then, a vital question, so long as so many thousands, so many millions of people are still consecrating their time, their money, their energy, in the attempt to do that which does not need to be done?

Let us turn, now, and for a little while face another theory of human life; try to find out, or to suggest, what we are here on this planet for, what may be accomplished, how much of grand and true may be wrought out as the result of our attempt.

The philosopher Kant has somewhere said that there are three things needed to the success of a human life, "something to do, some one to love, something to hope for." The old Catechism says that the chief end of man is "to glorify God and enjoy him forever." I indorse the words of Kant; I agree most heartily and thoroughly with the Catechism. Philip James Bailey, the author of that once famous poem "Festus," has said,

"Life's but a means unto an end; that end, Beginning, mean, and end to all things, God."

This also I indorse. I believe that life is something inner, something deeper than that which we ordinarily think of as constituting the matters of chief concern regarding it. Let me quote two or three lines again from Bailey's "Festus," familiar to you because so fine.

We live in deeds, not years; in thoughts, not breaths; In feelings, not in figures on a dial.

We should count time by heart-throbs. "He most lives Who thinks most, feels the noblest, acts the best."

What is human life, then? What is it for? The object of life is living. But what does living mean? Most people cannot answer that question, because they have never more than half lived, and consequently have never appreciated its depth and significance. As I have had occasion over and over and over again, to say to business men, and I like to say it on every opportunity, it seems to me, as I look over the face of society, that most people live only in some little fragmentary way, some corner of their being.

Most men spend their lives in the attempt to accumulate the means to live, and forget to begin to live at all. Sometimes, as you are riding through the country on a winter evening, you come to a silent farm- house, and you see one window lighted; and, if you should go and knock at the door, you would probably find out that the light is shining from the kitchen, where the family is gathered in the evening, perhaps as a matter of economy to save fire, perhaps to save trouble. And, if you examine the lives of these people, you would find that they live chiefly in the kitchen. They may have a sitting-room where they spend a few leisure hours; perhaps they have the beginning of a library; but they do not spend much time in that. They have little opportunity for the life of the parlor, representing the expansive, social human life which comes into contact with other lives. And so you will find that this, which is a figure, represents that which is true of most of us. We have only begun to live; and we live in the lower ranges of our nature, or perhaps we have touched life on a higher level in some tentative sort of way. But the most of us are only partly alive, have only developed a little of what is possible in us, have only come in contact with some fragments of this wonderful universe that is all around us on every hand.

What, then, is the meaning of life? What shall we try to do? What are we here for? I do not attempt to go into the profound explanation of mysteries too deep for me to answer, as to what must have been in the mind of God when he planned and created this universe of which we are a part. My task is a humbler one. Let us see if I can help you comprehend a little part of it. Take an illustration.

An immensely wealthy man suddenly dies, leaving his estates to a little boy seven or eight years of age. He has wide stretches of land, hill and valley, river, woods, all that is beautiful as making up a landscape. The house represents the accumulated resources of the experiences and the intelligence of a lifetime. There are not only beautiful drawing-rooms, telling of taste, but there is a library in which is all that the world has been able to accumulate of learning, of literature in every department. Here is another room containing instruments of music and the works of the great composers. There is an art gallery, containing some of the finest masterpieces in the way of painting and sculpture; and then there is a room devoted to scientific experiments,— chemistry, the microscope, the telescope. Here are means and opportunity for finding out what the world has so far developed.

Now has this young boy come into possession of these things? He has inherited them, he is his father's heir. We say they belong to him; but do they belong to him? In what sense and to what extent do they belong to him? They belong to him just in so far and just as fast as he develops himself into capacity of comprehension and enjoyment, no faster, no farther. As he enters upon his inheritance then he is put under tutors. Some man comes to teach him the languages which he does not comprehend; and by and by that part of the library which is composed of books written in other speech than his own begins to belong to him. It belongs to the tutor a good deal more than it does to the child, until the child has learned the lessons of the tutor. And so another teacher comes to instruct him in art; and the masterpieces of art belong to the person of taste, of culture, with appreciation, to the teacher again, to any one who knows and who feels, instead of to the boy, who merely has possession of the title-deeds.

Do you see the suggestion of the picture? Man wakes up here on this planet what sort of a being? Not at first "a little lower than God," as the old Psalmist says of him, but only a little higher than the animals, ignorant of himself, ignorant of his surroundings, weak, undeveloped in every faculty and power. He begins, we say, to live; and what does that mean? He begins to explore this wonderful world, which is his heritage; and do you not see that along with this exploration there goes of necessity a process of self- development? I would pit against that statement of Kant's a phrase something like this. The object of life is threefold: it is to become all possible, it is to serve all possible, it is to enjoy all possible. But I cannot outline completely either one of these suggestions; for they blend, they intermingle, as you will see in a moment. They are like different notes in a piece of music that are so blended together that they constitute one tune, while separate they are only fragments, or discords.

The first thing, then, if a man wishes really to live, is that he should develop himself, unfold the faculties and powers which lie dormant in him. He is a child of God. He is capable of comprehending within his limit that which is divine. He is capable of being touched, played on, by all the phases and forces of the universe surrounding him. He is an instrument of ten thousand strings; and marvellous may be the music of his life.

First, he should be as complete an animal as possible. Then he should develop himself as a being capable of thinking, of knowing. How many men are there that take possession of the intellectual realm that lies around them on every hand? Just think. Let me hint suggestions, illustrations, in one or two directions. A man goes out for a walk in the park, or, better yet, into the country. The park is too artificial, perhaps, to carry just the meaning that I have in mind. Let it be a walk in the country, then. How much do the grasses and the flowers have to say to him?

I have a friend in Washington, a famous botanist, a botanist not only of all things that live and grow to-day, but who has pushed his researches back and down into the prehistoric ages so as to understand and explain the records, the prints, the leaves and twigs, the forms of every kind that are on the rocks and left to tell the story of a life that has passed away many thousands on thousands of years ago. How much of all this marvellous realm, or even a suggestion of it, is revealed to the ordinary man as he walks through the field?

Look in the direction of geology a moment. Here is a river course; here is the shape of a hill top; do they say anything to the ordinary man who walks with his head down, and occupied with some problem of Wall Street, perhaps? Here are marvels of creative power. God shaped the slope of that hill as really as though he smoothed it down with his hand. And he who understands the methods of world building, of landscape-sculpture, may stand in wonder and awe and reverence before the forces that have been at work for millions of years, and are at work the same to-day. How many men have even a conception of the wonders of the microscopic world? To how many men do the star have anything to say at night? A man looks at a bowlder, unlike any other rock there is to be found anywhere in the neighborhood, and perhaps he does not even ask a question about it; while a man who has made a careful study of these things sees spring up before him in his imagination that long ice age before man lived on the planet, when this bowlder was swept from some far-off place by the glacial power, deposited where it is, scraped on its surface by the passing of the ice, as if God himself had left his sign-manual here, his autograph, that he, in after- ages who might make himself capable of reading, might understand.

These merely as fragmentary, brief hints of what it is to live in the intellectual realm.

Go up to that realm where the intellect is blended with the emotions, the glamour of pictures, poetry, sculpture, music, beauty of color and form and sound. What a world this is, infinite resources of an infinite universe, appealing to, and, if a man responds, calling out the faculties and powers of his own nature that are capable of dealing with these things, so that a man may feel that he is thinking over the thoughts of God, tracing his footsteps, listening to the marvellous music of his words! This is one of the results of self-development, if a man is unfolding, developing himself, becoming as much as possible.

Now let us turn sharply to one of these other phases which I spoke of, of doing what we can to help the world. And now note, this universe is so cunningly contrived that a man cannot possibly be successful as a selfish man. It is one of the most conclusive proofs, it seems to me, not only of the divine goodness, but of the moral meaning and scope of the world. Selfishness is not wicked only, it is the most outrageous folly on the face of the earth. If a man develop himself, if he develops that which is finest in him, that which is best and sweetest and truest, he develops not only his power to think, but his capacity to love, his capacity to enjoy, and to bestow enjoyment; and he cannot possibly succeed in the long run, and in the best ways, on selfish lines.

People used to have a notion that he who grasped and retained everything he could get hold of was the fortunate, the successful man. People had an idea in politics, for example, that that nation was happiest which humbled other nations; and, if it was superior to all the rest, by as much as they were poor and devastated, this nation was fortunate. We know now that a nation finds its prosperity in that of other nations, in its ability to exchange, to trade, to carry on all the grand avocations of life with them. If a man writes a book, he wants the world intelligent enough to understand and appreciate it. If a man paints a picture, he wants artistic ability on the part of the public, so that they will appreciate and buy his pictures. If a man carves a statue, he wants the people to appreciate glory of form enough to see how great and true his work is, and reward him for his endeavor. In other words, no man would write a book, and go off with it alone by himself. No man would paint a picture, and hide it. No man would carve a statue, and conceal it from his fellows.

We have learned, and are learning constantly in every direction, that our happiness is involved in the happiness of other people. The world is haunted to-day and I thank God that it is with the thought of the unhappiness, the misery, of men. What does it mean? It means that men have developed so on their sympathetic side that they cannot be happy themselves while the world is unhappy. So you see that this self- development, which I placed as the chief thing at the outset in the meaning of life, carries with it the necessity on the part of those who are developed, of doing everything they can to develop and lift up everybody else; so that making the most of yourself means making the most of everybody else.

And now, if I turn for a moment to that other point, merely to distinguish it by itself, although I have been dealing with it all the while, the end and aim of life once more is to be happy. I am perfectly well aware that the old Puritan theology has taught otherwise, so far as this life is concerned. I was brought up with the feeling that, if I wanted to do anything, the chances were it was wrong, that it was a good deal more likely to be in the way of virtue if it was something that was disagreeable to me. And yet, curiously enough, this old Puritan theology invented and held up before men, as a lure to lead them to virtue, the most tremendous bribe that ever entered into the imaginations of men, eternal felicity on the one hand, and eternal woe on the other. So that it conceded the very thing that it seemed to deny, that men naturally and necessarily sought happiness, and could not possibly do otherwise.

And so we learn to live, to think, to serve others. We are beginning to learn also that this desire for happiness is natural, is necessary, is right. If a man is not happy, you may be sure there is something wrong. If there is pain in the body, it means disease, difficulty, obstruction, something out of the way. It means that God's laws are not perfectly kept. If there is pain up in the mental realm, pain in the moral realm, pain in the spiritual realm, it means always something wrong. Man ought to be happy. He ought to seek happiness as the great end and outcome of human life.

And we are learning, as the natural and necessary result of our experiences in knowing and in serving, that just in so far as we know the laws of God, just in so far as we obey the laws of God, just in so far as we help others to know and obey, just in so far there comes into our lives the blessedness of the blessed God.

The end of life, then, the object of life here on earth, is to develop ourselves to the utmost. It is to learn to know, take possession of our inheritance, this earth, control all its forces for the service of civilization. It is to rejoice in all this self-development, in all this help, in all this knowledge, in all this power. It is to feel ourselves thrilling with the consciousness that we are sons of God, and are co-operating with him in bringing about the grand result of the ages, the perfection of man.

And then what? Death? This is only one stage of our career. We are here at school; we learn our lessons or we do not; we attain the ends we seek after or we only partly attain them or do not attain them at all; and then we go on. Does that mean that it ends there? I do not believe it. I believe that it simply means that we go out into a larger opportunity, from the planet to the system, to the galaxy, to the universe, wider knowledge answering to more magnificent resources in the infinite universe. We, with undeveloped powers that may increase and advance forever, and a universe so complete, so exhaustless, that it may match and lure and lead and rejoice us forever; we being trained as God's children in God's likeness and helping others to attain the same magnificent ends, this I believe to be the significance, the meaning, the purpose, of life.

Are there any here this morning who think or fear that the taking away of the old idea concerning the results of Lying may remove moral motive, may undermine character, nay make people less careful to do right? It seems to me hat, if people understand the significance of this universe, and their relation to it, they will find that all the carelessness of motive, the ease of salvation, as they call it, is with the old idea. Our theory is a more strenuous and insistent one. Children are learning as they become wiser that evil is not only evil, but it is folly. A man wishes life, health, happiness, prosperity, all good. He learns, as he goes on, that the universe is in favor of the keeping of its own laws; and that, f he flings himself against the forces of the universe, he is only broken for his pains. If you wish to be healthful, sappy, strong, wish to attain any desirable thing, it is to be bound not in defiance of the laws of the universe, but in loving and tender obedience.

And, then, if you only remember that in this universe and coder the universal law of cause and effect you are building to-morrow out of to-day, and next week and next year, and all he future, that every thought, every word, every action, is cemented together as a part of this structure that you build, hat you can make your own future for good or ill, and that you cannot build it successfully except in accordance with he eternal laws of things, then you find that here are the most insistent and tremendous motives it is possible for the human mind to conceive.

This life of ours, if we lead it nobly and truly, then, we shall find to be a growth into the likeness of the Divine, a growth into an increasing opportunity to share the work of our Father in building and helping men, and that, as the result of this, joy, infinite joy, is to fill our hearts until we share the very blessedness of our Father.

God made our lives to be a song Sweet as the music of the spheres, That still their harmonies prolong For him who rightly hears. The heavens and the earth do play Upon us, if we be in tune: Winter shouts hoarse his roundelay, And tender sweet pipes June. But oftentimes the songs are pain, And discord mars our harmonies: Our strings are snapped by selfish strain, And harsh hands break our keys. But God meant music; and we may, If we will keep our lives in tune, Hear the whole year sing roundelay, December answering June. God ever at his keyboard plays, Harmonics, right; and discords, wrong: "He that hath ears," and who obeys, May hear the mystic song.

SIN AND ATONEMENT.

For the sake of clearness, and in order that you may definitely comprehend the doctrine of sin and atonement which I believe to be the true one, I need in the first place to outline as a background that which lies at the foundation of all the popular theologies of Christendom. I am perfectly well aware that at least a part of the time, while I am doing this, I shall be traversing ground with which you are already familiar. Some of it, however, I think may be somewhat strange to you.

The tradition begins with the story of a war in heaven. In some way rebellion began among the angels; and he who had been Lucifer, the light-bearer, prince among the glorious sons of God, took up arms of rebellion against the Almighty. Naturally, he failed in this inevitably losing battle, and was cast out into the abyss, with a third part of all the angels, who had followed him. Then the tradition goes on: God decided to create the world, that the sons of men born and trained here might ultimately take the places that had been held by the angels who had been cast out on account of their sin. But Satan, seeing this fair and beautiful earth, this wondrous handiwork of God, determined, if possible, to thwart and defeat the purposes of the Almighty. He therefore invades this beautiful world. He finds Adam and Eve in their condition of perfect felicity, innocent, but inexperienced; and they fall a ready prey to his intention.

They then share his rebellion, accept him instead of God as king. Henceforth they are followers of him in his age-long warfare against light and truth, and, unless in some way saved, are to be sharers of his eternal destiny, cast out into chains and darkness forever.

Now comes the necessity for noting for a moment the nature of sin on this theory. You see it is not ignorance, it is not weakness merely, it is not inherited passion only: it is conscious and purposeful rebellion against God, putting yourself at enmity with his truth, his righteousness, his love. In action it is some specific deed done against God or against his truth or his right. As a state of mind, it is a heart perverted, choosing always that which is evil, a heart at enmity with God and with all that is good; and the theologians have always been obliged, as a matter of consistency, to hold, no matter how noble, how unselfish men might appear to be, that the natural man has inherently, always, necessarily been evil. He carries about with him the taint of original sin; that is, sin of constitution, ingrained, inherited, that which is of the very fibre of his being. This is the character of man as required by the old theological systems; and this is how it happened to come about. Evil is not something natural, not imperfection, not something undeveloped, not yet outgrown. Sin originated outside of this world, invaded it, and worked its ruin and destruction.

Now comes the device that has been called the Atonement, by which it is supposed that God is going to be able to save at least a part of this rebellious humanity. There have been a good many different theories of the atonement that have been held, eighteen or twenty varieties of the doctrine, three or four of which I must outline, in order to make them clear to your mind, that you may see what have been the devices by which the theologians have supposed that they could find a way for the deliverance of man from this condition of loss, and fit him to share the felicity for which he was originally intended.

Of course, the main point in the whole scheme is that the Second Person of the Trinity becomes incarnate, comes down here to this world, is born, grows up, teaches, suffers and at last is put to an ignominious death. This is the central idea of the doctrine of the atonement; or, rather, the Christ is the central figure in that doctrine. But how is it supposed to work out the atonement that is necessary, in order that man may be saved? You will see that the world, according to the ideas I have been delineating, is in a condition of rebellion. What men need is to be persuaded that they are wrong, convinced of sin, in theological language, and then made repentant, and in some way be forgiven for the wrong which they have done.

Now it is supposed that God must invent some scheme by which to make it possible for him to save these lost and fallen men. If you read the parable of the Prodigal Son as Jesus has so tenderly, touchingly, beautifully outlined it for us, you will see that there is no thought or plan or necessity for either in that. The son left his home, followed the impulses and passions of youth, had gone among those that were degraded, had soiled his character, done despite to his father's love, injured his own nature, degraded himself by his associations and actions. But when at last he awakes, becomes conscious of his father's love and righteousness and truth, and says, "I will arise, and go to my father," there is no talk of God's not being ready to receive him, or not being able to receive him, or needing to have something done before he can receive him, no thought of anybody's suffering any more in order that he may be forgiven. You see all these elements that are associated with the popular doctrines of atonement are not once thought of, never even alluded to. He simply arises, and goes to his father; and his father is so anxious to help him that he goes to meet him before he reaches the father's house, and gladly falls on his neck and kisses him and folds him in his arms. It only needs that the son should recognize the righteousness and goodness of his father, and should wish to go back. That is the doctrine of Jesus as taught in this wonderfully sweet and beautiful parable.

Now what are the theories of atonement as outlined in the popular theology? For the first thousand years of Christian history one of the strangest conceptions possessed the ecclesiastical mind that has ever been dreamed of. It was held literally that through the sin of Adam the human race had become the rightful subjects of Satan, that they belonged to him. He was their king, their emperor, their ruler, and had a right to them in this world and the next. And so some diplomatic negotiations must be entered into with the Devil, in order to deliver a certain part of these his subjects, and open the way for them to be saved. So the Church Fathers taught that Satan recognized in Christ his old adversary in heaven, and he entered into a bargain with God that, if he could have Christ delivered over to him, in exchange for that he would give up his right to so many of the souls of men as were to be saved as the result of this compact. So the work of the atonement used to be preached as being this sort of bargain entered into with Satan.

But note what quaint, naive ideas possessed the minds of people at that time. Satan did not know that Jesus possessed a divine nature, and that, consequently, he could not beholden of death; and so, when he entered into this bargain, he was cheated, he found out to his dismay that he had lost not only humanity, but Christ also, had been defrauded of them both. This was the doctrine of the atonement that was preached during the early centuries of the Christian Church, at least in certain parts of Europe.

But later there came another doctrine, the belief that the sufferings of the Christ were a substitute offered to God for what would have been the sufferings of the lost. He was made sin for us, he who had known no sin, as the New Testament phraseology has it. So that he, being infinite, in a brief space of time during his little earthly career, during his suspension on the cross and his descent into hell, was able to suffer as much pain as all the lost would have suffered throughout eternity. And this suffering of the Christ was supposed to be accepted on the part of God as the substitute for that which he would have exacted on the part of the souls of those that for his sake were to be saved.

There is still another theory that I must mention briefly, that which is called the governmental theory, that which I was taught during my course of theological instruction. The idea was that God had a moral government to maintain, not only on this earth, but throughout the range of the universe among all his intelligent creatures, and, if he permitted his laws to be broken without exacting an adequate penalty, then all governmental authority would be overthrown. In other words, men took their poor human legal devices, their political ideals, and lifted them into the heavens, made them the models after which it was supposed God was to govern his great, intelligent universe.

So they said God would be willing to forgive, he would like to forgive, he was loving and tender and kind, but it was not safe, safe for the interests of his universal government, for him to forgive any one until an adequate penalty had been paid in expiation of human sin.

You see, according to this theory, it does not apparently make much difference who it is that suffers, whether it is the person who has committed the sin or not; but somebody must pay an adequate penalty, and Jesus volunteered to do this, to be the victim, and so to deliver man from the righteous deserts which he had incurred as a transgressor of the law of God.

Gradually, however, as the world became civilized, as wider and broader thoughts manifested themselves in the human mind, as tenderer and truer feelings took possession of the human heart, these theories receded into the background; and there came to the front I remember the bitter controversies over it in my younger days what was called the Moral Theory of the Atonement. The originator and sponsor for this theory was the famous Dr. Horace Bushnell, of Hartford. He taught that God did not need the punishment of anybody to uphold the integrity of his moral government. He taught that God was not angry with the race, and did not care to exact a penalty before he was ready to forgive human sin. He taught that the inner nature of God was love, and that in the Second Person of the Trinity he came to earth, was born, grew up, taught, suffered, died, as a manifestation to the world of his love, of his goodness, of his readiness to forgive and help, and that the efficacy of the atonement as thus wrought on the part of the Christ was in its revelation to men of the love and saving power of righteousness.

This was the moral theory of the atonement. It was not supposed to work any result in the nature of God or his disposition towards men. Its effect was to work along the lines of human thought and human action: it was to affect men, and make them willing to be saved instead of making God willing to save them. This was the moral theory of the atonement; and you will see how it gradually approaches that which intelligent and free men, it seems to me, must hold to-day in the light of their careful study of human history and human nature. It is almost the theory which is being held by the freest and noblest men of to-day. The difference between it and that which I shall in a moment try to set forth is chiefly that Dr. Bushnell confines this work of the atonement to the person and history and character of one man instead of letting all men share in this divine and atoning work which is being wrought out through all the ages.

Let me now come to set forth what I believe to be the simple and demonstrated truth. My objections against this old theory are threefold. I will mention them, and have done with them in a word.

In the first place, the supposed origin of sin in heaven seems to me so absurd as to be utterly unthinkable. This idea of war in heaven, rebellion against God, smacks too much of the Old World traditions, of the mythologies of Greece and Rome and of other peoples. Jupiter could dethrone his father, the god Saturn, because Saturn was not almighty and all-wise. These gods of the ancient time were merely exaggerated types of human heroes and despots. There could be war among them, and one of them overthrown; and Jupiter could divide the universe, after he had conquered and dethroned his father, with his two brothers.

All this is reasonable, when you are talking about finite creatures; but try to think for one moment of an archangel, a pure and clear-eyed intelligence, deliberately choosing to rebel against Omnipotence! He must have known it would be utterly, absolutely, forever hopeless! Intelligent creatures do not rebel under conditions like that, particularly when you combine with the absolute hopelessness of the case the fact that he knew he was choosing misery, suffering, forever.

As I said, the whole conception of the origin of evil that implies the rebellion of a spiritual being who knew what he was doing is inexpressibly absurd, so absurd that we may dismiss it as impossible. If there were any such rebellion, if you waive the absurdity for the moment and consider the possibility, God would be responsible; for he made him. The whole theory is not only absurd: it is unjust in its implications towards both God and man. And then, and perhaps we need not say any more about it, we know that it is not true. It did not even originate in the Bible, it did not even originate among the Jews: it is nothing in the world but a pagan myth imported into Jewish tradition just a few hundred years before the birth of Jesus. It is of no more authority in rational human thought than the story of Jason or Hercules, not one particle.

Let us now turn, then, to what we know, from the history of man and the scientific study of the universe, to be something approaching the reality of things. People have always been talking about the origin of evil. It is not the origin of evil that we have to face or deal with or explain at all. Let me ask you to consider for a moment the condition of the world when man first appeared on this planet. Here among the lower animals were what? All the vices and all the crimes that we can conceive of, only they were not vices nor crimes at all. There were all the external actions and all the internal feelings and passions; but they were not vices, and they were not crimes. Why? Because there was no moral sense which recognized anything better, no moral standard in the light of which they might be judged.

Here, for example, in this lower world, were all hatreds, jealousies, envies, cruelties, thefts, greeds, murders, every kind of action that we speak of as evil in man. And yet I said there was no evil there, no moral evil there, because there was no consciousness, no recognition, of the distinction between the lower and the higher. This was a part of the natural and intended order of the development of life, not an accident, not an invasion from the outside, not a thwarting of the will of God, not an interference with his purpose, all of this a part of the working out of his purpose.

Now, when man appeared, what happened? The origin, not of evil, but the origin of goodness. A conscience was born. Man came into possession of a moral ideal, in the light of which he recognized something higher than this animalism that was all around him, and became conscious of the fact that he must battle against that, and put it under his feet. So that the life of the world, from that day to this, has been the growth, the gradual increase, and the gradual conquest of good over that which was in existence before.

There is no fall of man, then, there is no conscious and purposeful rebellion against God to be accounted for, there is no need of any devil to explain the facts. He is only an encumbrance, only in the way, only makes it difficult and practically impossible to solve our problem.

The old story was that, after the rebellion, pain and death and all evil came into the human world; and the natural world was blighted. Thorns and briers and thistles sprang up on every hand; and animals which before had been peaceful began to fight and destroy each other. We all know this to be a childish myth, and pagan. The actual history of the world has been something entirely other than that.

Now I do not wish that you should suppose that I minimize evil, that I make light of sin, that I do not properly estimate the cruelties and the wrongs that have devastated the world. I need only suggest to you that you look in this direction and that to see how hideous all these evils may be; how bitter, how cruel, is the fruit of wrong thoughts and of wrong actions. Look at a man, for example, divine in the possibilities of his being, but through vice, through drink, through habits of one kind and another, corrupted until it is an insult to a brute to call him brutal. We do not deny all this. Notice the cruelties of men towards each other, the jealousies, the envies, the strifes, the warfares. How one class looks down upon and treats with contempt another that is a little lower! How masters have used their slaves; how tyrants like Nero and Caligula have made themselves hideous spectacles of what is possible to humanity, on a stage that is world-wide and illuminated by the flash-lights of history!

I do not wish you to suppose for a moment that I belittle, that I underestimate these evils, only we do not need anything other than the scientific and historic facts of the world in order to account for them. What is sin, as science looks at it and treats it? Not something consciously and purposely developed, not something originating in a rebellion in some other world than this. It seems to me that we can very easily account for it when we recognize that man has been gradually coming up from the lower orders of life, and that he still has in him the snake and the hyena, the wolf, the tiger, the bear, all the wild, fierce passions of the animal world only partly sloughed off, not yet outgrown; when you remember how ignorant he is, how he does not understand yet the meaning of these divine laws and the divine life, glimpses of which now and then attract his attention and lure him on; when you remember that selfishness, misguided by ignorance, can believe that one man can get something for his behoof and happiness and good at the expense of the welfare of somebody else, and harm come only to the person that is defrauded. Right in here, if I had time to treat it in still further detail, it seems to me we have a simple and adequate explanation of all the evil that has ever blasted, blighted, and darkened the history of man.

Now, man being this kind of a creature, having an animal origin as well as a divine one, gradually climbing up out of this lower life and looking towards God as his ideal, what is it that he needs? Is there any need of atonement? All need of atonement! What does atonement mean? The word itself carries its clearest explanation. In its root it means "atonement," healing the division, whatever its nature or kind, bringing man into one-ness with God and men into one-ness with each other.

Now let me suggest to you a little as to the things that keep man and God apart, keep men away from each other; and they will suggest the atonement that is needed to heal all these divisions, and bring about that ideal condition of things that we dream of and pray for and talk about, when men shall perfectly love God, and when they shall love each other as themselves.

What is it that keeps man from God? First, it seems to me, it is ignorance. What man needs in order to bring him into oneness with God is first to have some clear conceptions of the divine, some high, sweet, noble thoughts of God, some knowledge of the laws of God as embodied in himself and in the universe around him. Man needs intelligence, then, to help him, needs education.

In the next place, he needs such a picture of God as shall; make him seem lovable. You cannot make the human heart love that which seems hateful. The picture of God, as he has been outlined to the world in the past, has repelled the human heart; and I do not wonder. I do not think it strange that humanity should be at enmity with that conception of the divine. Make God the ideal of all that is noble and sweet and lovely, and the heart will be as naturally attracted and drawn to him as a flower is toward the sun.

Then man needs to have his spiritual side developed, that in him which is akin to God, so that he shall naturally live out the divine love. Education, then, is all on man's side, you will see. God does not need to be changed: we need to know him, to love him, to come into conscious relationship with him. This is what we need, so far as our relation to God is concerned.

Now for the more important side; for it is infinitely the more important practically. Let me speak a little while of the work of atonement between man and man. If we trace the history of humanity, we find that men were scattered in groups all over the world, isolated, separated from each other, ignorant of each other, misunderstanding each other, hating each other, fighting each other; and the work of some other world than this. It seems to me that we can very easily account for it when we recognize that man has been gradually coming up from the lower orders of life, and that he still has in him the snake and the hyena, the wolf, the tiger, the bear, all the wild, fierce passions of the animal world only partly sloughed off, not yet outgrown; when you remember how ignorant he is, how he does not understand yet the meaning of these divine laws and the divine life, glimpses of which now and then attract his attention and lure him on; when you remember that selfishness, misguided by ignorance, can believe that one man can get something for his behoof and happiness and good at the expense of the welfare of somebody else, and harm come only to the person that is defrauded. Right in here, if I had time to treat it in still further detail, it seems to me we have a simple and adequate explanation of all the evil that has ever blasted, blighted, and darkened the history of man.

Now, man being this kind of a creature, having an animal origin as well as a divine one, gradually climbing up out of this lower life and looking towards God as his ideal, what is it that he needs? Is there any need of atonement? All need of atonement! What does atonement mean? The word itself carries its clearest explanation. In its root it means "atonement," healing the division, whatever its nature or kind, bringing man into one-ness with God and men into one- ness with each other.

Now let me suggest to you a little as to the things that keep man and God apart, keep men away from each other; and they will suggest the atonement that is needed to heal all these divisions, and bring about that ideal condition of things that we dream of and pray for and talk about, when men shall perfectly love God, and when they shall love each other as themselves.

What is it that keeps man from God? First, it seems to me, it is ignorance. What man needs in order to bring him into oneness with God is first to have some clear conceptions of the divine, some high, sweet, noble thoughts of God, some knowledge of the laws of God as embodied in himself and in the universe around him. Man needs intelligence, then, to help him, needs education.

In the next place, he needs such a picture of God as shall: make him seem lovable. You cannot make the human heart: love that which seems hateful. The picture of God, as he has been outlined to the world in the past, has repelled the human heart; and I do not wonder. I do not think it strange that humanity should be at enmity with that conception of the divine. Make God the ideal of all that is noble and sweet and lovely, and the heart will be as naturally attracted and drawn to him as a flower is toward the sun.

Then man needs to have his spiritual side developed, that in him which is akin to God, so that he shall naturally live out the divine love. Education, then, is all on man's side, you will see. God does not need to be changed: we need to know him, to love him, to come into conscious relationship with him. This is what we need, so far as our relation to God is concerned.

Now for the more important side; for it is infinitely the more important practically. Let me speak a little while of the work of atonement between man and man. If we trace the history of humanity, we find that men were scattered in groups all over the world, isolated, separated from each other, ignorant of each other, misunderstanding each other, hating each other, fighting each other; and the work of civilization means to bring men together, to work out an atonement between nation and nation, religion and religion, family and family, man and man.

Here, again, as in the case of God, the first thing that needs to be overcome is ignorance. Look back no further than our late war. I think every careful student of that tremendous conflict is ready to say to-day that, if the North and South had been acquainted with each other, known each other as they know each other now, the war would have been impossible. We need to know other men. As you go back, you find curious traditions illustrating this ignorance of different nations and different peoples of each other. Plato, for example, taught it as a virtue that the Athenians should hate all other peoples except the Greeks and all other Greek cities except Athens; and they spoke of the outside nations that did not speak Greek as barbarians, people who could not talk, people who, when they essayed to speak, said, "Ba, ba," misusing words and expressions. They had traditions of men who carried their heads under their arms, who had only one eye, which was in the middle of their forehead, all sorts of monstrosities in human shape, antagonistic to the rest of mankind.

Even in modern times those ignorances, misconceptions, and prejudices are far from being outgrown. Lord Nelson counted it as a virtue in an Englishman that he should hate a Frenchman as he did the devil. How many people are there to- day who look with an unprejudiced eye upon a foreigner?

The things, then, that keep nations apart are ignorance. Then there is the lack of sympathy. You will find people walking side by side here in our streets, people in the same family, who find it impossible to understand each other.

They cannot put themselves in the place of another; they cannot comprehend something which is a little different from what they are accustomed to hear; not only cannot they understand it, they cannot lovingly or patiently look at it. Think of the things that have kept people apart in physical and mental and spiritual realms, the rivers, the mountain chains, the oceans; differences of religion, differences of language, differences of civilization; different ethical ideas, until people of the world have sat looking at each other with faces of fear and antagonism instead of with the dawning in their eyes of love and brotherhood.

Now what the world needs is something to atone, to bridge over these differences, to bring men into sympathetic and loving acquaintance with each other. I wish to note two or three things that have wrought very largely and effectively in this direction. Does it ever occur to you that commerce is something besides a means for the accumulation of wealth? Commerce has played one of the largest parts in the history of this world in atoning the differences, the antagonisms, between nation and nation and man and man. It has taught the world that there is a community of interests, and that, instead of fighting each other, they are mutually blessed and helped by coworking, co-operating, exchanging with each other.

So the inventors, the discoverers, have helped to bring about this sense of human brotherhood, this community of human interests. How much, for example, was wrought when the electric wire was placed under the seas, and, instead of allowing weeks and weeks for a misunderstanding to grow and for ill-feeling to ferment between England and this country, puts us in such quick relations that a misapprehension could be corrected in an hour. All these things have helped bring the world together, are engaged in this magnificent religious service of atonement, of making nations one, making humanity one, a family.

I do not wish you to suppose that I misunderstand or underestimate the work of the Christ in this direction. He has done a grander work of atonement than any other figure in the history of the world. He revealed to us the glory, the tenderness, the love, of God, and so lifted the heart of the world towards the Father as no other one man has done who has ever lived. And, then, he lived out and manifested the glory, the tenderness, the wonder, of human character and human life as hardly any other man who has ever lived; and on so world- wide a stage did he do this that the influence of his work has overrun all national barriers, and is rapidly coming to be world-wide, and in admiration of, and love for him, Jew and Greek, and barbarian, Scythian, Arabian, European, and Asiatic, all the nations of the world are becoming one. For no matter what their theory may be about him, whether they hold him to be God or man, they hold the ideal that he set forth and lived to be spiritually human and nobly divine. So Jesus is more and more, as the ages go by, helping us to one-ness with God, helping us into sympathetic one-ness with each other.

But I would not have you think that Jesus is the only one who has wrought atonement for the sin of the world. Every man in his degree, in so far as he has been divine and human, patient, faithful, has rendered service to the world, has done his part in bringing about this magnificent consummation.

Look for a moment at Abraham Lincoln. Think what he did by the atoning sacrifice of his life for liberty, for humanity, for truth. On the one hand, his murderer showed what sin may come to in its ignorance, its misconception, its antagonism to whatever is right and good and true. And, on the other hand, he, with words of forgiveness on his lips, words of human love, with all tenderness and charity in his heart, illustrated again and lived out the sweetness of divinity and the tenderness of humanity.

As another illustration, human, simple, natural, just let me say a word concerning the act, the attitude, of General Grant at Appomattox. He did more at the surrender of Lee to send a thrill of brotherly sympathy through North and South and help wield this nation into one than he could have possibly done by the most magnificent achievement of arms, when he refused to take his opponent's sword; when he let the officers go away with their side-arms; when he told each man that his horse or his mule was still of right his because he would need it to begin the new life again that was before him.

Facts like these suggest the naturalness, the humanness, as well as the God-likeness of the work of atonement that is going on all over the world, as it climbs and swings slowly up out of the darkness and into the light of life. Jesus the great atoning sacrifice? Yes, but thousands on thousands of others atoning in just the same divine way, just the same human way, just as naturally, just as necessarily. Every man who does an honest day's work, every man who is kind and loving in his family, every man who is helpful as a neighbor, every man who stands faithfully by his convictions of truth, every man who shows that he cares more for the truth than he does for worldly success, that he knows that in that truth only is immortality, and that it is greater and better and sweeter than even life, every man who consecrates himself in this way is doing his part towards working out the atonement of human sin, the reconciliation of man with God, the reconciliation of men with each other.

Let us, then, while loving Jesus, while reverencing him for the grandeur of his work and the beauty of his life, let us rise and claim kinship with him, rise to the dignity and glory of the thought that we are sons of God as he was, and that we may share with him the grandest service that one man can render to his time, the helping of people to find and love and serve God, the helping of people to discover and love and serve each other. The outcome of this atoning work is simply the coming of that time which we speak of familiarly without half comprehending it, when the world shall recognize the universal Fatherhood of God and the universal brotherhood of man.

PRAYER, AND COMMUNION WITH GOD

SOME years ago I heard a minister, then widely known throughout the country, say in a public address, "Prayer is the power that moves the arm that moves the world." Can we accept that to-day as a definition of a rational view of the relation in which we stand to God? Many of you will remember that not long ago the churches and the scientific men of England and America were much stirred and roused over a discussion concerning the practical efficacy of prayer. There was much talk of what was called the "prayer-gauge." I think it was Professor Tyndall who proposed to test the question as to whether prayer was a real power in the physical world; and his test, if I remember rightly, was something like this. He said: You churchmen claim that prayer is able to heal the sick. Now, he said, let us take a certain hospital. We will divide it, a certain number of wards on one side, and a certain number of wards on the other, equalizing so far as we can the nature of the illnesses which afflict the patients. You now concentrate as much as you please, and as many as you please, the prayers on certain wards in the hospital, and we will commit the rest to the ordinary treatment of the physicians; and we will see if you are able to produce any results.

Against a certain type and theory of prayer I suppose a test like that is legitimate enough; and this type, this theory, is the one that has prevailed throughout Christendom largely for a good many hundreds of years. I suppose you can remember in your boyhood some of you are as old as I that it was not an uncommon thing for the minister to pray earnestly for certain things that intelligent men would hardly think of praying for in the same fashion to-day. It was not an uncommon thing, a few years ago, to have a special prayer- meeting during a drought in the endeavor to prevail upon God to send the rain; and there was certainly a Scriptural warrant for it; for Elijah is represented in the Old Testament as having, by the power of prayer, shut up the heavens for three years and a half, and then as bringing rain again as the result of his petition. If you study the Book of James, and remember, when you do study it, that it was not written by the apostle, but by some unknown author towards the middle of the second century, you will see that he teaches that, if any one is sick, you are not to send for a physician. The brethren are to assemble, the invalid is to be anointed with oil, they are to pray over him, and the explicit and unqualified promise is given that the prayer of faith shall save the sick. And yet we have been confronted for ages with the spectacle of people breaking their hearts in pleading prayer for those that were sick, and seeing them fade and vanish from their sight in spite of their petitions.

41

I have heard it said a good many times that the fame of the Cunard line of steamships touching the matter of the safety of its passengers was to be explained by the piety of the founders of the line, and the fact that they prayed every time a ship sailed that it might safely cross the seas and land its passengers without accident in the wished-for haven. Are there no prayers for other lines? Has no one ever prayed on behalf of a ship that did meet with an accident? But this would be explained on this theory by saying that the prayer was not the prayer of faith or that there was some defect in it somewhere.

I refer to these things simply by way of illustration to recall to your mind that prayer used to be supposed to be a power touching the winds, the waves, the prosperity of the crops, insuring safety during a dangerous journey; that it was a power that was able to heal disease, that could accomplish all sorts of strange and startling effects in the physical realm.

And now I simply wish to call your attention to the naturalness of that kind of prayer in the olden time. To some of us this thought may seem strange, it may seem almost absurd, to-day; but remember it was not strange, it was not absurd, in the times when the old theory of the universe was thoroughly believed in, not only by church members, but by scientific men as well.

What was that old conception? I have had occasion to refer to it in one connection or another a good many times; and now I shall have to refer to it again, so that you may clearly see what is involved in this question of the efficacy of prayer. God was supposed to be up in heaven, away from nature. Nature was a sort of mechanism, a machine that ordinarily ran on after its own fashion. God had made it, indeed, in some sense, God supported it continually; but it went on apart from him, and he was away from it. He was, as Carlyle used to say, looked upon as an absentee God. He was up in heaven. He ruled this world as the Kaiser rules Germany, arbitrarily. He was not even always supposed to know everything that was going on, at least, if you are to judge by the tone of the prayers of a good many people such as I have heard. He needed information concerning matters. He needed to be pleaded with, that he might interfere and accomplish some results that would not otherwise take place. He ruled the world arbitrarily and from a distance.

Now, if any German wishes a certain thing accomplished that would not happen in the ordinary course of nature and human life, he knows that the Kaiser has almost unlimited power; and, if he can persuade him to undertake it, it may be accomplished. So he will send a petition to the Kaiser; and he will back that petition with all the influence that he is able to bring to bear upon it. If there is a prime minister who stands specially high in favor with the Kaiser, do you not see how much might be accomplished by winning his ear, and getting him to intercede on behalf of the petitioner? Do you not see right in there the parallel to the old idea that used to dominate us in regard to the government of the universe? If only we could get God interested in the matter, if we could bring to bear upon him an adequate amount of influence, if we could get Jesus to intercede with him, then something might be accomplished.

Are these antiquated ideas? I received a letter only a little while ago. It told me nothing new; but it came to me with a shock, roused me to a recognition of ideas still dominant and popular in the common mind. It was from a Catholic. He said: We do not worship Mary; but she is in the spirit world, and she is in sympathetic relation with this world's sorrow and trouble. We pray to her, asking her to intercede with her son, because a mother's influence is efficacious. Think for a moment of the implications of this theory of governing the universe. God is away off, has forgotten us, or does not care, at any rate, is not doing for us the things we need. If we can get Jesus to intercede! But, according to this Catholic theory, Jesus had perhaps forgotten or was not attentive. So he pleads with his mother, and gets the mother to exert her influence on Jesus so he may exert his influence on God, and at last something may be done. I confess to you, friends, that this theory of things does not seem piety to me, but the precise opposite.

I ask you now to follow me while I attempt to point out some of the difficulties that confront us in this old-time theory of prayer. Why is it that we cannot pray to God to change the order of the natural world? Why cannot we believe that prayer is the power that moves the arm that moves the world??? Why cannot I consistently pray to God to heal my disease or the disease of a friend, or to save the soul of some friend who would otherwise be neglected by the divine care? Why cannot I any longer pray to God to send his light and truth to the heathen world? Why cannot I pray to him to insure my safety in mid-Atlantic, to do something to prevent my colliding with a derelict, as the Van-dam has done during the last few days? Do you think there was no one on that ship that prayed? What is the difficulty in the mind of the intelligent, modern thinker when he faces this conception of prayer?

Let us think a little clearly just a moment; and I imagine I can make it plain. We no longer think of God we cannot think of him as outside the system of nature, and as possibly interfering with it to produce a result that would not otherwise take place. Why? Because God is the soul, the mind, the heart of nature. The forces of the universe, acting according to their changeless and eternal laws, are simply God at work. And, when I pray to God to interfere, I am praying him to interfere with himself, I am praying him to contradict his own wisely and eternally and changelessly established methods of controlling the world.

The question is sometimes asked, but a man can interfere with the course of nature, and produce a result that would not be naturally produced without it? Certainly, because man does not stand in this relation to natural forces. But man, however, does not change any law, he does not interfere with any law. He simply discovers some law and obeys it, and in that way produces a result that would not otherwise be produced. But man does not stand, I say, in this vital relation to the forces of the universe and their laws. When you remember that these forces working, as I said, changelessly, eternally, after their methods, when you remember that these are God in his ceaseless and wise and loving activity, then do you not see that he cannot contradict or interfere with himself? Here is the great difficulty in regard to this old method, this old conception of prayer which confronts the intelligent, the educated, the thoughtfully devout man.

When I was first struggling out into the light? as it seems to me now from my old theological training, I met another difficulty that I think will appeal to you. It seemed to me an impertinence for me to be telling God, as I heard so many people on every hand, all sorts of things that he knew before. I reconsidered the words of Jesus, You are not to give yourself to much speaking in your prayers, for your Father knoweth what you have need of before you ask him. And then there was another difficulty which troubled me more than any of the others, a delightful, splendid difficulty it has seemed to me since those days. It was connected with the thought of God's goodness and love. There are heathen, they tell us, who have got a glimpse, from their point of view, of this fact about God. It is said they do not bring any offerings, except some flowers, to the deities they regard as good, because, they say, they do not need to be persuaded. They bring all their costly offerings to the bad gods, the ones they are afraid of; and they attempt to buy their favor or buy off their anger.

When I waked up to the free and grand conception of the eternal love and the boundless goodness of the Father, then it seemed to me that many of my prayers in the past had been so far from reasonable that they were absurd, and so far from piety that they were wrong. To illustrate what I mean. When I was minister of an orthodox church in the West, a lovely, faithful lady came to me to raise some question touching this matter of prayer. It had been suggested, I suppose, by something I had said; and I asked her this question: What would you think of me if I should come to you, and with pathos in my voice, and perhaps with tears in my eyes, plead with you to be kind to your own children, beg you to give them something to eat, beseech you to furnish them with clothes, entreat you to educate them, to do the best for them that you knew how? What would you think of it? I asked. She said, I should feel insulted. And I replied, Do you not think that God is almost as good as you are?

If you are anxious and ready, do you think that God needs to be pleaded with and entreated and besought in order to make him willing, in order to make him kind, in order to bring some sort of pressure to bear upon him so that he will do the things for his children of which they most stand in need? No scientific difficulty, no question of theories of the universe, has ever affected my practice in the matter of prayer so much as this overwhelming, blessed thought of the loving-kindness and care of the infinite Father. He does not need to be informed, he does not need to be persuaded. Has not Jesus told us that your heavenly Father is more ready to give the things which you need than you are to give good gifts to your children?

And so I came to have a difficulty with the kind of prayer- meetings in which I was brought up as a boy, and which I used to lead as a young and earnest minister. I have heard kinds of prayers which have seemed to me reflections on the goodness and the kindness of our Father in heaven. I remember one man I used to hear him over and over again, week by week who would pray, It is time for thee, O God, to work! And, as I came to think of it, it hurt my sense of reverence. I shrank from it. And I could not believe that God was going to let thousands of souls in China or Africa perish merely because Christians in America did not pray hard enough and long enough for their salvation. Why should they meet with eternal doom on account of the lack of enthusiasm or devotion of people of whom they have never heard?

So I used to find myself troubled about this question of praying so hard for the salvation of other people's souls. If, as the old creeds tell us, it is settled from all eternity as to just who is to be saved and who is to be lost, there would hardly seem place for a vital prayer; and if, as a friend of mine, a minister, and a very liberal and broad one, though in one of the older churches, said to me, "I believe that God will save every single soul that he can save," then do you not see again that it touches this kind of prayer? If he cannot save them, then why should I beg him to do it? If he can, and loves them better than I do, again, why should I plead with him after that fashion to do it?

These, frankly and freely spoken, are some of the difficulties connected with a certain theory of prayer.

I gladly put all that now behind my back, and come to the grand and positive side of my theme. I wish to tell you what I myself believe in regard to this matter of prayer. And, in the first place, let me suggest to you that prayers, even the prayers of the past, any of them, the most objectionable types, are not made up only of petition; they are not all begging, teasing for things. There enter into their composition gratitude, adoration, reverence, aspiration, a sense of communion with the spiritual Being, a longing for higher and finer things; a sense of refuge in time of trouble, a sense of strength in time of need, a sense of hope, uplift, and outlook as we glance towards the future. A prayer, then, you see, is a very composite thing, not a simple thing, not merely made up of the element of pleading with God to give us certain things that we cannot come into possession of by ordinary means.

Right here let me stop long enough to ask you to attend a little carefully to the teaching of Jesus on the subject of prayer. You will see he chimes in almost perfectly with the things I have been saying. If we followed his directions literally, we should never pray in public at all. He says, Enter into your chamber, and shut to the door, and commune with the Father in secret. He does not advocate long prayers, nor this kind of pleading, begging prayers that I have referred to. Do you remember the story of the unjust judge? Jesus tells this parable on purpose to enforce the point I have been speaking of. He says: Here is an unjust judge: a widow brings her case before him. She pleads with him until she tires him out; and at last he says, although I am an unjust judge, and fear neither God nor men, because with her continual praying she wearies me, I will grant her petition. Jesus does not say you are to weary God out in order to get your petitions granted, but just the opposite. How much more shall God give good gifts unto those that ask him Read once more that other story of the man who rises at night and goes to a neighbor for assistance. The neighbor, for the sake of being gracious and kind, will rise, although it gives him trouble and he does not wish to, and grant his request. But God is not like that neighbor: he does not need to be wearied or roused to make him care for our interests. This is the teaching, you will notice, of Jesus. If there is anything that appears like contrary teaching, you will find it in the supposed Gospel of John, written by an anonymous author, in which quite different doctrines are taught in regard to a good many things from those that are reported of Jesus in the other gospels.

Now I wish to come to my own personal position concerning the subject of prayer. It is fitting is it not that we should open our hearts with gratitude to God, no matter what has come to us of good or bright, of beautiful, sweet and true things, no matter through what channel, by the ministry of what friend, as the result of the working of no matter how many natural forces. Trace it to its source, and that source is always of necessity the one fountain, the one eternal Giver. And, if there be no more than courtesy in our hearts, ought it not to be easy and fitting for us to think, at least, if we do not say, Thank you, Father? Not only thanksgiving, but adoration.

Any uplook to something beautiful and high and fine above you partakes of the nature of worship. So that prayer which is worship, is it not altogether fitting and sweet and true? Only as we look up do we ever rise up, do we ever attain to anything finer and better.

And then there is communion. Is it true that God is Spirit, and that he is Father of his children, also spirit? Are we made in his likeness? Is there community of nature between him and us? I believe that he is human in all essential qualities, and that we are divine in all essential qualities. I believe the only difference between God and man is a difference not of kind, but of degree, and that there is, possibility of constant interchange of thought, of feeling, communion, between God and his children. Profound, wonderful truth it seems to me is expressed in those beautiful words of Tennyson's:

"Speak to him thou, for he hears, And spirit with spirit may meet.
Closer is he than breathing, And nearer than hands and feet."

Communion then possible, the very life of that which is divine within us!

Then I do not believe for one moment that prayer is only a sort of spiritual gymnastics, that it produces results in us merely by the exercise of spiritual feelings and emotions. I believe that in the moral and spiritual realms prayer does produce actual results that would not be produced in any other way. This, however, mark you carefully, not by producing any change in God, only changing our relations towards God. Can I illustrate it? I have a flower, for example, a plant in a flower-pot in my room. It seems to be perishing for the lack of something. It may be that the elements in the air do not properly feed it: it may be that it is hungry for light. At any rate, I try it: I take it out into the sunshine, I let the air breathe upon it, the dews fall upon it, the rains touch it and revive it and the plant brightens up, grows, blossoms, becomes beautiful and fragrant. Have I changed natural laws any? Not to one paruncicle. I have changed the relation of my plant and the air; and I have produced a result of life and beauty where would have been ugliness and death.

So I believe in prayer in that sense, that it may and does change the spiritual attitude of the soul towards God so that we come into entirely new relations with him, and the spiritual life in us grows, unfolds, becomes beautiful and sweet, not because we have changed God, but because we have got into a new set of relations with him.

If I thought that I could change God by a prayer, that I could interfere in the slightest degree with the working of any of the natural forces, I would never dare to open my lips in prayer again so long as I live. We do not need to change God: we need simply to change our attitude towards him, change our relations to him. Is not this true in every department of human life? How is it that you produce results anywhere? You wish a mountain stream to work for you. Do you change the laws of motion? You adapt your machinery to those laws of motion, and all the power of God becomes yours. You do not change him, you change yourself, your attitude towards him. And so in every one of the discoveries, in every one of the revolutions, that have come to the world, simply by discovering God's methods, and humbly adapting our ways to those methods Thus the forces of God, which are changeless and eternal, produce for us results which they would not have produced but for adapting our lives to the working of their ways.

A great many people do not think they ever pray. I have never seen a man yet who did not pray. You cannot live, and not pray: you cannot escape it if you try. Take Montgomery's famous old definition, "Prayer is the soul's sincere desire, Uttered or unexpressed, The motion of a hidden fir That trembles in the breast."

Soul's sincere desire. Yes, the body's desire, the mind's desire, the heart's desire, any desire, any outreach of life, is a prayer, an appeal for something that only the universe, that only God, can bestow. So, no matter whether you think you are religious or not, you are a praying man so long as you are a living man; and you cannot escape the fact if you try. It is merely a question whether you are a loving praying man or some other kind.

There is another aspect of prayer to which I wish to call your attention. Prayer is the refuge of a soul in trouble. It does not mean here, again, that you change God any. Can you not understand what it means to go to God, as it were, and fling yourself, like a child, against his breast and feel yourself folded in the everlasting arms? Your sorrow may not be removed, the burden may not be taken away, the life of your friend may not be saved, the sickness may not be healed; but there is comfort, there is strength, there is peace, there is help. Why, even in our human life do you not know how it is? You go to some friend you trust and love with your trouble. Perhaps he cannot lift it with one of his fingers; but he can tell you that he loves you, he cares, he would help you if only he were able. He can put his arm around you, he can say, God bless you; and you are stronger. You go away with lifted shoulder and with head that fronts the heavens; and you are able to bear the burden. Is there nothing akin to this in the sense of coming into intimate relations with the eternal Father, when troubled, pressed, when the outside world is dark, and feeling that here is refuge in a love deeper, higher, unspeakably more tender than that of the dearest friend that ever lived?

And this suggests another point. I have no doubt that sometimes, in my attempts to lead the devotions of this congregation, I use words which, if I were to sit down and critically analyze, I could not logically justify. I do not mean to; but, perhaps, sometimes I do. What of it? When my children were small, and my little boy came and climbed up in my lap and expressed himself in all sorts of illogical and foolish ways, telling me every sort of thing he wanted, impossible things, unwise things, things I could not get for him, things I would not get if I could, because I thought myself wiser than he, did these things trouble me? I loved to have him pour out his whole little soul into mine, because he was my child and because I did not expect him to be over-wise. It was this simple touch of kinship, this simple communion of father and child, which was sweet and tender and true.

So I believe with my whole soul that God loves us, his little children, with an unspeakable tenderness, a tenderness infinitely beyond that with which any earthly father ever loved a child, and that we can go to him freely and pour out our hearts, whether it is wise in expression or unwise; only let us do it with the feeling, "Not my will, Father, but Thine, be done," not as though we were trying to persuade him to do things for us that he would not otherwise do, but merely as the pouring out of our gratitude, our tenderness, our love.

There is another thing that needs just a word of suggestion. I believe that we ought to pray to God, not in the sense of begging for things, but sympathetically bringing in the arms of our sympathy all those we love and all those we hate, if there are any, and all things that live on the face of the earth. There is a hint of what I mean in those beautiful words of Tennyson's:

"For what are men better than sheep or goats That nourish a blind life within the brain, If, knowing God, they lift not hands in prayer Both for themselves and those who call them friend? For so the whole round earth is every way Bound by gold chains about the feet of God."

Let us reach out our arms of sympathy to all the world and bring the world sympathetically into the presence of our Father. So our own hearts and loves will broaden, until they, too, are divine.

And, then, there is one other thing. What a strength prayer has been to the grandest souls of the ages! Never was truer, finer truth written than those magnificent words of Isaiah: "Even the youths shall faint and be weary, and the young men shall utterly fall: but they that wait upon the Lord shall renew their strength; they shall mount up with wings as eagles; they shall run, and not be weary; they shall walk, and not faint!"

Take Jesus in his hour of agony, take Savonarola with his struggle, take Huss, Wyclif, Luther, take all the grand souls of the ages when they have simply stood with the feeling, One with God is a majority, and ready to face the world, if need be, in the conviction that they spoke for and represented the truth. The times of which Lowell speaks:

"Truth forever on the scaffold, Wrong forever on the throne, Yet that scaffold sways the future, and, behind the dim unknown, Standeth God within the shadow, keeping watch above his own."

This sense that God is for the truth and right, and, if you are standing for the truth and right, the Almighty Power is backing you up, the ground you stand on impregnable, because of that position. You do not expect God to work miracles, you do not expect him to do anything; but simply the sense that you are in his presence, that you are on his side, re- enforces you more than a thousand men could re-enforce an army in the time of its need. This is the great sense of surety that the poet Clough had in mind, when he wrote those wonderfully fine words:

"It fortifies my soul to know That, though I perish, Truth is so; That howsoe'er I stray or range, Whate'er I do, thou dost not change. I steadier step when I recall That, if I slip, thou dost not fall." Here is the confidence, the strength, that comes from prayer, from communion with God, from the sense of being in his presence, from a feeling of fellowship with the Divine.

The truest and finest, the sweetest prayer must come oft of the loving, the sympathetic, the tender soul. No selfish prayer can expect to enter into the heart of God. You will note in the words that Jesus teaches his disciples, it is not "My" Father, it is "Our" Father. And, if we wish to pray in the divine spirit, we shall broaden that "Our" until it includes not only our family, our church, our city, our State, our nation, our humanity, but until it includes all life that swims or walks or flies, feeling that it is the one life of the Father that is in us all. For, as Coleridge has finely put it, He prayeth best who loveth best All things, both great and small; For the dear God who loveth us, He made and loveth all.

45

THE WORSHIP OF GOD

THERE are those who in religious matters, as well as in all other departments of life, are content to walk unquestioningly the path which the footsteps of previous generations have made easy and familiar. But there are others and these among the more thoughtful and earnest minds to whom it is not enough to utter earnest words concerning enthusiasm and devotion, consecration and worship. These spiritual attitudes and exercises must first be made to appear reasonable to them, fitting, fitting to their conception of God, fitting to their ideas of that which is highest and finest in man.

So there are many things that pass to-day as forms of worship, many ideas connected with worship, which this class of minds cannot heartily and fully accept. Some of them do not seem to them fitting, as they look upward towards God. They cannot, for example, believe that God cares for flattery, cares to sit on his throne, and be told by his creatures how great and how wonderful he is. They cannot think that he cares to have presents brought to him, gifts offered on his altar, as men say. They cannot believe that he really is anxious for many of these external forms and ceremonies, which seem to the onlooker to constitute the essential element of much that passes as popular worship.

And then, on the other hand, man has grown into a sense of dignity. He has a higher and loftier idea of his own nature and of what is fitting to a man; and he cannot any longer heartily enter into the meaning of words which speak of him as a worm of the dust, which seem to him to intimate that God cares to have him prostrate himself in utter humiliation, to speak of himself always as a miserable sinner, as one without any good in him.

Many of these things from the point of view of the man himself no longer constitute the real conviction, the real feeling of the noblest hearts; and so there are many who are troubled over this question of worship, who are not quite sure as to how much spiritual significance it may any longer retain, not quite sure as to how vital a part it may play in the development of the religious life of man.

We find an adequate and perfectly natural explanation of some of these phases of worship that trouble us to-day, as we look back and note some of the steps in the religious development of the race. I shall not raise the question as to how or where or in what way the act of human worship began. I will simply say that one of the first manifestations of that which came to be religious worship which we are able to trace at the present time is to be found in the burial-mounds of the dead. Men reverenced the memory of the chief of the tribe who had passed into the invisible. They did not believe that he had ceased to exist: they rather looked upon him as having become, because invisible, a higher ruler. They thought of him as still interested in the welfare of the tribe, still its guardian, still its avenger, still demanding of the tribe the same reverence that it paid to him while he was yet alive; and his followers clothed him with all the human attributes with which they were familiar during the time he was among them. He was still hungry, he was still thirsty, he still wanted his old-time weapons, all those things he was familiar with during his earthly career. And so they brought food, and laid it on the burial-mound above his body; and they poured out their libations of drink to quench his spiritual thirst.

These were very real beliefs on the part of man universally during a certain stage of his mental, his moral, his spiritual growth. It was a very natural step beyond this to the origin of sacrifices. All sacrifice began right here. It was a religious meal, in which God and his worshippers equally shared. Some animal, supposed to partake of a life similar to that which distinguished the god and the worshipper, too, is sacrificed. It is cooked, and the worshippers partake of the meal; and they fully believe that the god joins in it also. And then the drink they partake of, and pour out their libation for the invisible spirit.

So the first sacrifice was a meal eaten together; and just as, for example, to-day you see a remnant of this idea when a man eats with an Arab, although the Arab may discover five minutes after that it was his bitterest foe, he finds himself at least during a little time bound to amity and peace by the fact that they have shared this sacred meal together, so in the act of sacrifice it was believed that the worshipper consecrated himself in loyalty to his God, and that the God consecrated himself in faithfulness to his worshippers as their guardian and protector. Here is given the central significance of sacrifices that have made so large a part of the religious ceremonial of the world.

These are not peculiar to what we call pagan people. Do you remember the story of how, after the flood, Noah offers a sacrifice, and God up in heaven is represented as smelling the flavor of the burning meat and as rejoicing in it, accepting the offering, and pledging himself to guard and care for his worshippers? Do you remember, also, that story of Jacob, how, when he is on his journey, he falls asleep, and has his wonderful dream, and sees the ladder starting at his feet and ending at the throne of God, up and down which the angels are passing? When he wakes in the morning, he says, "Surely, this is holy ground"; and he takes the stone on which he slept, and sets it up as an altar, and pours out the sacred oil as an offering to his God.

All the way through the Old Testament, in the history of the Hebrew people, you trace these same ideas that you find in the life of almost all the other nations of the world. It was only a step beyond this to the idea of presenting gifts to God, no matter what the nature of that gift might be. And, as men came to make him these sacred offerings, they came also to believe and in the most natural way in the world that, the more costly the gift, the more likely it was to be accepted on the part of its sublime recipient.

So human sacrifices arose; for there could be no more sacred gift than for a man to offer his own child or his own wife to God. The gods were looked upon as sometimes demanding these tremendous sacrifices as the

46

conditions of their mercy or their care. I refer you for illustration to one of the most striking and touching of Tennyson's poems. I think it is entitled "The Victim." There had been famine in the land, and the priests have announced that they have learned that the gods demand as an offering that which is most sacred and most dear to the heart of the king; and the question is as to whether it is his son, his boy, or his wife. They think it must be the boy, because he was the one that would continue the kingly line; but the wife detects the gladness of her husband when he sees that the boy is to be selected, and knows by that sense of relief that passes over his face that the priests have made a mistake, and that she herself is to be the victim. And so, in her love for him and for the people, she rushes upon the sacrificial knife.

All these ideas, you see, are perfectly natural in certain stages of human development, logically reasoned out in view of their thought of the gods and of their relations to them and of what these gods must desire at their hands. It is not only among the very early beliefs that you find these ideas controlling the thought and action of men. Study the ancient classical times as they are reflected in the Iliad, in the Odyssey, or in Virgil's Aeneid, and you will find that the gods were very human in all their feelings, their thoughts, their passions. As, in the Old Testament, Yahweh is reported to have been a jealous God, not willing that respect should be paid to anybody but himself, so you find the old Greek and Roman deities very jealous as to what were regarded as their rights, as to what the people must pay to them; and, if they are angry, they can be appeased if an offering rare and costly enough be brought by the worshipper. You can buy their favor; you can ward off their anger, if only you can offer them something which is precious enough so that they are ready to accept it at the worshipper's hands.

These are not merely Old Testament ideas, nor only pagan ideas. Some years ago, when I was in Rome, I visited among others one of the many churches dedicated to Mary under one name or another; and there was a statue of the Virgin by the altar, and it impressed me very much to see that it was loaded down with gifts. Every place on the statue itself to which anything could be attached, anything on the altar around it, was weighted down with gold chains, with jewels, with precious gifts of every kind. These had been brought as thank-offerings, expressions of worship, or pledges connected with a petition, because I have brought thee this gift, have mercy, do this for me which I need.

So these old ideas are vital still, and live on in the modern world. And yet modern and magnificent are those utterances of the old Hebrew prophet, who had so completely outgrown the common customs even of his time, when he represents God as saying that he is weary of all these external offerings. He says: I do not want the cattle brought to my temples. Those that wander on a thousand hills are already mine. If I were hungry, I would not ask thee. He does not want the rivers of oil poured out. What does he want? The old prophet says, What doth the Lord require of thee but to do justly, to love mercy, and to walk humbly with God? And some of the later writers caught a glimpse of the same spiritual truth when they said, Not burnt-offerings, not calves of a year old; when they cry out, Shall I bring the fruit of my body for the sin of my soul? No, it is a broken and contrite heart, a heart sorry for its sin, a heart consecrating itself to righteousness and truth, this inner, spiritual worship.

The prophets, you see, were climbing up to that magnificent ideal so finely set up by Jesus as reported in the Gospel from which I read our lesson this morning. They had not only believed that God was to be worshipped after these external fashions, but that there was some special place, not only where it was easier to think of him, but where he demanded the offering should be brought. He said to the woman at the well: You think it is Mount Gerizim where the people ought to worship, and the Jews think it is Mount Moriah; but I say unto you that neither in this mountain nor yet at Jerusalem shall men worship the Father. God is spirit, the universal spirit, every place a temple, every spot hallowed, if only those that worship him do so in spirit and in truth.

You see, then, how up these stairways of gradual approach the human race, in the person of its highest and finest representatives, has climbed, how near it has come to the spiritual ideal of God and the spiritual thought of that which he requires at our hands.

Is worship, then, so far as external form is concerned, to pass away? By no manner of means, as I think. As you analyze any one of these old primitive acts of worship, no matter how crude, no matter how cruel, how bloody, how repulsive it may be to-day from the outlook of our higher civilization, you will note that it has in it an element which, I believe, is permanent, and can never be outgrown. Whatever else there is, there is always the sense of a Presence, Invisible, mighty, high, and, from the point of view of the worshipper, holy and set apart. There is always the feeling of being in the shadow of the high and lofty One who inhabiteth eternity. There is always the sense of uplooking, of worship, in the higher sense of that term. Always, at any rate, the germ of these; and this, it seems to me, we may be sure and certain, however it may clothe itself in the future, shall never pass away.

I wish now, if there are any who think it is not befitting the greatness, the nobleness of man that he should bow himself in the presence of the highest, humiliate himself, if you choose to use that term, in acts of worship, I wish now, I say, to consider worship under two or three aspects, and see what it means. And, in the first place, I ask you to note that the ability to worship is always the measure of the rank of a being, it is the test and the standard of greatness.

As you look over the animal world, which one of them are we accustomed to think of as coming the nearest to man? What one do we love to have most with us, to associate most with our joys, with the peace of our homes? Is it not the dog? And as you examine the dog, study carefully his nature and characteristics, do you not note that there is in his nature a hint, a suggestion, of that which is the root of all worship? The dog is the one animal with which man is accustomed familiarly to associate himself, who looks up with an incipient reverence, love, almost worship, to his master. And it is this quality in the dog that enables him to look up, and, however dimly, feel the life of some one that is above him, that lifts him into our society, and makes us feel this tenderness of heart-kinship with that which is finest in his nature.

And man is man simply because he is able to look above himself. The old Greeks had an anticipation of that idea when they called man anthropos; for the meaning of the word is the upward-looker. As in imagination you go back and down to the time when man first appeared, developed from the lower life which preceded him, the first thing you can think about him as human is the opening of his eyes in wonder, the lifting of his face in curiosity and question, and the birth of adoration in his soul. This is that which made him man.

You go and study the lowest type of barbaric life to-day; and you will find that the barbarian has very little curiosity as compared with the civilized man. You will find that it is very difficult to astonish him with anything. He does not wonder. He takes everything for granted. He does not see clearly and deeply enough to appreciate the marvel. Let me illustrate from a specimen of barbaric life itself. A few years ago the chief of an Indian tribe was brought from the plains of the West to visit Washington. The idea was to impress him as much as possible with the idea of our civilization, so that he might report it to his people when he went home. After they had crossed the Mississippi on their way to the West, the gentleman in whose care he was travelling asked the chief what the one thing which he had seen during his trip was which had impressed him the most; and he said at once the St. Louis bridge. But his companion said, Are you not astonished at the Capitol of Washington? "Yes," he said, "but my people can pile stones on top of each other; but they cannot make a cobweb of steel hang in the air."

You see how that perception lifted him above the average level of his people? He was showing his capacity for higher and nobler civilization. It is just this ability in the man to wonder, to see something to wonder at, to worship, to admire, which lifts him one grade higher than that of the average level of his tribe. So that which makes man a man is the capacity in him to admire. All admiration is the essence, the root, of worship. And, the more things a man admires, the greater and nobler type of man he is seen to be. If he can admire music, if he can admire painting, if he can admire sculpture, if he can admire poetry, if he can admire literature of every kind, if he can admire grand architecture, the beautiful monuments of the world, we say, Here is a large, all-round type of man. We estimate his dignity, his greatness, by the capacity that he shows for worship in its lower type; for worship is simply looking up with admiration.

There is another quality about this worship that I wish to speak of. It is the power that is capable of transforming a man, making him over into the likeness of that which he admires. You find the man without this capacity, and you know it is hopeless to appeal to him, hopeless to set up ideals, hopeless to place before him enticing examples. There is nothing in him to which these things appeal. Take Alexander the Great. It is said he carried around with him a copy of the Iliad, and that Achilles was his ideal of a hero. Do you not see how this admiration transformed the life of the young king, and made him after the type of that which he admired? It does not make any difference what this special admiration may be. Let a man admire Beethoven, and he will cultivate instinctively the qualities that make the beauty and greatness of Beethoven's character and the wonders of his career.

This ideal may be in a book, it may be embodied in fiction. I have liked always, either on the walls of my room or on the walls of my heart, to have certain portraits of persons whom I have loved, who are no longer living; and they are to me constant stimulus. They speak to me by day, and in my dreams at night their eyes follow me, and seem to look into my soul; and in their presence I could not do a mean, an unmanly thing. I love, I reverence, I worship these lofty ideals. And the quality of these characters filters down through and permeates the thought and the life.

You remember how the other aspect of this thought is illustrated by Shakspere. He says, "My nature is subdued To what it works in, like the dyer's hand." If that with which you keep company, that you admire, is below you, it degrades; if it is above you, it lifts. In any case you are transformed, shaped into the likeness of that which you admire.

There is another aspect of this close akin to that which I have just been dealing with. It is only the worshipper who has in him any promise, any possibility, of growth. Whether it is the individual or the nation, it makes no difference. If you find no capacity to admire that which is above and beyond you, then there is no hope of progress. Take the young man who thinks he has exhausted the possibilities of the world, who has reached the stage, who prides himself on not being surprised, not being over whelmed, not admiring anything. The careful outside observer knows that, instead of having exhausted the possibilities and greatness and wonders of the universe, he has simply exhausted himself.

The man who knows how full the world is of that which is beautiful and great and true and noble walks through the universe with his head bared and bowed, and feels, as did Moses when standing in the presence of the burning bush, that he ought to take off his shoes from his feet, for the place where he is standing is holy ground. Wherever you are standing in this universe, which is full of God from star to dust particle, is holy ground; and, if you do not feel it, if you are not touched, if you are not bowed, if you are not thrilled with wonder, it is defect in you, and not lack of God.

If the musician admires his great predecessors and strives to emulate them; if the painter in the presence of the Sistine Madonna feels lifted and touched, so that he never can be content with poor work again; if the sculptor is ready to bend his knees in the presence of the Venus of Melos, as he sees her standing at the end of the long gallery in the Louvre; if the lover of his kind admires John Howard, and can never be content unless he is doing something for his fellow- men again; if we can be touched by lives like Clara Barton's, like Florence Nightingale's, like Dorothea Dix's, like the great and consecrated ones of the earth; if in any department of life we can be lifted, humbled, thrilled, at the same time with the thought of the greatness and glory and beauty that are above and beyond us, then there is hope of growth, then there is life that can come to something fine and noble in the future.

I wish, in the light of these illustrations of what worship means, to note the thought that a great many men conscientious, earnest, simple who have never been accustomed to think of themselves as religious, and perhaps would deny it if a friend suggested to them that they had in them the possibilities of worship, that perhaps they are worshippers, even if they know it not. A great many persons have thrown away the common ideals of worship, and perhaps have settled down to the idea that they are not worshippers at all, while all the time the substance and the beauty and the glory of worship are in their daily lives and always in their hearts. I want to suggest two or three grades of worship, to show that this worship climbs; and I want to call attention to the fact that on the lowest grade it is worship of God just the same as on the highest, that all worship or admiration for truth, for beauty, for good, wherever, however, manifested, is really worship of God, whether we think of it or call it by that name or not, because they all are manifestations of God.

Take the man who is touched and lifted by natural beauty, the sense of natural power; the man who loves the woods, who turns and stands to see the glory of a sunset, who is lifted by tides of emotion as he hears the surf beat on the shore, who feels bowed in the presence of the wide night sky of stars, who is humbled at the same time that he is uplifted in the presence of the mountains, who is touched by all natural scenes of beauty and peace and glory. Are not these men in their degree worshippers?

Take the feeling that is expressed in those beautiful lines of Byron. We do not think of Byron as a religious nature, but certainly he had in him the heart of worship when he could write such thoughts as these:

"'Tis midnight.
On the mountains brown
The cold, round moon shines deeply down;
Blue roll the waters; blue the sky
Seems like an ocean hung on high,
Bespangled with those isles of light,
So wildly, spiritually bright.
Whoever looked upon them shining
And turned to earth without repining,
Nor wished for wings to flee away
And mix with their eternal ray?"

And Wordsworth says he feels a Presence that "Disturbs him with the joy of elevated thought, A sense sublime of something far more deeply interfused."

And so you may run all through the poets, these simply as hints, specimens, every one of them worshippers, touched by the beauty, glory, uplift of the natural world.

And then pass to the next stage, and come to the worship of the human, to the admiration of the highest and finest qualities that are manifested in the lives of men and women. Who is there that is not touched and thrilled by some story of heroic action, of heroic self- sacrifice, of consecration to duty in the face of danger and death? And no matter what this manifestation of human goodness may be, if you can be thrilled by it and lifted by it, then you have taken another step up this ladder of worship which leads you into the very presence chamber of the Divine.

Let a boy read the life of Lincoln, see his earnest thirst for knowledge, the sacrifice he was willing to pay for it, his consecration to his ideals of truth, the transparent honesty of the man, the supreme contempt with which he could look down upon anything poor or mean or low, the firmness and simplicity with which he assumes high office, the faithfulness, the unassuming devotion, that he carries into the fulfilment of the trust. Take him all the way through, study his character and admire, and you are a worshipper of that which is divine.

So in the case of Jesus, the supreme soul of history in its consecration to the Father, its simple trust in the divine love, its superiority to fear, to question, to death. When we bow ourselves in the presence of the Nazarene, we are not worshipping another God. We are worshipping his Father and our Father as lie shines in the face of Jesus, as he illumines and beautifies his life, as he makes glorious the humble pathways of Galilee, and so casts a reflected glory over the humblest pathways any of us may be called upon to tread.

The next step in our ascent brings us to the conscious worship of God himself. We cannot grasp the divine idea. The finite cannot measure or outline the infinite; and so, when we say God, we mean only the grandest ideal that we can frame, that reaches on towards, but can never adequately express the Deity. And so we worship this thought, this ideal, growing as our capacity develops, advancing as the race advances, and ever leading us Godward, as when we follow a ray of light we are travelling towards its source. And the attitude of our souls in the presence of this which is divine is truest worship. The humility of it, the exaltation of it, is beautifully phrased in two or three lines which I wish to repeat to you from Browning's Saul: "I but open my eyes, and perfection, no more and no less, In the kind I imagined, full-fronts me, and God is seen God In the star, in the stone, in the flesh, in the soul and the clod. And, thus looking within and around me, I ever renew (With that stoop of the soul which in bending upraises it, too), As by each new obeisance in spirit I climb to his feet!"

Here is the significance of the thought I had in mind at the opening. We talk about humbling ourselves. When we can bend with reverence in the presence of that which is above us, the very bending is exaltation; for it indicates the capacity to appreciate, to admire, to adore. Thus we climb up into the ability to worship God, the infinite Spirit, our Father, in spirit and in truth.

Now to raise one moment the question suggested near the opening, Are forms of worship to pass away? The reply to this seems to me perfectly clear. Those forms which sprang out of and are fitted to only lower ideals of worship, ideals which humanity outgrows, these must be left behind, or else they must be transformed, and filled with a new and higher meaning. But forms will always remain. But note one thing: they sometimes say that we Unitarians are too cold, and do not have form enough. You will see that, the higher men rise intellectually, the less there is always of outward expression.

For example, before men were able to speak with any large vocabulary, they eked out their meaning by all kinds of motions and gestures. But the most highly cultivated men to- day, in their conversation, are the ones who get the least excited and have the least recourse to gestures, because they are capable of expressing the highest, finest, and most varied thoughts by the elaborate power of speech which they have developed. And perhaps the highest and finest worship of the world will not be that which has the most elaborate ceremonial and ritual; but it will have adequate and fitting ceremonial and ritual, because it will naturally seek to express in some external way that which it feels.

I sometimes wish and perhaps you will pardon me for saying it here and now that we Unitarians were a little less afraid of adequate posture and gesture in our acts of public worship. God is, indeed, everywhere as much as he is here; but this is the place we have specially consecrated to thinking about him and to going through our stated forms of worship. And if, when you enter the house of a friend, you take off your hat, you bow the head, it seems to me it would be especially fitting to do it, when one enters a Christian church. And, in the attitude of prayer, I wish that all might find it in their hearts to sit with bended brow and closed eyes as in the presence of the Supreme, shutting out the common, the outside world, and trying to realize what it means to come consciously to the feet of the eternal One.

I love these simple, fitting, external manifestations of the worshipful spirit; and, if we do not substitute them for the worship, and think we worship when we bend the knee, this appropriate expression of the spirit, or feeling, it seems to ought to help cultivate the feeling and the spirit, and make it easier for us to be conscious of the presence of the Divine.

We are men, then, in the highest sense of the term, only as we are worshippers. And the more worshipful we are, in high and true sense of that word, the nobler and higher manhood, and the grander the possibilities in us of de intellectual, moral, spiritual growth.

Let us, then, cultivate the admiring, the wondering, the worshipful attitude of heart and mind, and recognize on lowest steps of this ladder that lifts to God, the presence of the same divine power and beauty and glory as that which we see clearly on the highest, and know that always, when we are worshipping any manifestation of God, we are shipping Him who is spirit, in spirit and in truth.

When on some strain of music Our thoughts are wafted high; When, touched with tender pity, Kind teardrops dim the eye; When thrilled with scenes of grandeur, Or moved to deeds of love, Do we not give thee worship, O God in heaven above? For Thou art all life's beauty, And Thou art all its good: By Thy tides are we lifted To every lofty mood. Whatever good is in us, Whatever good we see, And every high endeavor, Are they not all from Thee?

MORALITY NATURAL, NOT STATUTORY.

IT is very common for people to identify their special type of religion or their theological opinions with religion itself, and feel that those who do not agree with them are in the rue sense not religious. Not only this. It is perhaps quite less common for them to identify their particular type of religion with the fundamental ideas of morality, and think that the people who do not agree with them are undermining the moral stability of the world. For example, those who question the absolute authority of the Catholic Church are looked upon the authorities of that Church as the enemies, not only of religion, but as the enemies of society, the enemies of humanity, as doing what they can to shake the very foundations of he social order. You will find a great many Protestant theologians who seem to hold the opinion that, if you dare to question the authenticity or authority of some particular nook in the Bible, you are not only an enemy of religion, but you are an enemy of morality. You are doing what you can to disturb the stability of the world.

But, if we look at the matter with a little care, we shall see that we ought to turn it quite around, look at it from another point of view. Though every Bible, every particle of religious literature, every hymn, every prayer on the face of the earth, were blotted out of existence to-day, religion would not be touched. Religious books did not create religion, did not make man a religious being. It is the religious nature of man that made the Bibles, that uttered itself in prayers, that created the rituals, that sung the hymns and chanted the anthems. It is man, a religious being, who makes religious institutions, who creates all the external aspects and appearances of the religious life. And the same is true precisely in regard to moral precepts. If the Ten Commandments were blotted out of the memory of man, if every single ethical teaching of Jesus should perish, if the high and fine moral precepts of Epictetus and Marcus Aurelius and all the great teachers of the pagan world should cease to exist, if there were not a printed moral precept on earth, morality would not be touched. It is not these that have created morality. It is the natural moral nature of man that has written all the commandments, whether they have come to us by the hand of Moses or of Gautama or Mohammed or Confucius or Seneca, or no matter who the medium may have been.

Man is a moral being, naturally, essentially, eternally, and this is a moral universe, inherently, necessarily, eternally; and, though all the external expression of moral thought and feeling should be lost, the human race would simply reproduce them again.

It is sometimes well for us to get down to the bed-rock in our thinking, and find how natural and necessary the great foundations are. The Hindu priests used to tell their followers that the earth, which was flat, rested on certain pillars, which rested again on some other foundation beneath them, and so on until thought was weary in trying to trace that upon which the earth was supposed to find its stability. And they also told their followers that, if they did not bring offerings, if they did not pay the special respect which was due to the gods, if they were not obedient to heir teachings, these pillars would give way, and the earth would be precipitated into the abyss.

But we have found, as a result of our modern study of he universe, that the earth needs no pillars on which to rest; but it swings freely in its orbit, as the old verse that used to read in my schoolboy days says, "Hangs on nothing in the air," part of the universal system of things, stable in its eternal sound and motion, kept and cared for by the power that lever sleeps and never is weary. So, by studying into the foundations of the moral nature of man, we have discovered a last that it needs no artificial props or supports, but that morality is inherent, natural and eternal.

I shall not raise the question, which is rather curious than practical, as to whether there are any beginnings of moral feeling in the animal world below man. For our purpose this morning it is enough to note that the minute that man appears conscience appears, and that conscience is an act which springs out of social relations. In other words, when the first man rose to the ability to look into the face of his fellow and think of the other man as another self, like himself in feelings, in possibilities of pleasure or pain, when this first man was able imaginatively to put himself in: he place of this other, then morality as a practical fact was Dorn.

We may imagine, for the purpose of illustration, this man saying: Here is another being who appears to be like myself. He is capable of suffering pain, as I am. He does not like pain any better than I do. Therefore, I have no right to make him suffer that which I do not wish to suffer myself. This other man is capable of pleasure. He desires certain things, similar things to those which I desire. If I do not wish him to take these things away from me, I have no right to take them away from him.

I do not mean that this was thought out in this clear way, but that, when there was the first dim perception of this other self, with similar feelings, similar possibilities, similar pleasures, similar pains, then there became a conscience, because there was a consciousness of this similarity of nature. Morality, then, is born as a social fact.

To go a little deeper, and in order to trace the natural and historical growth of the moral ideal, let me say that morality in its deepest and truest sense is born of the fact of sex, because it is right in there that we find the root and the germ of permanent social relations. And I wish you to note another very significant fact. You hear people talking about selfishness and unselfishness, as though they were direct contraries, mutually exclusive of each other, as though, in order to make a selfish man unselfish, you must completely reverse his nature, so to speak. I do not think this is true at all. Unselfishness naturally and necessarily springs out of selfishness, and, in the deepest sense of the word, is not at all contradictory to that.

For example: A man falls in love with a woman. This, on one side of it, is as selfish as anything you can possibly conceive. But do you not see by what subtle and divine chemistry the selfishness is straightway transformed, lifted up, glorified, and becomes unselfishness? The very love that he professes for her makes it necessary for his own happiness that she should be happy, so that, in seeking for his own selfish gratification, he is devoting himself unselfishly to the happiness of somebody else.

And, when a child is born, do you not see, again, how the two selfishnesses, the father's and the mother's, selfishly, if you please, brooding over and loving the child, at once go out of themselves, consecrating time and care and thought and love, and even health or life itself, if need be, for the welfare of the child?

Right in there, then, out of this fact of sex and in the becoming of the family, are born love and sympathy, and tenderness and mutual care, all those things which are the highest and finest constituent elements of the noblest developments of the moral nature of men.

51

Imagination plays a large part in the development of morality; for you must be able to put yourself imaginatively in the place of another before you can feel for that other, and in that way recognize the rights of that other and be ready to grant these rights to that other. So we find that morality at first is a narrow thing: it is confined perhaps to the little family, the father, the mother, the child, bound together by these ties of kinship, of love, of sympathy, devoting themselves to each other; but they may look upon some other family as their natural enemies, and feel no necessity whatever to apply these same principles of love and tenderness and care beyond the limits of their own little circle.

So you find, as you study the growth of the moral nature of man, that it is confined at first to the family, then to the patriarchal family, then the tribe; but the fiction of kinship is still kept up, and, while the member of the primeval tribe feels he has no right to rob or murder within the limits of his tribe, he has no compunction whatever about robbing or injuring the members of some other tribe. So the moral principle in its practical working is limited to the range of the sympathy of the tribe, which does not go beyond the tribal limits. We see how that principle works still in the world, from the beginning clear up to the highest reaches which we have as yet attained.

Take the next step, and find a city like ancient Athens. Still, perhaps, the fiction of kinship is maintained. All the citizens of Athens are regarded as members of the same great tribe or family. But even in the time of Plato, whom we are accustomed to look upon as one of the great teachers of the world, there was no thought of any moral obligation to anybody who lived in Sparta, lived in any other city of Greece, and less was there any thought of moral obligation as touching or taking in the outside barbarian. So when the city grew into a nation, and we came to a point where the world substantially stands to-day, do you not see that practically the same principle holds, that, while we recognize in some abstract sort of fashion that we ought to do justice and be kind to people beyond our own limits, yet all our political economy, all our national ideas, are accustomed to emphasize the fact that we must be just and righteous to our own people, but that aggression, injustice of almost any kind, is venial in our treatment of the inhabitants of another country? And it may even flame up into the fire of a wordy patriotism in certain conditions; and love of country may mean hatred and injustice towards the inhabitants of another country, or particularly towards the people of another race.

Let me give you a practical illustration of it. What are the relations in which we stand to-day towards Spain? I have unbounded admiration for the patience, on the whole, for the justice, the sense of right, which characterize the American people. I doubt if there is another nation on the face of the earth to-day that would have gone through the last two or three years of our experience, and maintained such an attitude of impartiality, of faithfulness, of justice, of right. And yet, if we examine ourselves, we shall find that it is immensely difficult for us to put ourselves in the place of a Spaniard, to look at the Cuban question from his point of view, to try to be fair, to be just to him. It is immensely difficult, I say, for us to look at one of these international questions from the point of view of another race, cherishing other religious and social ideas, having another style of government.

And there is another illustration of it that has recently occurred here in our country, which is sadder still to me. Only a little while ago a postmaster in the South was shot by a mob. The mob surrounds his house, murders him and his child, wounds other members of the family, burns down his home; and why? Under no impulse whatever except that of pure and simple race prejudice, the utter inability of a white man to put himself in the position of a black to such an extent as to recognize, plead for, or defend his inherent rights as a man.

I am not casting any aspersion on the South in what I am saying, none whatever. Were the conditions reversed, perhaps we should be no better. It is not a practical problem with us. If there were two or three times as many colored men in the State of New York as there are white men, then we might understand the question. Let us not mentally cast any stones at the people across the line. I point it out simply as illustrating the difficulty that we have in recognizing the rights, the moral rights, of people beyond the limits of that sympathy to which we have been accustomed and for a long period trained.

I believe the day will come when we shall be as jealous of the right of a man as we are now of the right of an American. We are not yet. There have been foregleams and prophecies of it in the past. Long ago a Latin writer said, I am a man, and whatever is human is not foreign to me. But think what a lone and isolated utterance that has been for hundreds of years. Jesus taught us to pray, not my Father, but our Father, and we do pray it every day in the year; but how many are the people in any of the churches that dream of living it? A hundred years ago that heretic, who is still looked upon as the bugaboo of all that is fine and good, Thomas Paine, wrote, "The world is my country, and to do good is my religion," a sentence so fine that it has been carved on the base of the statue of William Lloyd Garrison on Commonwealth Avenue in Boston, as being a fitting symbol of his own philanthropic life.

How many of us have risen to the idea of making these grand sentiments the ruling principles of our lives? But along the lines of moral growth it is to come. The day will be when, as I said, we shall feel as keenly whatever touches the right of any man as to-day we feel that which touches the right of one of our own people; and the moral growth of the world will reach beyond that. I love to dream of a day when men will no longer forget the inherent rights of any inhabitant of the air or of the waters or of the woods or any of the domesticated animals that we have come to associate with our lives.

We feel towards them to-day as in the old days a man felt towards another man who was his slave, that he had a right to abuse, to maltreat, even to kill, if he pleased. We have not yet become civilized enough, so that we feel it incumbent upon us to recognize the fact that animals can suffer pain, that animals can enjoy the air or the sunshine, and that that they have a right to each when they do not trespass upon the larger rights of humanity. I was something of a boy when it first came over me that it was not as amusing to animals to be shot and killed as it was to me to shoot and kill them. From the time I was able to lift a gun I had always carried one; but I soon learned that for me there was no pleasure in taking needlessly the life of anything that lived. We are only partially civilized as yet in the treatment of our domesticated animals. How many people think of the torture of the curb bit, of the check, of neglect in the case of cold, of thirst, of hunger? How many people, I say, civilized and in our best society, are careful yet as to the comfort, the rights, of those that serve them in these humble capacities?

The time will come when our moral sympathetic sense shall widen its boundaries even farther yet, and shall take in the trees and the shrubs, the waters, the hills, all the natural and beautiful features of the world. I believe that by and by it will be regarded as immoral, as unmanly, to deface, to mar, that which God has made so glorious and so beautiful. As soon as man develops, then, his power of sympathy, so that it can take the world in its arms, so soon he will have grown to the stature of the Divine in the unfolding of his moral nature.

I wish now to raise the question, for a moment, as to what is to be our guide in regard to moral facts and moral actions. I was trained, and perhaps most of you were, to believe that I was unquestioningly to follow my conscience, that whatever conscience told me to do was necessarily right. The conscience has been spoken of as though it were a sort of little deity set to rule man's nature, this little kingdom of thought and feeling and action. But conscience is nothing of the kind. Half of the consciences of the world to-day are all wrong.

Let me hint by way of illustration what I mean: Calvin was just as conscientious in burning Servetus as Servetus was in pursuing that course of action which led him to the stake. One of them was wrong in following his conscience, then. You take it to-day: some people will tell you there is a certain day in the week that you must observe as sacred. Your conscience tells you there is another day in the week that you must observe as sacred. Can both be right? Many of the greatest tragedies of the world have come about through these controversies and confusions of conscience. The Quaker in old Boston went at the cart's tail, in disgrace, because he followed his conscience; and the Puritan put him there because he followed his conscience. Were both of them right? The inquisitor in Spain put to death hundreds and thousands of people conscientiously; and the hundreds and thousands of people conscientiously went to their deaths.

What is conscience, then? Conscience is not a moral guide. It is simply that monitor within that reiterates to us forever and forever and forever, Do right. But conscience does not tell us what is right. We must decide those questions as a matter of calm study and judgment in the light of human experience. It is the judgment that should tell us whether a thing is right or wrong. And how shall we know whether it is right or wrong? Simply by the consequences. That which helps, that which lifts man up, that which adds to the happiness and the well-being of the world, as the result of human experience, is right. That which hurts, that which injures men and women, that which takes away from their welfare and happiness, that is wrong. All these things, as we shall see before I get through, are inherent in the nature of things, not created by statute, not the result of the moral teaching of anybody.

This leads me to extend this idea a little farther, and to raise the question as to what is the standard by which you are to judge moral action. If you will think it out with a little care, you will find that the standard of all moral action may be summed up in the one word "life." Life, first, as continuance; second, to use a philosophical term, content, that which it includes. Life, this is the standard of right and wrong.

To illustrate, take me physically, leave out of account all the rest of my nature now for a moment, and consider me as an animal. From the point of view of my body, that which conduces to length of life, to fullness, to completion, to enjoyment of life, is right, the only right, from this physical point of view. That which threatens my life, that which takes away my sum of strength, injures my health, takes away from my possibility of enjoyment, that, from a physical point of view, is wrong; and there can be no other right or wrong from the point of view of the body.

But I am not simply body. So this principle must be modified. Come up to the fact that I am an intellectual being. In order to develop myself intellectually, I may have to forego things that would be pleasant on the bodily plane. I sacrifice the lower for the higher; and that which would be right on the physical plane becomes relatively wrong now, because it interferes with something that is higher and more important.

Rise one step to man as an affectional being. If you wish to develop him to the finest and highest here, you may not only be obliged under certain conditions to sacrifice the body, but you may be obliged to sacrifice his intellectual development. In order that he may be the best up here, he must put the others sometimes, relatively, under his feet. So, again, that which would be right on the physical plane or the intellectual plane becomes relatively wrong, if it interferes with that which is higher still.

And so, if you recognize man as a spiritual being, a child of God, then you say it is right, if need be, to put all these other things under his feet, in order that he may attain the highest and best that he is capable of here. But you see it is life all the way, it is the physical life or it is the mental life or it is the affectional life or it is the spiritual life; and that which is necessary for the cultivation and development of these different grades of life

53

becomes on those grades right, and that which threatens or injures one or either of these grades becomes, so far as that grade is concerned, wrong.

Life, then, continuance, fullness, joy, use, this is the standard of right and wrong; a standard which no book ever set up, which no book can ever overthrow; a standard which is inherent, natural, necessary, a part of the very nature of things.

I wish now for a moment I must of course do it briefly to consider the relation of religion to this natural morality. And perhaps you will hardly be ready some of you, at any rate for the statement which I propose to make, that sometimes, in order to be grandly moral, a man must be irreligious. I mean, of course, from the point of view of the conventional religion of his time, he must be ready to be regarded as irreligious. In the earliest development of the religious and moral life of a tribe, very likely, the two went hand in hand, side by side; for the dead chief now worshipped as god would be looked upon as in favor of those customs or practices which the tribe had come to regard as right. But religion perhaps you will know by this time, if you have thought of it carefully is the most conservative thing in the world. Naturally, it is the last thing that people are willing to change. This reluctance grows out of their reverence, grows out of their worshipful nature, grows out of their fear that they may be wrong.

But now let me illustrate what I mean. Religion, standing still in this way, has become an institution, a set of beliefs, of rites and ceremonies, which do not change. The moral experience of the people goes right on; and so it sometimes comes to pass that the moral ideal has outgrown the religious ideal of the community. And now, as a practical illustration to illume the whole point, let us go back to ancient Athens for a moment in the time of Socrates. Here we are confronted with the curious fact that Socrates, who has been regarded from that day to this as the most grandly moral man of his time, the one man who taught the highest and noblest human ideals, is put to death as an irreligious man. The popular religion of the time cast him out, and put the hemlock to his lips; and at the same time his teaching in regard to righteousness and truth was unspeakably ahead of the popular religion of his day.

Let us come to the modern Athens for a moment, to the time of Theodore Parker in Boston. We are confronted here, again, with this strange fact. There was not a church in Boston that could abide him, not even the Unitarian churches; and in the prayer-meetings of the day they were beseeching God to take him out of the world, because they thought he was such a force for evil. And at the same time Theodore Parker stood for the very highest, tenderest, truest moral ideal of his age.

There was no man walking the earth at that time who so grandly voiced the real law of God as did Theodore Parker. And yet he was outcast by the popular religious sentiment of his time.

This, then, is what I mean when I say that we ought to be careful, and study and think in forming our religious ideals, and see that we do not identify our own unwillingness to think with the eternal and changeless law of God. This is what I have meant in some of the strictures which I have uttered during the last year upon some of the theological creeds of the time. The people have grown to be better than their creeds, but they have not yet developed the courage to make those creeds utter the highest and finest things which they think and feel. This is what I have meant when I have said that the character of God as outlined in many of these creeds is away behind and below the noblest and finest and sweetest ideals of what we regard as fitting even to humanity to-day.

Religion, then, may be ahead of the moral ideal or it may be behind it. The particular type of religion I mean, of course, which is being held at any particular time in the history of the world. But the moral ideal of necessity goes on, keeping step with the social experience of the race.

I must touch briefly now just one other point of practical importance that we need to guard, in order to be tender and true in our dealings with our fellow-men. You will find, if you look over the face of society, that there are two kinds of morality, frequently quite inconsistent with each other; and sometimes the poorer of the two kinds is held in higher esteem than the better. I mean there is conventional morality, and there is real morality.

As a hint of illustration: An American woman goes to Turkey to-day; and she is shocked by the customs of the women and their style of dress. It seems to her that no woman can possibly be moral who, although she covers her head, can appear on the street with feet and ankles bare. But this same Turkish woman is shocked beyond the possibility of utterance to know that in Europe and America women carefully cover their feet, but expose their faces and their shoulders. It seems terrible to her, and she cannot understand how a European or American woman can have any regard for the principles of delicacy and morality.

Do you not see how, in both cases here, it is purely a matter of convention? No real question of morality is touched in either case? I speak of this to prepare you to note how conscience can be as troubled over things which are purely conventional as it can over things which are downright and real. Let me use another illustration, going a little deeper in the matter. Here is a man, for example, who is terribly shocked because his neighbor takes a drive with his family on Sunday afternoon. It seems to him an outrage on all the principles of public and social morality; and he is eager to get up a society to abolish such customs, that seem to him to threaten the prosperity of all that is good in the world. But this same man, perhaps, has been trained in a way of conducting his business that, while legal, is not strictly fair. This man may be hard and cruel towards his employees. He may cherish bitter hatreds towards his rivals. In his heart he may be transgressing the law of vital ethics, while fighting with all the power of his nature for that which does not touch any real question of right or wrong at all.

Or take a woman who, while shocked at the transgression of some social custom in which she has been trained from her childhood, or, for example, has come to think that a certain way of observing Lent, on which we have just entered, is absolutely necessary to the safety of religion and morals both, is yet quite willing, and without a qualm of conscience, on the slightest hint of a suspicion, to tear into tatters the character of one of her neighbors or friends, does not hesitate to slander, perhaps is unjust or cruel to the servants that make the house comfortable and beautiful for her; in other words, transgressing the real laws of right and wrong, she is shocked and troubled over the transgression on the part of others of some purely conventional statute, the keeping or breach of which has no real bearing on the welfare of the world.

A good many of our social judgments are like the case of the old lady pardon me, if it should make you smile, but it illustrates the case who criticised with a great deal of severity a neighbor and friend who wore feathers on her bonnet. Somebody said to her, But the ribbons on your bonnet are quite as expensive as the feathers that you criticise. "Yes," she said, "I know they are; but you have got to draw the line somewhere, and I choose to draw it at feathers." So you find a great many people on every hand in society who are choosing to draw these lines purely artificial, purely conventional in regard to matters of supposed right or wrong, while they are not as careful to look down deeply into the essential principles of that which is inherently right or wrong.

And now at the end I wish to suggest what is a theme large enough for a sermon by itself, and say that these laws of righteousness are so inherent that they are self-executed; and by no possibility did any soul from the beginning of the world ever escape the adequate result of his wrong-doing. The old Hebrews, as manifested in the Book of Job, the Psalms, and all through the Old Testament, taught the idea, which was common at that time in the world, that the favor of God was to be judged by the external prosperity of men and women. The Old Testament promises long life and wealth and all sorts of good things to the people who do right; and I find on every hand in the modern world people who have inherited this way of looking at things. I have heard people say: I have tried to do right, and I am not prosperous. I wonder why I am treated so? I have heard women say, I have tried to be a good mother: why is my child taken away from me? As though there was any sort of relation between the two facts. I hear people say, Don't talk to me about the justice of God, when here is a man, who has been dishonest all his life long, who has prospered, and become rich and lives in a fine house, drives his horses, and owns a yacht. As if there was any sort of connection between the two, as though a man merely because he had a fine house and owned a yacht was escaping the punishment of his unjust and selfish life.

Remember, friends, look a little below the surface. There is no possibility of escape. I break some law of my body; do I escape the result? I break some law of my mind; do I escape the result? I break some law of my affectional nature; is nothing to happen? I break a law of my spiritual nature; does nothing take place as the result of it? You might as well say that the law of gravity can be suspended, that a man can fling himself over the edge of a precipice, and come to no harm. The precipice over the edge of which you fling yourself may be a physical one, may be a mental one, an affectional one, a spiritual one; but the moral gravity of the universe is never mocked, and the man who breaks any of God's laws never goes free. He may discover that he has broken it, be sorry for it, begin to keep it again, and recover himself; but the consequences are sure, inevitable, eternal.

You look at a man who is externally prospering, and because of this you say he is not suffering the result of the evil he has done. Go back with me to Homer's Odyssey at the time when Ulysses and his companions fell into the hands of the sorceress, and his companions were turned into swine. Would you go and look at these swine, and say they are not suffering anything? See how comfortable they are. See with what gusto they eat the food that is cast into their troughs. See how happy they are as swine. They are not suffering anything Is it nothing to become swinish, merely because you have your beautiful pen to live in? Is a not suffering the result of his moral wrong when he debases and degrades and deteriorates his own nature, and becomes less a man, because he is surrounded with all that is glorious and beautiful that art can supply? Look within whatever department of nature where the law has been disobeyed, and there forever and forever read the result, the inevitable law, that the soul that sinneth, in so far as it sinneth, it shall die.

REWARD AND PUNISHMENT.

Two WEEKS ago I preached a sermon, the subject of which was "Morality Natural, not Statutory." Judging by the conversations which I have had and letters which I have received, it has aroused a good deal of question and criticism in certain quarters. This must be for one of three reasons. In the first place, the position which I took may not be a tenable one. In the second place, it is possible that the views expressed, being somewhat new and unfamiliar, were not found easy of apprehension and acceptance. In the third place, it is possible that, in endeavoring to treat so large a subject, I did not analyze and illustrate enough to make myself perfectly clear.

At any rate, the matter seems to me of such supreme importance as to make it worth my while this morning to continue the general subject by a careful and earnest treatment of the great question of reward and punishment as applied to feeling, to thought, to conduct, the whole of human life.

Let me say here at the outset, as indicating the point towards which I shall aim as my goal, that in the ordinary use of language, in the popular use of language, I do not believe in either reward or punishment: I believe only in causes and results. This, as I said, is the point that I shall aim at. Where shall I begin?

I need to ask you to consider for a moment the state of mind of man, so far as we can conceive it, when he first wakes up as a conscious being, and begins to look out over the scene of nature and human life with the endeavor to interpret facts as they appear to him. Of course, he knows nothing whatever of what we mean by natural law: he knows nothing of natural cause and of necessary result. So far as we can discover by our researches, all the tribes of men about whom we have been able to gather any information have had a belief, if not in God, at least in gods, or in spiritual existences and powers that controlled within certain limits the course of human events. It may have been the worship of ancestors, it may have been the worship of some great chief of the tribe; but these invisible beings have been able to help or hurt their followers, their worshippers; and of course they have been thought of as governing human life after substantially the same methods that they used when they were living here in the body.

That is, it has been a magical or arbitrary government of the world that has been for ages the dominant one in the human mind. People have supposed that these invisible beings desired them to do certain things, to refrain from doing certain other things, and they have expected them to reward or punish them how? By giving them that which they desired, on the one hand, or sending them something which they did not desire, on the other. They have brought the gods their offerings, their sacrifices, their words of praise, and have asked that they might be successful in war, that they might bring home the game which they sought when they went on a hunting expedition. When there have been disease, pestilence, famine, drought, no matter what the nature of the evil, they have been regarded as allotments of these divine powers sent on account of something they have done or omitted to do. It never occurred to them to interpret these as part of a natural order, because they knew nothing about any natural order. They reasoned as well as they were able to reason at that stage of culture in any particular age of the world's history which they had reached. But this has been the thought of men time out of mind concerning the method of the divine or spiritual or unseen government of the world.

Is this way of looking at it confined to primitive man, confined to pagan nations? Do we find something else, some other condition of mind, when we come to study carefully the Old Testament? Let us see. Take the first verse which I read as a part of my text. The author of this Psalm we do not know who he may have been says, "I have been young, and now am old; yet have I not seen the righteous forsaken, nor his seed begging their bread." As I have read this a great many times in the past, I have wondered as to the strange experience that this man must have had in human life, if this is a correct interpretation of that experience. I have been young: I do not like to admit that as yet I am old; but, whether I am or not, I have a good many times seen the righteous forsaken, and his seed begging their bread.

It seems to me that the writer of this verse was trained in a theory of the government of human affairs that does not at all match the facts. He has this magical, this arbitrary theory in his mind. It was the general conception I think, as any one will find by a careful reading of the Old Testament or study of Jewish history, the ordinary conception among the Hebrews, that God was to reward people for being good by prosperity, long life, many children, herds of cattle, distinction among his fellow-men, positions of political honor and power; and the threat of the taking away of these is frequently uttered against those that presume to do wrong. In other words, it seems to me that the ordinary theory of the government of human affairs as set forth in the Old Testament is precisely this same one that I have been considering as the natural and necessary outcome of the ignorance and inexperience of early man.

As time went on, now and then some deeper, more spiritual thinker begins to question this method of reasoning, begins to wonder whether it is quite adequate; and we have a magnificent poetical expression of this kind of critical thought in the Book of Job. This Book of Job is any way and every way worthy of your careful attention. It is the nearest to a dramatic production of anything in the Bible. James Anthony Froude said once in regard to it that, if it were translated merely as a poem and published by itself, it would take rank as a literary work among the few great masterpieces of the world.

But the thing that engages our attention this morning is not its power as a dramatic production, but its criticism of God's government of the world. It has been assumed, as I have said, and we are not through with that assumption, that, if a man suffered, if he was ill, if his wife or children were taken away from him, if his property was destroyed, somehow he had offended God, and that this was a punishment for the course of wrong-doing in which he had been engaged. But the author of the Book of Job conceives that this does not quite match the facts; so he gives us this magnificent character that he declares upright, spotless, free from wrong of any kind, who yet is suffering. He has lost his property, it has been swept away, his children have been put to death, almost everything that he cared for he has lost, and he from head to feet is sick of a loathsome disease; and he sits in the midst of his deprivation and sorrow. His friends gather around him; and with this old assumption in their minds some of them begin to taunt him. They say, Now, Job, why not confess, why not own up as to what you have been doing? Of course, you have been doing something wrong, or all this would not have happened. This is the tone that one of his critics takes. This is the kind of comfort that he receives in the midst of his sorrow. But Job protests earnestly and indignantly that it is not true. He says he is innocent, there are no secret wrongs in his life; and he wishes that he might find some way by which he could come into the presence of the great Ruler of the universe, and openly plead his cause. But his friends do not believe him.

Now the writer of the book lets us into the explanation he has thought out for this: God for a special reason is testing Job, to see whether he will be true to him in spite of the fact that he does not get the ordinary

56

blessings that the people were accustomed to look for as the rewards of their conduct. But the writer is not consistent with the wonderful position that he makes Job assume; for, after the trial is all over, he falls in with the popular theory, and shows us Job, not with the old children who could not be brought back, but with a lot of new ones, with herds and cattle again in plenty, with honor among his fellow-citizens, with all that heart could wish in the way of worldly prosperity and peace.

So I say the writer is not quite consistent, for he falls back at the end on the old theory, and he lets us gain a glimpse behind the scenes, just enough to see that there are cases, special cases, where the popular theory does not hold; but he still seems to assume that, in a general way, we are to accept it as correct, and as explaining the facts of human life.

The Jews acted on this theory in their political history. Their prophets, their great teachers, asserted over and over again that, if they were true to their God, if they were faithful in their obedience to the law, if they lived out all these highest and finest ideals of ceremonial as well as heart righteousness, that they would be mighty as a nation, that their enemies would be put under their feet, that they would have political success and power; and yet their increasing insistence on this ceremonial and interior righteousness of thought and life was found to be no adequate defence against the Roman legions. Political success did not come to them. In spite of all their obedience, they were swept out of existence as a nation.

Now do we find any difference in teaching in the New Testament? We do; and we do not. The teaching of the New Testament is not consistent in this matter. If Jesus be correctly reported, his own teaching is not quite consistent on this subject. Let me give you one or two illustrations, that you may see what I mean. John tells us that a certain man, who had been born blind, was brought to Jesus to be cured; and the people stood about, and said to Jesus, "Who is it, this man himself or his parents, that sinned, so that he was born blind?" You see it does not occur to them that there is any natural cause for a man's being blind, apart from some sin on the part of somebody. Who is it, then, his father or mother, or he himself, that has sinned, that is the cause of it? Jesus says, "Neither this man nor his parents have sinned," and you think at first that you are going to get an adequate explanation; but he straightway adds that the man was blind in order that the works of God might be manifest in him; which we cannot accept to-day as quite an adequate explanation.

Then take the case of the man who was lying at the pool of Bethesda, and was reported as cured. Jesus meets him, after a good deal of question and criticism on the part of the Jews, and says, "Now you have been healed, see to it that you sin no more, lest a worse thing come to you," seeming to imply again that sin might be punished by lameness, by affliction of this kind or that.

So it seems to me that we do not get, even in the New Testament, entirely free from this old conception. Indeed, there are the verses which I read as a part of our lesson from the fifth chapter of Matthew, one of which for a clear or more spiritual insight I have quoted as a part of my text, "Blessed are they that do hunger and thirst after righteousness, for they shall be filled" with what? Filled with righteousness; not filled with health, external prosperity, many children, friends, political position, honor. Blessed are the pure in heart, for they shall what? See God. "Blessed are the merciful, for they shall obtain mercy. Blessed are they that are persecuted for righteousness' sake, for theirs is the kingdom of heaven."

You see these beatitudes strike down to the eternal principle of natural, necessary causation and result, just as does the last verse which I have quoted from Galatians, "Be not deceived; God is not mocked; for whatsoever a man soweth, that shall he also reap," not something else, that. Here is a clear and explicit annunciation of the eternal, universal law of cause and effect, of the idea that those things which happen are not arbitrary infliction, but natural and necessary result.

Let us, then, consider this matter for a little as we look over the face of human life as it is manifested to us at the present time. I suppose hardly a week passes that, either by letter or in conversation, I do not come face to face with this same old problem, showing that only partially and here and there have men and women even to-day come to comprehend the real method after which this universe of ours is governed. For example, let me give you a few illustrations.

I have a friend in Boston, one of the noblest men I ever knew, sweet, gentle, true: he came to me one day, and said: "Mr. Savage, I have tried all my life to be an honest man. I do not own an ill-gotten dollar. I have tried to be kind and helpful to people in need, in trouble; and yet," and then it began to dawn on him that he was not on a very logical track, for he smiled, "and yet I have not got on very well in the world; I have not made a great deal of money; I have not been specially prosperous in business." And the implication was that here, next door or in another street, was a man who had a good many ill-gotten dollars, and who had not been generous or kindly or humane or tender, but who had prospered and become rich, as he had not. And he raised this as a serious objection against the justice of the government of the world.

I have had mothers; I presume a thousand times, say to me: "I have tried to take the best possible care of my child. I loved my child, I watched over it night and day, I have money enough to give it a good education, I could train it into fitness for life; and yet my child is taken away." Here is somebody else who has not the means to educate her child, perhaps whose character and intelligence are a good deal below the average level. Her child is spared, spared for what? Spared for a career for which it will be entirely unfitted; and the question is, Why does God do such things, why is the universe governed in this fashion?

57

And I have had persons say to me: "I have been ill all my life, I have suffered no end of pain and trouble: I wonder why? What have I done that I must be burdened and afflicted after this fashion?" So these questions are coming up perpetually, showing that underlying the ordinary surface of our common daily life is still this theory that God arbitrarily governs the world, and rewards people for being good with health and with money and with children and with all sorts of prosperity. There is no end of talk in regard to judgments, as they are called. I remember when I was living in the West I take this as an illustration as good as any a neighboring small city was badly devastated by fire. All the ministers around me in my city began to preach about it as a judgment of God for the supposed wickedness of this city. One peculiar thing about this particular judgment, which I noticed as reported in the papers, was that the last thing which the fire burned was a church; and it left standing next door, and untouched, a liquor saloon. It seemed to me a very peculiar kind of divine judgment, if that is what it really was.

And so, as you look into these cases of supposed divine judgments, which people are so ready to see in regard to their neighbors, you will find that it has some serious defect of this sort almost always that makes you question whether a wise man would be guilty of that method of conducting his affairs.

This, perhaps, is enough by way of setting forth the popular method of looking at these problems. I want to ask you now to go with me for a little while, as I attempt to analyze some of these cases, and get at the real principle involved as to what it is that is really going on.

Now take this case of the mother whose child is taken away from her, as she says. Let us see if we can find out what is really being done. It is possible, of course, that the child has inherited, it may be from a grandfather or great-grandfather, from somewhere along the line, a tendency to a particular kind of disease. It may be that, without anybody's being to blame for it or anybody's knowing it, the child was exposed to some contagious disease on the street or at school. It may be that the mother, through a little otherwise pardonable vanity, wishing to display the beauty of the child rather than to dress it in the healthiest manner, has been the means of exposing it to cold. It may be any one of a dozen things has caused the death of this child. And do you not see that in every case it has nothing whatever to do with the mother's moral goodness or spiritual cultivation? It is absurd to think that the mother, in this case, is being punished for something that she is entirely unconscious of having been guilty of. Do you not see that there is no logical connection between an inherited disease, between exposure, between taking cold, between any of these natural causes and the goodness of the mother? Is it not absurd to talk about their having anything whatever to do with each other?

I remember hearing a famous revivalist preach some years ago; and in this particular sermon he represented God as using all means to try to turn such a man from his path of evil, as he regarded it, into the way of right and truth and salvation; and he said: First, perhaps, God takes his property away from him; and that does not change him. And by and by he takes his wife; and that does not change him. And then he takes one of his children; and, as he expressed it, he lays these coffins across his pathway in order to warn him of his sinful condition, and turn him into the right way.

Think of a God who kills other people on account of my wrong!

I had a friend in Boston once, a lady, a school-teacher, who in all seriousness told me, when her sister died, that she was afraid God had taken her sister away because she had not been sufficiently faithful in attending church services during Lent. Think of it! Not only the lack of logic in linking things like these together, but the practical impiety of attributing to God such feelings and action in regard to his dealings with his children!

Let us take the case of a man who, not being highly elevated in character, becomes rich. Let us see if we can get at the principles involved here. Perhaps you can call to mind one or another case that you may be thinking of while I speak. Of course I shall mention no names. Here is a man who possesses remarkable natural business ability, power to read the commerce, the business of his times. He deals with these in a practical way. He complies with the conditions of accumulating wealth. No matter for the present whether he does wrong in doing it or not, that is, whether he is unjust or hard or cruel; but he complies with the conditions for the obtaining of money in this particular department of life. Now do you not see that, no matter what his moral character may be in other directions, whether he is kind to his wife, whether he is loving towards his children, whether he is generous in a charitable way, whether he is politically stanch or corrupt, do you not see that these questions are entirely irrelevant, have nothing whatever to do with the question of success in the money field? He sows according to the laws of the product which he wishes to raise, and the product appears.

Or take the case of a farmer: Here is a certain tract of land adapted to a particular crop. He sows wisely in this field. He cultivates it: the rain and the sun do their part; and in the fall he has a magnificent result. Now has that anything whatever to do with the question whether the man was a good man or not, as to whether he went to prayer-meeting or not, as to whether he read his Bible or not, as to whether he was profane or not, as to whether he was a good neighbor or not? Whatsoever a man soweth, that shall he reap, and reap it where he sows it. Is it not perfectly plain? So in any department of human life, I care not what, trace it out, and you will find that precisely the same principle is involved, and that you get results, not arbitrary bestowal's of reward or punishment.

Now I must come having, I hope, made this sufficiently clear, though after this fragmentary fashion to deal a little more with some of the ethical sides of this question. I have had no end of persons tell me, first and last, that it seemed to them that the universe could not be a moral universe, that it was not governed fairly, that reward and punishment were not meted out evenly to people; and they based their criticism on statements of fact similar to those with which I have been dealing.

Now let us look into the matter a little deeply; and let us see if we can find any hint of light and guidance. I have had a person within a week say to me, "I do not feel at all sure that it means much that people get the moral results of their moral action in a particular department of life. If a person becomes a little bit callous and hard, wisely selfish and prudent, and so prospers in the affairs of this life, I am not sure that he is not as well off as anybody, perhaps a little better off, perhaps a little better off than a person who is sensitive, and worries because he does not reach his ideals; and it is possible that he serves the world after all quite as well." This is a kind of criticism, I say, that has been made to me in the last week.

Let us look at it for just a minute. People do not seem able as yet to understand that a man is really "punished," in the popular sense of that word, unless they can see him publicly whipped. It does not seem to them to mean anything because a man deteriorates, because the highest and finest qualities in him atrophy and threaten to die out. I used an illustration in my sermon two weeks ago to which I shall have to recur again, to see if I can make it mean more than it did then. It is the story of Ulysses who fell into the hands of the famous sorceress, and whose companions were turned into swine. Now would you be willing to be turned into a pig, merely because, being a pig, you would not know anything about it, and would not suffer? Would you be willing to be reduced to the life of an oyster, merely because, being an oyster, you would be haunted by no restless ideals, and, so far as you had any sense at all, would probably be very comfortable indeed? Is there no "punishment" in this deprivation of the highest and finest things that we can conceive of?

It seems to me that a person who has deteriorated, who has become selfish, who has become mean, who has lost all taste for high and fine and sweet things, and is unconscious of them, is having meted out to him the worst conceivable retribution. If a man is mean and knows it, if a man is selfish and is conscious of it, if a man is unjust and is stung by the reflection, there is a little hope for him, there is life there, there is moral vitality, there is a chance for him to recuperate, to climb up into something higher and finer; but, if he has not only become degraded and mean, but has become contented in that condition, it seems to me that he is worse off than almost anybody else of whom we can dream.

Let us see for a moment on what conditions a man who has deteriorated is well off. There are three big "ifs" in the way, in my thought of it. If a man really is a spiritual being, if he is a child of God, if there are in him possibilities of unfolding of all that is sweet and divine, then he is not well off when he is not developing these, and is content not to develop them. Browning says, in his introduction to "Sordello," "The culture of a soul, little else is of any value."

If we are souls, and if the culture of a soul is of chiefest importance, then cursed beyond all words is the man who has deteriorated and become degraded and is content to have it so. Blessed beyond all words is the soul that is haunted by discontent, haunted by unattained and unattainable ideals, who is restless because of that which he feels he might be and yet is not, he who is touched by the far-off issues of divinity, and cannot rest until he has grown into the stature of the Divine!

And then, once more, if it be true that it is worth our while to help our fellow-men in the higher side of their nature, to help them be men and women, to help them realize that they are children of God, and to grow into the realization of it, if, I say, this be worth while, then lamentable beyond all power of expression is the condition of that man who does not feel it and does not care for it, and does not consecrate himself to its attainment. Look over the long line of those who have served mankind. Who are they? From Abraham down, the prophets of Israel; Jesus, Paul, Savonarola, Huss, Wyclif, Luther, Channing, Parker, who have these men been but the ones who were ready at any price to do something to lift up and lead on the progress of mankind? These are the ones who have felt the meaning of those sublime words of Jesus: "He that loseth his life shall save it." If there is any meaning in that splendid passage from George Eliot, that is so trite because it is so fine,

"Oh may I join the choir invisible
Of those immortal dead who live again
In minds made better by their presence: live
In pulses stirred to generosity,
In deeds of daring rectitude, in score
For miserable aims that end with self,
In thoughts sublime that pierce the night like stars,
And with their mild persistence urge man's search
To vaster issues.
So to live is heaven:
To make undying music in the world,
Breathing as beauteous order that control
With growing sway the growing life of man.
This is life to come,
Which martyred men have made more glorious
For us who strive to follow.

May I reach That purest heaven, be to other souls
The cup of strength in some great agony,
Enkindle generous ardor, feed pure love,
Beget the smiles that have no cruelty,
Be the sweet presence of a good diffused,
And in diffusion ever more intense.
So shall I join the choir invisible
Whose music is the gladness of the world."

If, I say, there is any meaning in that magnificent song, then indeed it is worth while to be miserable, if need be, worth while to suffer, worth while to sacrifice for the sake of planting seed in the spiritual fields, and looking for its spiritual results, and not finding fault with the universe because we do not get results of spiritual goodness in material realms.

There is one other "if." If it be true, as I believe it is, that this life goes right on, and that we carry into the to-morrow of another life the precise and accurate results that we have wrought out in the to-day of this; if it be true that, when we get over there, it will be spiritual facts and spiritual things with which we shall deal, then the man who has cultivated his spiritual nature and has reaped spiritual results has no right to find fault with the universe because it has not paid him with material good.

Let us remember, then, that we get what we sow. God has not promised to pay you in greenbacks for being good; God has not promised to give you physical health because you are gentle and tender; God has not promised to give you long life because you are generous; God has not promised to give you positions of social or political honor because you are kind to your neighbors, faithful to your wife, true to your children. Can you not see that whatsoever a man sowest, that shall he reap; and that he will reap in the field where he sows, and not in some other; and that God is dealing fairly, justly, tenderly, truly, with you in giving you the results at which you aim, and not the results at which you do not aim?

So, if you really care to be a man, if you care to be a woman, honest, noble, tender, true, then be these, and be grateful that you reap the reward where you sowed, and do not find fault with God or the universe because he does not pay you for things that you have not done, because he does not make a crop grow in some field that you have not cultivated, because it is eternally true that God is not mocked, and that whatsoever a man soweth, that shall he also reap.

THINGS WHICH DOUBT CANNOT DESTROY.

THE critical and investigating work of the modern world threatens to shake not the earth only, but also heaven. And there are large numbers of people who are disturbed and afraid: they are troubled lest certain things that are precious, that are dear to them, may be taken away. Not only this, they are troubled lest things of vital importance to the highest life of the world be taken away. I propose, then, this morning to run in rapid review over a few of the changes that are caused by the investigating spirit of the time, and then to point out some things that are not touched, that cannot be shaken, and that therefore must remain. And I ask you to have in mind, as I pursue this line of thought, the question whether doubt has taken away anything really valuable from mankind. The negative part of my theme I shall touch on very lightly, and dispose of as briefly as I may.

What has doubt, what has investigation, done concerning the universe of which we are a part? In the old days, before doubt began its work, before men asked questions and demanded proof, we lived in a little, petty, tiny world, which the imagination of the superstitious and the fear of ignorant men had created. But the cycles and epicycles which Ptolemy devised, and by means of which he explained, as well as he knew how, the movements of the heavenly bodies around us, these have passed away. The breath of doubt has blown upon them; and they have gone, like mists driven by the wind.

But has doubt quenched the light of any star? Has doubt taken away from the glory of the universe? Rather, as the result of the work of these myriad investigators, whose one aim and end was truth, at last we have a universe worthy to be the home of an infinite God, a universe that matches our thought of the Divine, a universe that thrills and lifts us, fills us with reverence, and bends us to our knees in the attitude of worship.

The same spirit has raised no end of questions concerning God. What has been the result? We have lost the old thought of God in the shape of a man sitting on a throne located in the heavens just above the blue or on some distant star. We have lost the thought of a God as a tyrant, as a jealous being, as angry every day with his children, as ready to punish these children forever for their ignorance, for their intellectual mistakes, for their sins of whatever kind. We have changed our conception of him; but have we lost God? I will not answer that question at this stage of the discourse, because I wish merely to suggest it now, and dwell on it a little more when I come to the positive treatment of our morning's theme.

Let us glance at the Bible a moment. Doubt and investigation have been at work there. What has been the result? Have we lost the Bible? No. We have gained it. We have lost those things about it which were intellectual burdens because we could not believe them, which were a moral burden because they conflicted with our highest and noblest sense of right. We no longer feel under the necessity of reconciling human mistakes with divine infallibility. Professor Goldwin Smith has told us recently that these old theories of the Bible were a millstone about the neck of Christendom, and that they must be gotten rid of if Christianity was to live. This is all that doubt and investigation have done to the Bible. They have cleared away the things that no sane and earnest and devout mind wishes to keep; and they have restored to us in all their dignity and beauty and sweetness and power the real human Bible, the Bible which poured out of the heart of the olden time, and which is in all its truth and sweetness, so far as they go, a revelation of the divinest things in human thought and human dream.

Preachers tell us every little while that those who ask questions have taken away our Lord, and they know not where he has been laid. What has this spirit done concerning Jesus? Has it taken him away from us? Rather, as the result of all this question and criticism, at last we have found him, found him who has been hidden away for ages, found the man, divine son of God, son of man, brother, friend, inspirer, companion, helper. It has done for Jesus the grandest service of which we can conceive.

And now one more point. People used to suppose they knew all about the next world. They knew where heaven was and where hell was, and who were to be the inhabitants of either place, and why. Doubt and question have been at work here, and now we do not know where heaven is; and we do not know where hell is, except that it is within the heart of those that are not in accord with the divine life. Where the places are, we know not; but blessed beyond all words be ignorance like this! We know because we believe in righteousness and truth that there is no hell except that which we create for ourselves; and that is in this world, in any world where there is a breach of a divine law. But has the great hope gone? Has doubt touched that, so that it has shrivelled and become as nothing? That I shall have occasion to touch on a little more at length in a moment; and so I leave it here with this suggestion.

I wish you now to note, and to note with a great deal of care, that doubt, criticism, question, investigation, have no power to destroy anything. People talk as though, if you doubted a thing, it disappeared, as though doubt had magical power to annihilate in some way a truth. If you really do doubt an important divine truth, it may disturb and trouble you for a while; but the truth remains just the same. I remember some years ago a parishioner came to me, an intelligent lady, and said, "Mr. Savage, I have about lost my belief in any future life." I smiled, and said: "I am sorry for you, if it interferes with your comfort and peace; but remember one thing, neither your doubt nor my belief touches or changes the fact." The eternal life is not something to be puffed away with a breath, if it be real. So rest right there in the firm assurance that whatever is true is true, and rests on the eternal foundation of the permanence of God; and asking questions about it, digging away at its foundations, testing it in any and all sorts of ways, cannot by any possibility injure it. Enforce thus this idea, simple as it seems, because thousands of men and women at the present time are made to tremble by utterances from the pulpit, as though doubt were really a destroyer. Of course, it seems commonplace the moment you think of it; and, still for your peace and for the restfulness of your mind as you look on the things that are taking place about us, hold fast to this simple idea.

There is one other point which I wish to raise. What is the use of criticism? What is the use of all this investigating? Why indulge in all this doubt? And now let me give you an illustration which will lead me to answering this question and enforcing the point I have in mind. A farmer, if he selects a favorable piece of ground, plants good seed, cultivates it properly, if the rain falls and the sun shines, and the weather is propitious, will have a successful crop. Does it make any difference now whether the farmer has correct ideas about soil and seed and cultivation? Does it make any difference whether he has any true conception of the nature and work of the sunshine in producing this crop? In one sense, No. In another, a very important sense, Yes. Suppose the farmer, having gotten into his mind the idea that the sun is the source of all the life and growth of the things that he plants and the crops he cultivates, should say, "Well, now, it does not make any difference whether I have correct scientific theories about the sun or not: the sun carries on his work just the same." I have heard people say, over and over again, using an illustration like this: "What difference does it make what your theories are about the spiritual life, about the origin and nature of religion, about morality? If you live a good life, the results are just the same, whatever your thinking may be." And I grant it. But now suppose the farmer should say to himself: "The sun is the source of all the life that I am able to produce, that I see growing around me; and now I will worship him as a god. I will pray to him, I will sing songs of praise to him, I will bring birds and animals and burn sacrifices to him; and so I will win his favor, and get him to produce these wonderful results for me." Suppose he should so seek his results, and pay no attention to the character of the soil, to the kind of seed he planted, or to proper cultivation: would that make no difference?

Do you not see that theory may be of immense practical importance in certain contingencies? Whether he has any knowledge of the sun or not, if he complies with the laws, the conditions, if he is fortunately obedient, then his results will be produced. But, if his ignorance, his superstition, lead him to neglect the natural forces with which he deals, then it may make all the difference in the world. So, as I study the history and development of religious thought, I see everywhere that men and women, through their ignorance in regard to the real nature of the universe and of God and of their own souls, are going astray, wasting time, wasting thought, wasting effort, misdirecting all these instead of complying with the real natural universal conditions on which these noblest and highest results which they desire depend.

If a man, for example, believes that he is to please God by a sacrifice, by an offering, by swinging incense, by going through a certain ceremony, instead of being righteous and true, does it make no difference? Carry out the idea as far as you please, I think I have made plain the thought I had in mind.

So it does make a difference what our thoughts, our theories, may be; and, therefore, there is good in this work of investigation which proposes to sift and test and try things, and find out the real nature of the forces which confront us and with which we have to deal.

Now, then, I come to the positive answering of our question. Are there some things that doubt cannot touch? And are these things the most important ones, the ones that we need to feel solid under our feet? What do we need? We do not need to be able to unravel all the mysteries of the universe. Any quantity of the questions we ask are not practical ones. We do not need to wait for an answer to them. Any number of the things that are in doubt are of no practical consequence; and we need not wait for their settlement before we begin to live and to help our fellowmen and to do what we can to bring in the coming kingdom of our Father.

I wish to note now a few of the things that seem to me very stable things, that doubt cannot disturb. And first I will say that which I mean when I use the word "God." I wish you to learn to separate between the word and the reality. Sometimes people are quarrelling over a label instead of the reality that is back of all. I care very little for a name. I care for things, for the eternal truths of the universe. May we then feel that modern doubt does not touch our belief in God? I ask you to consider a moment, and see. As we wake up, assuming nothing, and look abroad, what do we find? We find ourselves in the presence of a Power that is not ourselves, another Power, a Power that was here before we were born, a Power that will be here after we have died, a Power that has produced us, and so is our father and mother on any theory you choose to hold of it, a Power out of which we have come. Now suppose we look abroad, and try to find something in regard to the nature of this Power. We can conceive no beginning: we can conceive no end. And let me say right here that, as the result of all his lifelong study and thinking as an evolutionist, Mr. Herbert Spencer has said that the existence of this infinite and eternal Power, of which all the phenomenal universe is only a partial and passing manifestation, is the one item of human knowledge of which we are most certain of all.

An Infinite Power, then, an eternal Power, shall I say an intelligent Power? At any rate, just as far as our intelligence can reach, we find that the universe matches that intelligence, responds to it, so that we must think of it, it seems to me, as intelligent. Out of that Power, as I have said, we have come; and who are we? Persons, persons that think, persons that feel, persons that love, persons that hope; and we are the children of this Power, and, according to one of the fundamental principles of science, nothing can be evolved which was not first involved, the stream cannot rise higher than its source, that which is produced must be equal to that which produces it.

This Power, then, eternal, infinite, intelligent, must be as much as what we mean by person, by thought, by love, by hope, by all that makes us what we are. Shall we call a Power like this God? Shall we call it Nature? Shall we call it Law? Shall we call it Force? It seems to me that, if we take any name less and lower than God, we are indulging in a huge assumption, and a negative assumption at that. Suppose that, looking at one of you, I should call you body instead of calling you man. I should be assuming that you are only body, which I have no right to do. If I call this Infinite Power, then, Nature, Force, Law, Matter, I am indulging in a negative assumption which is scientifically unwarranted. As a reasonable being, then, I think I am scientifically warranted in saying that belief in God is something that all investigation only affirms, and affirms over and over again, and with still greater and greater force.

I have not time to go into this at any further length this morning; but I believe that we are scientifically right in saying that all the doubt, all the investigation, all the questioning of the world, have only given us a stronger and more solid assurance that we have a divine Power around us, and that we are the children of that Power.

In the next place, to carry the idea a little farther, we want, if we may, to believe that this Infinite and eternal Power manifested in the universe is a good Power. If it be not, we are hopeless. I hear reformers sometimes in their zeal picturing the dreadful condition of affairs socially or industrially or politically, and saying that the world is getting worse and worse, that the rich are getting richer, and the poor are getting poorer, and the republic is becoming more corrupt week by week and year by year, giving the impression that the world in general is on the down grade. If I believed that, I should give it up, I should see no reason for struggle and effort. If an Infinite Power is against me in my efforts to do good, what is the use of my making the effort?

We want to know, then, as to whether a belief in the goodness of this Infinite Power is a thing that doubt and investigation have not touched and cannot disturb. Let us consider just a moment one or two thoughts bearing upon it.

The pessimist tells us that the universe is bad all the way through, that this is the worst possible kind of world. When a man makes a statement like that, I always wish to ask him a question which it seems to me absolutely overturns his position, how did he happen to find it out? If the universe is bad all through, essentially bad, where did he get his moral ideal in the light of which to judge and condemn it? How does this bad universe produce an amount of justice and truth and love to be used as a measuring-rod in order to find out whether it will correspond with these ideals or not? That one question seems to me enough to turn pessimism into nonsense.

Let us look at it in another way. As we look back, as far as we can towards the beginning of things, we find this fact: when man appeared on the earth, conscience was born, as I told you the other day, a sense of right came with him, and since that day he has been struggling to attain and realize an ever and ever enlarging and heightening ideal. This, then, the conscience, the sense of right, the ideal, must be a part of the nature of the universe that has produced them. And we notice that these have been growing with the advance of the ages. Before dwelling on that a little farther, let me touch another consideration which is germane to it.

If you look over the face of human society, you get proof positive, scientific demonstration unquestionable, that good is in the majority, love is the majority power of the world. How do I know? You draw up a list of all those things that you call evil, and you will note, as you analyze them, that they are the things that tend to disintegrate, to separate, to tear down; and you draw up a list of those things that you call good, and you will find that they are the things that tend to build up, that bind human society together, and help on life and growth and happiness.

Now the simple fact that human society exists proves that the things that tend to bind together are more powerful than the things that tend to disintegrate and tear down. Just as, for instance, if you see a planet swinging in the blue to-night, you will know that the centripetal power is stronger than the centrifugal, or there would be no planet there. That which tends to hold it together is mightier than that which tends to disintegrate and fling its particles away from each other. So the simple fact that human society exists proves that good is in the majority.

And then, as we trace the development of human society from the far-off beginning, we find that justice, truth, tenderness, pity, love, helpfulness, all these qualities have been on the increase, and are growing; and, since the Power that has wrought in lifting up and leading on mankind is unspent, we believe that that Infinite Power of which we have been speaking is underneath this lifting, is behind this progress, and that the end may reasonably be expected to issue in that perfection of which we dream and whose outlines we dimly see afar off.

An infinite power, then, a power that is good, a power that we may study, partially understand, at any rate, and co-operate with. We can help on this progress instead of hindering it. We can do something to make the world better. Here are two things then, God and goodness, that no doubt, no investigation, have ever been able to touch or destroy.

A third thing. We want to believe that there is a meaning in these little individual lives of ours. Sometimes, when we read of pestilences or the great wars of the world, when we think of children born and dying so soon almost as they are born, when we note the brevity of even the longest life and take into account the sweep of the ages, we sometimes find ourselves depressed with the thought that these human lives of ours mean so little. It sometimes seems as though nature cared nothing for us, and swept us away as the first cold and the frost sweep away the millions of flies that had been buzzing their little hour of sunshine.

We need to feel, then, if we are to live manly, womanly lives, that there is some plan, or may be some purpose in our being born, in our little struggle of a few years, in our being thwarted, in our succeeding, in our being sick or well, in our being rich or poor, in our being learned or ignorant. Does it make any difference how we live these lives of ours? Is there significance in them, any purpose, any plan, any outcome, to make it worth while for us to struggle and strive? We need to know this; and what do the investigation and the doubt and the struggle of the world say to us concerning these? If there is anything which science teaches us, it is that the infinite God, the Power, whatever we name it, that is the thought and life of this universe, is expressed just as perfectly in the tiniest atom as in the most magnificent galaxy. There is no such thing as an imperfect atom in this universe. The infinitesimal atoms below us, and the tiny orbits through which these atoms and molecules sweep, are as much in the grasp of the Eternal Law as the movements of the stars over our heads.

Things are not lost in this universe out of the eternal purpose because they are little. So our apparent littleness, the weakness, feebleness of our lives, need not disturb the grandeur of our trust in this direction.

Then as we study ourselves, as we see the good that has been growing through the ages, and as we note the fact that I hinted at a moment ago, that we can plant ourselves in the way, and hinder the working of the Divine, so far as our tiny strength goes, or that we can study the conditions of this growth and co-operate and help it on, and so be just as truly a builder of the highest and finest humanity of the future as God is himself, as we note this, are not our little lives raised into dignity and touched with glory? And why should I cringe and humiliate myself in the presence of a planet a thousand times larger than our earth, or a sun a million and a half times larger than the planet that shakes to its centre as I stamp my tiny foot? I, or one like me, has measured the sun, weighed it as an apothecary can weigh a gram in his scales. I have untangled the rays of his light, and am able to tell the substances that are burning those ninety millions of miles away, in order to send down that ray of light to our earth. I have untangled the mysteries of the heavens, and find these only aggregations of matter like those of which my body is composed; but I deal with all these and overtop them, speeding with my thought with the rapidity that leaves the lightning behind. And I know that, because I can think God and can trace his thoughts after him as he goes through his creative processes, so I am more than these,— a child of the Creator. I may feel as a little boy feels who stands beside his father who is the captain of some mighty ship. The ship may be a million times greater than he; but the captain's intelligence and hand made it, shaped it, rules it, turns it whithersoever he will. And I am the captain's child, like him, and capable of matching his masterly achievement.

And so I may believe that I, as a child of the infinite Father, am of infinite importance to him in this universe of his; and I can live a grand and noble life. Nobody can harm me but myself. Place an obstacle in my path, and, whether it be insurmountable or not, I may show myself a coward or a hero as I face it. Tell me I have made a mistake, I can repair it. Tell me I have committed some moral error, am guilty of sin, I confess it. But I can make all these mistakes and sins stairways up which I can climb nearer and nearer to God. You may test me with sorrows, affliction, take away my property, take away my health, take away my friends; and the way in which I receive these may either make me nobler or poorer and meaner, as I will. The sun shines upon the earth. It turns one clod hard, makes it incapable of producing anything. It softens and sweetens another, the same sun: the difference is in the way in which it is received. So these influences may touch me, may make me hard and bitter and mean and rebellious, or I may stand all, and say, as the old Stoics used to, "Even if the gods are not just, I w ill be just, and shame the gods."

So man may say, Whatever comes upon me, I will meet it like a man, and like a child of the Highest, and so make my life significant, a part of the divine plan, something glorious and real.

One thought more. When we have got through with this life, and stand on the shore of a sea whose wavelets lap the sands at our feet, and the ships of those that depart go out into the mist, and we wonder whither, what has doubt done, what has investigation done, touching this great hope of ours, as we face that which we speak of as the Unknown? So far as the old-time and traditional belief is concerned, I hold that doubt has been of infinite and unspeakable service. Certainly, I could rather have no belief at all than the old belief. Certainly, I would rather sink into unconsciousness and eternal sleep than wake to watch over the battlements of heaven the ascent of the smoke of the torment that goeth up forever and ever. But is there any rational ground for hope still? I cannot stop this morning even to suggest to you the grounds for the assertion that I am about to make. I believe that, if we have not already demonstrated eternal life, we are on the eve of such demonstration. I believe that another continent is to be discovered as veritably as Columbus discovered this New World. As he, as he neared the shore, saw floating tokens upon the waters that indicated to him that land was not far away, so I believe that tokens are all about us of this other country, which is not a future, but only a present, unseen and unknown to the most of us.

But grant, if you will, that that is not to be attained, modern investigation and doubt have done nothing to touch the grounds of the great human hope that springs forever in the breast, that hope which is born of love, born of trust, born of our dreams, born of our yearning towards the land whither our dear ones have departed.

Let me read you just a few lines of challenge to those that would raise a question as to the reality of this belief:

What is this mystic, wondrous hope in me, That, when no star from out the darkness bore Gives promise of the coming of the morn, When all life seems a pathless mystery Through which tear-blinded eyes no way can see; When illness comes, and life grows most forlorn, Still dares to laugh the last dread threat to scorn, And proudly cries, Death is not, shall not be? I wonder at myself! Tell me, O Death, If that thou rul'st the earth, if "dust to dust" Shall be the end of love and hope and strife, From what rare land is blown this living breath That shapes itself to whispers of strong trust, And tells the lie, if 'tis a lie, of life? Where did this wondrous dream come from? How does it grow as the world grows?

It must be a whisper of this eternal Being to our hearts; and so, in spite of all the advance of knowledge, all the criticism, it remains untouched, brightening and growing. And so there is reason, as we gaze out on the future, why we should look with contempt, if you will, upon the conditions that trouble us in this life, the burdens, the sorrows, the illnesses, when all that life means at its highest is that out of the conditions, whatever they are, I should shape a manhood, cultivate a soul, make myself worth living, fitting myself for that which gleams through the mist a promise, if you will, of something there beyond.

Now I wish simply to call your attention to the fact that doubt does not touch this eternal Power, does not touch the fact that this is a good Power, and that it is on the side of goodness, does not touch the fact that we are the children of that Power and may co-operate with it for good and share its ultimate triumph, does not touch the great hope that makes it worth while for us to suffer, to bear, to dare all things. And these great trusts, are they not all we need to be men, to be women, to conquer the conditions of life and prove ourselves children of the Highest?

EVOLUTION LOSES NOTHING OF VALUE TO MAN.

I TAKE two texts, one of them from the New Testament. It may be found in the fifth chapter of the Gospel according to Matthew, the seventeenth verse, "Think not that I came to destroy the law or the prophets: I came not to destroy, but to fulfil." The other text is from Emerson: "One accent of the Holy Ghost The heedless world hath never lost."

The theory of evolution to-day, in the minds of all competent students, is quite as firmly established as is the law of gravity or the Copernican theory in astronomy. But, when it was first propounded in its modern form by Herbert Spencer, when he issued his first book, and when Darwin's "Origin of Species" was published, there was an outcry, especially throughout the religious world. There was a great fear shuddered through the hearts of men. They felt as though the dearest things on earth were threatened and were likely to be destroyed. Essayists declared that this theory undermined the foundations of morals. They said that it took away, not only the Bible, but God and all rational religion. They told us that, in tracing the ancestry of man back and down to the animals, humanity was being desecrated, and that the essential feature of man as a child of God was being taken away.

If I believed that any of these things were true, I might not be an enemy of evolution, if indeed it be established; for there is very little reason in a man's setting himself against an established truth. But I should certainly be very sad, and should wish that we might hold some other theory of things. But I believe that it will appear, as we study the matter a little while carefully, that not only are these charges that have been brought against the theory baseless, but that right here is to be found not only the real progress of the world, but the true conservatism. Evolution is the most conservative theory that has ever been held. It keeps everything that has been found serviceable to man. It may transform it. It may lift it to some higher level, on to some loftier range of life; but it keeps and carries forward everything that helps. This inevitably and in the nature of things.

There are two great tendencies which are characteristic of that method of progress or growth which we call by the name of evolution. One is the hereditary tendency, and the other is the tendency to variation. One, if it were in full force, would merely, forever and forever, repeat the past: the other, if it were in full force, would blot out all the past, and forever be creating something new. It is in the balance of these two tendencies that we discover the orderly growth of the world; and this orderly growth it is which constitutes evolution. Let me illustrate: Here is a tree, for example. The tendency that we call heredity would simply constantly repeat the past: the tendency to vary would vary the tree out of existence. The ideal is that it shall keep its form, for example, as an oak, but that, in the process of growth, the bark shall expand freely and sufficiently to make room for the manifestation of the new life. Now, if the bark had power to refuse expansion, of course, you know, the tree would die. If there were not power enough to maintain the form, then, again, the tree would cease to exist. This you may take as a type and illustration of the method of all life and all progress everywhere.

Those people who naturally represent the heredity tendency what we call the conservative people of the world are the ones who are always afraid of any change. They deprecate the utterance of new ideas. They hesitate to accept any new-fangled notions, as perhaps they call them. They are afraid that something precious, something sweet, something dear, that belonged to the past, may be lost.

This manifests itself in all departments of life. I suppose that there never was an improvement proposed in the world that somebody did not object to it in the interests of the established order. And yet, if these people that do not want any changes made had had control of the world ten thousand years ago, where should we be to-day? We should still be barbarians in the jungles. For it is because these people have not been able to keep the world still that we have advanced here and there in the direction of what we are pleased to call civilization. You remember, for example, as illustrating this opposition, how the workingmen, the laborers of the time, a few years ago, in England, fought against the introduction of machinery. They said machinery was going to take their work away, it was going to break down the old industrial order of the world, it was going to make it impossible for the laborer to get his living. A few machines were to do the world's work; and the great multitude were to be idle, and, not having anything to do, were to receive no pay for labor, and consequently were to starve. This was the cry. The outcome has been that there has been infinitely more done, a much larger number of laborers employed, employed less hours in the day, paid higher wages; and in every direction the condition of the industrial world has been improved. I speak of this simply as an illustration of this tendency.

When we come to religion, it is perfectly natural that the opposition here should be bitterer than anywhere else in the world; and it always has been. If you think of it just a little, if you read the history of the world a little, you will find that the last thing on earth that people have been willing to improve has been their religion. And this, I say, is perfectly natural. Why? Because men have instinctively felt and rightly felt, as I believe that religion was the most important thing in human life. They felt that it was the most sacred thing, that on it depended higher and more permanent interests than on anything else; and they have naturally been timid, naturally shrunk from change, with the fear that changing the theories and the practices and the thoughts was going to endanger the thing itself. They have said, We will hold on, at any rate, to these reverences, these worships, these precious trusts, these hopes; and we will hold on to the vessels in which we have carried them, because how do we know, if the vessels are changed or taken away, that we may not lose the precious contents themselves? This, I say, has been the feeling; and it has been a perfectly natural feeling.

I wish then, this morning, for a little while to review with you some of the steps in evolution that the world has taken, and let you see how it has worked in different departments of human thought and human life, so that you may become convinced if possible, as I am that evolution has never thrown away, has never lost, anything precious in any department of the world since human life began. If I believed it did, I would fight against it. For instance, here is a devout Catholic servant-girl. She believes in her saints. She counts her beads and recites her Ave Marias. She goes to the cathedral on Sunday morning. And this is her world of poetry and romance. Here is a source of comfort. This throws a halo around the drudgery of the kitchen, the service of the house in which she is an employee. Would I take away this trust, this poetry, this romance, untrue as I believe it to be in form, inadequate as I believe it to be? Would I take it away, and leave her mind bare, her heart empty, leave her without the comfort, without the inspiration? Not for one moment. I would take it away only if, in the process, I could supply her with something just a little better, a little more nearly true, something that would give her comfort, something that would be an inspiration to her, something that would buoy her up as a hope, something that would help her to be faithful and true in the work of her daily life. This is what evolution means. It means taking away the old, and, in the process, substituting therefore something a little bit better. I would not take away the idol of the lowest barbarian unless I could help him to take a step a little higher, so that he should see the intellectual and spiritual thing that the idol stood for, and so enable him to walk his pathway of life as firmly, as faithfully, as hopefully, as he did before.

I have been watching the work that has been going on in our streets during the last months. You, too, have seen how they will replace the track on an entire line of railway without stopping the running of the cars. They take away the old and worn and poorer, but constantly substitute something better for it; and human life moves right on. Everything is better; the change has come; but that change is; an improvement. This is what evolution does; for evolution is nothing new in the world. It is only the name for the method of God, which is as old as the universe itself, new to us because we have just discovered it; but as old as the light of a star that has been travelling for twenty-five thousand years, and has just come into the field of the astronomer's telescope, so that he announces it as a new discovery.. This is what it means.

Now let me call your attention to the fact that in the world below us the world of the trees and the shrubs and the flowers and the plants this evolutionary force is working after precisely the same method that I have just been indicating. All the fair, the beautiful things have been developed under this process, in accordance with this method, out of the first bare and rough and crude manifestations of vegetable life. Nothing has been thrown away that was of any value. Take it, for example, in regard to the wild weeds which have become the oats and the wheat and the barley and the rye of the world. All the old that was of value has been kept and has been developed into something higher and finer and sweeter. The aboriginal crab-apple has become a thousand luscious kinds of fruits; and the flowers all their beauty, all their fragrance, all their color and form? are the result of the working of this method of God's power that we have called evolution. Nothing of any value is left behind in the uncounted ages of the past. All that is of worth to-day has been transformed and lifted to some higher level and made a part of the wondrous life that is all around us.

So, when you come to the animal life, you find the same thing. The swift foot, the flashing wing, the beauty of color, all the wonders of animal life have simply been developed in accordance with this method and under this impelling force which we call evolution, which is only a name for the working of God.

When we come up to the level of man, what do we find? Man as an animal is not the equal of a good many of the other animals in the world. He is not as swift as the deer, he is not as strong as the lion, he cannot fly in the air like a bird, he cannot live in the sea like the fishes. He is restricted to the comparatively contracted area of the surface of the land. He is not as perfect as an animal; but what has evolution done? It has given him power of conquest over all these, because the evolutionary force has left the bodily structure, we need expect no more marked changes there, and has gone to brain. So this feeblest of all the animals physically speaking he would be no match for a hundred different kinds of animals that are about us is able to outwit them all, that is, to outknow, he has become the ruler of the earth. And not only has this evolutionary force gone to brain, it has gone to heart; and man has become a being whose primest characteristic is love. The one thing that we think of as most perfect, that we dream of as characterizing his future development, is summed up in his affectional nature. Then, too, he has become a moral being.

There are times, like the present, when it seems as though the animal were at the top, and the affectional nature suppressed, and the conscience were ruled out of court; and yet you study the methods of modern warfare as compared with those of the past, you see how pity and tenderness and care walk by the side of every gun, hide in the rear of every battlefield to attend to the wounded and suffering. And you know what talk there has been of pity for the hungry, the desire of the world to feed those that need; and the one dominant note in the discussion of the war all over the world has been the question as to its being right. No matter how we may have decided, whether the decision be correct or not, the civilized world bows itself in the presence of its ideal of right, and demands that no war shall be fought the issue of which is not to be a better condition of mankind.

Evolution, then, tends to the development of brain, heart, conscience, and the spiritual nature of man. It has left nothing behind that is of any value to us. It has transformed or sublimed or lifted all up into the higher range of the life that we are living to-day, and contains within itself a promise of the higher and the grander life that we reach forward to to-morrow.

I wish now, for a moment, to illustrate the working of this in regard to some of the institutions of the world. If I had time, I could show you that the same law is apparent in the development of the arts, sculpture, painting, poetry. I must pass them by, however. As illustrating what I mean, let me take the one art of music. From the very beginning man has been interested in making some sort of sounds which, I suppose, have been regarded as music by him. Most of those that are associated with the barbaric man would be anything but music to us. The music, for example, that they give in connection with a play in a Chinese theatre would not be acceptable to the cultivated ear of Americans. We have left behind much that the world called music. We have left behind any number of musical instruments. We do not now have those that the Psalmist makes so much of, the old-time harp, the sackbut, the psaltery. I do not know, though you may, what kind of instruments they were. The world has completely forgotten them, and left them out of sight. And yet no musical note, no musical chord, no musical thought, no musical feeling, has been forgotten or dropped along the advancing pathway of the world's progress; and in our organs all the attempts at instruments of that kind from the beginning of the world are preserved, transformed and glorified. In our magnificent orchestras all the first feeble beginnings are developed until we have a conception of music to-day such as would have been utterly incomprehensible to the primeval man. What I wish you to note is and this is the use of my illustration that the advancing growth of the music of the world has forgotten nothing that it was worth while to keep.

66

Let me give you one more illustration. Take it in the line of government. The first tribes were governed by two forces, brute force and superstitious fear. These were the two things that kept the primal tribes of the world in order, such order as was maintained in those far-off times. The world has gone on developing different types of government, different types of social order. I need not stop to outline them for you this morning: you know what they are; and I only wish you to catch the thought I have in mind. I suppose that every time one of the old types was about to pass away the adherents of that type have been in a panic lest anarchy was threatening the world. Believers in these types have said that it was absolutely necessary to keep them, in order to preserve social order. Take the attitude of the monarchy to-day, for example, as towards the republic. When we attempted to establish our republic here in this western world, it was freely said by the adherents of the old political idea in Europe that it would of necessity be a failure, that there was no possibility of a stable human order without a hierarchy of nobles with a king at the top; and I suppose they believed it. But we have proved beyond question that we can have a strong government, an orderly government, without either nobility or king. There is less government in the United States here to-day than in almost any other country of the world, a nearer approach to what the philosopher would call anarchy. Anarchy does not mean disorder, when a philosopher is talking: it means merely the absence of external government. And that is the ideal that we are approaching.

Paul says, you know, that the law was made for wicked people, for the disobedient and the disorderly, not for good people. How many people are there in New York to-day, for example, who are honest, who pay their debts, who did not commit a burglary last night, who do not propose to be false to wife and home, on account of the law, the existence of courts and police? The great majority of the citizens of America to-day would go right on being honest and kind and loving and helpful, whether there were any laws or not. They are not kept to these courses of conduct by the law. They have learned that these are the fitting ways of life that these are the things for a man to do; and they despise themselves if they are less than man. In other words, this governmental order, which exists as an outside force, at last gets written in the heart and becomes a law of life.

Now precisely the same process is going on in other departments of the world: it is going on in religion. And now let me come to religion, and illustrate the working of the law here. The old types of religious thought and life and practice, the first ones that the world knew, are long since outgrown. We regard them as barbaric, as cruel.

We have learned that there are not a million gods of whom we need stand in awe. We have learned that God is no partial God. We have learned that God does not want us, as universal man once believed, to sacrifice the dearest object of our love. We have learned that he does not want us to sacrifice our first-born child, as the old Hebrews used to, and the remains of which custom are plainly visible throughout the Old Testament everywhere. We have left behind these old types of religious thought and life; but the world has lost nothing in the process. The world has not left religion behind. The whole process of growth and development in the sphere of the religious life and the development of man has been one of outgrowing crude and partial and inadequate thoughts and feelings about the universe and God and man and duty and destiny.

We do not care so much about ceremony as the world did once. The most civilized people in the world are not so given to these things in their religious development. We do not care so much about creed as they did a thousand or five hundred years ago. We do not believe that God is going to judge us by our intellectual conceptions of him and of our fellow- men. And I suppose it is true, always has been true as it is to-day, that the adherent of any particular form or theory of the religious life has the feeling that, when that is threatened, religion is threatened; and he defends it passionately, fights for it, perhaps bitterly, feels justified in opposing, perhaps hating, those he regards as the enemies of God and his great and sacred and religious hopes. And yet we know, as we study the past, whether we can quite appreciate it as true in regard to the theories which I am voicing to-day, that the truth has never been in any danger, and the highest and finest and sweetest things in the religious life have never been in any danger, are not in any danger to-day.

Let me indicate in two or three directions. There has been a class of thinkers, which has done a good deal of talking and writing in this direction, who are telling us that the poetry, the romance, the wonder, the mystery, of the world those things that tend to bring a man to his knees and to lift his eyes in awe and reverence are passing away; that science is going to explore everything; that there is going to be no more unknown; and that, when we have completed this process, one of the great essentials of religious thought and feeling and life will have perished from among men. I venture to say to you that there has never been a time in the history of the world when there was so much of mystery, so much of wonder, so much of reverence, so much of awe, as there is to-day. We are apt to fool ourselves in our thinking, and, when we have observed a fact, and labelled it, to think we know it.

For example, here is this mysterious force that we call electricity, which is flashing such light in our homes and through our streets as the world has never known before. The cars, loaded, are speeding along our highways with no visible means of propulsion. We step up to a little box, and put a shell to our ear, and speak and listen, and converse with a friend in Boston or Chicago, recognizing the voice perfectly, as though this friend were by our side. We send a message over a wire, under the deep, and talk to London and all round the globe; and we have labelled this force electricity. And, instead of getting down on our knees in reverence, we get impatient if our communication is delayed two minutes or three. We fool ourselves with the thought that, because we have called it electricity, we know it, we have taken the mystery out of the fact. Why, friends, do you know anything about electricity? Do you know what it is? Do you know why it works as it does? I do not; and I do not know of anybody on the face of the earth who does. The wonder of the "Arabian Nights" is cheap and tame and theatrical compared to the wonder of this everyday workaday world of ours, in the midst of which and by means of which we are carrying on our business and our daily avocations. The wonder of the carpet that would carry the person through the air who sat upon it and wished is nothing compared with the power of electricity, steam, any one of these invisible, intangible powers that are thrilling through the world to-day. There never was so much room for mystery, for awe, for poetry, for romance, as there is in the midst of our commercial life in this nineteenth century.

This element of religion, then, is in no danger. We know nothing ultimately. Who can tell me what a particle of matter is? Who can tell me what a ray of light is, as it comes from a star? Who can tell me how the movements in the particles of air striking my eye run up into nerve and brain, and become translated into thought, into light, into form, into motion, into all this wondrous universe that surrounds us on every hand?

Then take the element of trust. People used to think they could trust in their gods. Rebecca, for example, stole her father's gods, and hid them in the trappings of her camel, and sat on them. She thought, then, that she had a god near her who would care for her. The old Hebrew, with an ox-team, carried his God, in a box that he called the ark, into battle, and supposed that he had a very present help in time of need. But we have the eternal stability and order of the universe, a God that never forgets, a God on whom we can lean, in whom we can trust, who is not away off in heaven, but here, closer to us than the air we breathe, a God in whom we live and move and have our being.

And has this evolution of the religious life of the world threatened the stability of truth? There never was a time on earth when there was such a passion for truth as there is today. What means all this intense activity of the scientific world? these men that devote their lives to some little fraction of the universe which they study through their microscope, not for pay, to find one little fragment of the truth of God; these critics that are rummaging the dust-heaps of the ages in the hope that they may find one little, bright-glittering particle of truth in the midst of the rubbish? There never was such a passion for truth as there is here and now.

Are we going to lose the sense of righteousness which is the very heart of religion? There never was a time since the world began when the average man cared so much for righteousness, when he laid so much emphasis on human conduct, on kindness, on help, on all those things that make this life of ours desirable and sweet. The ideal of character and behavior has risen step by step from the beginning, and is higher to-day than it ever was before. Not because men fear a whipping, not because they are threatened with hell in another world, not because a God of vengeance is preached to them, because they have grown to see the beauty of righteousness, because they know that obedience to the laws of God means health, means sanity, means peace, means prosperity, means well-being, means all high and good and noble things. This righteousness is not driven into one by blows from outside: it blossoms out from the intellect and the conscience and the heart, as the recognized law of all fine and desirable and human living.

What are we losing, then, as the result of this growth of the world in accordance with the law of evolution? Are we losing our hope of the future? The form of that hope is passing away. We no longer believe in an underground world of the dead, as the Hebrews did. We no longer believe in a heaven just above the blue, as Christendom has believed for so long. We no longer believe in a heaven where all struggle and thought and study and growth are left out, where there is to be only a monotonous enjoyment that would pall upon any living rational soul. The form of it is passing away; but there never was a time when there was such a great and inspiring hope, not simply for myself and my friends, not simply for my neighbors, not simply for my particular church. There never was a time when there was such a great hope, including humanity for this world and for the next, as that which inspires us now.

Nothing, then, in religion that is of any worth has the world forgotten or is it likely to forget. All the old reverences and loves and trusts and inspirations and hopes and tendernesses are here intermingled. They are in the highest and noblest people; and they are being carried on and refined and purified and glorified as the world goes on.

And now let me suggest one thought more that may be of comfort to some. A great many people have been accustomed to associate so much of their religion with the forms of their religious expression that they fancy that the world's outgrowing these means that religion is being outgrown. I said, you remember, when touching upon government as an illustration of the working of the law of evolution, that governmental forms were being outgrown just as fast as the world was becoming civilized. If this world ever becomes perfect, government will cease to be, in the sense of these external forms, simply because there will be no need of it; just as you take down a staging when you have completed a house. So I look forward to less and less care for the external forms of the religious life. I believe they will remain, and they ought to remain, just as long as they are any practical help to anybody; but, because a person ceases to need them, you must not think that he has ceased to be religious. When the world gets to be perfectly religious, there will be no need of any churches, there will be no need any more of preachers, there will be no need of any of the external ceremony of religion.

You remember what the old seer says in the book of Revelation, as he looks forward to the perfect condition of things. He is picturing that ideal city which he saw in his vision coming down from God out of

68

heaven. This was his poetical way of setting forth his idea of the perfected condition of humanity; and he said, speaking of that city, "And I saw no temple therein, for the Lord God was the temple of it."

The external forms pass away when the life needs them no more. Take, for example, the condition of things when Jesus came to Jerusalem. You know how they put him to death. And what did they put him to death for? They put him to death because he preached of a time when there would be no need of any temple, no need of any priesthood, no need of any of the external things that they regarded as essential to religious life. They thought he was blaspheming, they thought he was an enemy of God and of his fellowmen, because he talked that way. He said to the woman of Samaria, You think you must worship God on this mountain, Gerizim, and the Jews think they must worship him on Mount Moriah; but God is spirit, and the time will come when you will not care whether you are in this place or that, but will worship him in spirit and in truth.

You see it was just along these lines that Jesus was preaching and working in his day. So, when humanity becomes perfected, external forms, that have helped mould and shape man into his perfection, will be needed no more. They will fall off, pass away, and be forgotten; but that will not mean that humanity has forgotten or left behind any great essential to the religious life. It will mean simply that he has taken them up into his own heart, absorbed them into his life. He naturally drops them when he is no longer in need of external supports.

This law of evolution, then, is simply the method of God's progress from the beginning, the same method which was to be found in the lowest, the method which has lifted us to where we are, the method which looks out with promise towards the better things which are to come.

The one life thrilled the star-dust through,
In nebulous masses whirled,
Until, globed like a drop of dew,
Shone out a new-made world.
The one life on the ocean shore,
Through primal ooze and slime,
Crept slowly on from less to more
Along the ways of time.
The one life in the jungles old,
From lowly creeping things,
Did ever some new form unfold,
Swift feet or soaring wings.
The one life all the ages through
Pursued its wondrous plant
Till, as the tree of promise grew,
It blossomed into man.
The one life reacheth onward still;
As yet no eye may see
The far-off fact, man's dream fulfill?
The glory yet to be.

WHY ARE NOT ALL EDUCATED PEOPLE UNITARIANS?

THE religious opinions of the average person in any community do not count for much, if any one is studying them with the endeavor to find out their bearing on what is true or what is false. This is true not only of popular religious opinions, but of any other set of opinions whatever; and for the simple reason that most people do not hold their opinions as the result of any study, of any investigation, because they have seriously tried to find out what is true, and have become convinced that this, and not that, represents the reality of things.

Let us note for a moment and I do this rather to clear the way than because I consider it of any very great importance how it is that the great majority of people come by the religious opinions which they happen to hold. I suppose it is true in thousands of cases that a man or a woman is in this church rather than that merely as the result of inheritance and childhood training. People inherit their religious ideas. They are taught certain things in their childhood, they have accepted them perhaps without any sort of question; and so they are where they happen to be to-day. If you stop and think of it for just a moment, you will see that this may be all right as a starting-point, but is not quite an adequate reason why we should hold permanently, and throughout our lives, a particular set of ideas. If all of us were to accept opinions in this sort of fashion, and never put them behind us or make any change, where would the growth of the world be? How would it be possible for one generation to make a little advance on that which preceded it, so that we could speak of the progress of mankind? Then, when persons do make up their minds to change, to leave one church and go to another, it is not an uncommon thing for them simply to select a particular place of worship or a special organization for no better reason than that they happen to like it, to be attracted to it for some superficial cause. How many people who do leave one church for another do it as the result of any earnest study, or real endeavor to find the truth? And yet, if you will give the matter a moment's serious consideration, you will see that we have no sort of right to choose one theory rather than another, one set of ideas rather than another, because we happen to like one thing, and not something else. Liking or disliking, a superficial preference or aversion, is an impertinence when dealing with these great, high, and deep questions of God and the soul, of the true or the false.

Then I have known a great many people in my life who went to a particular church for no better reason than mere convenience. It was easily accessible, it was just around the corner, they did not have to make any long journey, and did not have to put themselves out any to get up a little earlier on Sunday morning, which they would otherwise need to do. A mere matter of convenience! And this is so many times allowed to settle some great question of right or wrong. Then you will find those who select a particular church or a particular church organization, become identified with it, merely because on a casual visit to the place they were taken with the minister, happened to like his appearance, his method of speaking, the way he presented his ideas. Or perhaps they were attracted by the music. There are persons who decide these great questions of God and truth and the soul for no more important a reason than the organization and the capacity of the church choir.

It is not an uncommon thing for people to attend some particular church because it promises to be socially advantageous to them. It is fashionable in a particular town. I have a friend, I still call him friend, a Boston lawyer, who told me in conversation about this subject one day that he deliberately went to the largest church he could find, and that, if in the particular city in which he was residing the Roman Catholic Church was in the majority, he should attend that. There are thousands of persons who wish to be in the swim, and who are diverted this way or that by what seems to them socially profitable. Think of it, claiming to be followers of the Nazarene, who was outcast, spit upon, treated with contempt, on whom the scribes and Pharisees of his day looked down with bitterness and scorn, and who led the world for the sake of his love for God out into a larger truth, who made himself of no reputation, claim to be followers of him, and let a matter of fashion decide whether they will go this way or walk in some other path I Think of the irony of a situation like that!

Then, again, there are those who attach themselves to some one church rather than to another because, after looking over the ground, they made up their minds that it would be to their business advantage. They will become associated with a set of people who can help them on in the world. It is all very well, if there be no higher consideration, for a person to be governed in his action by motives like these; but is it quite right to decide a question of truth or falsehood, of God or duty, of the consecration of the human soul, of the service of one's fellow- men, on the basis of supposed financial advantage? There is hardly a year goes by that persons do not come to me, considering the question as to whether they will attend my church. I can see in a few minutes' conversation with them that they have some purpose to gain. They wish to be helped on in the prosecution of some scheme for their own advancement. If they succeed, they are devout Unitarians and loyal followers of mine. If not, within a few weeks I hear of them as devoted attendants somewhere else, where they have been able to make their personal plans a success.

These are some of the reasons there are worthier ones than these which influence the crowd. There are, I say, worthier ones. Let me hint one or two. I do not think it is any sacrilege, or betrayal of confidence, for me to speak a name. The late Frances E. Willard, one of the ablest, truest, most devoted women I have ever known, frankly confessed to me in personal conversation that she was more in sympathy with my religious ideas than of those of the Church with which she was connected, but her love, her tender love and reverence for her mother and the memory of her mother's religion were such that she could not find it in her heart to break away. She loved the services her mother loved, she loved the hymns her mother sung, she loved the associations connected with her mother's life. All sweet, beautiful, noble; but, if nobody from the beginning of the world had ever advanced beyond mothers' ideas where should we be to-day? Is it not, after all, the truest reverence for mother, in the spirit of consecration she showed to follow the truth as you see it to-day, as she followed it as she saw it yesterday?

So much to justify the statement I made, that the average popular belief on any subject is not a reliable guide to a person who is earnestly desiring to find the simple truth.

Now let us come to the answer of the specific question which I have propounded. Why are not all educated people Unitarians? I ask this question, not because I originated it, but because it has been put to me, I suppose, a hundred times. People say, You claim to have studied these matters very carefully, you have tried to find the truth, you think you have found it. You have followed what you regard as the true method of search. If you have found the truth, and if other people, using this same method and being as unbiased as you, could also find it, how does it happen that Unitarians are in the minority? Why do not all persons who study and who are educated accept the Unitarian faith? This question, I say, has been asked me a great many times; and it is a question that deserves a fair, an earnest and sympathetic answer. Such an answer I am now to try to give.

In the first place, let me make a few assertions. I have not time to prove them this morning; but they are capable of proof. The advantage of a scientific statement is that, though you do not stop to prove it, you know it can be proved any time, whenever a person chooses to take the time or trouble. For example, if I state the truth of the Copernican system, or that the earth revolves around the sun, and you challenge me to prove it in two minutes, I may not be able to; it may take longer than that; but I know it can be demonstrated to-morrow or next week or any time, because it has been demonstrated over and over again.

I wish now to assert the truth of certain fundamental principles; and these principles, you note, are those which constitute the peculiarity of the Unitarian people as a body of theological believers. For example, that this which is all around us and of which we are a part is a universe is demonstrated beyond question. It is one, the unity of the universe. The unity of force, the unity of substance or matter, the unity of law, the unity of life, the unity of humanity, the unity of the fundamental principles of ethics, the unity of the religious life and aspiration of the world, these, I say, are demonstrated. And do you not see that demonstrating these carries along with it the unquestioned, the absolute demonstration of the unity of the power that is in the universe and manifests itself through it? The unity of God? The Lord our God is one! And this is no question of speculation, it is demonstrated truth. Now, as to any speculative or metaphysical division of God's nature into three parts or personalities, there is not, and there cannot be, in the nature of things, one slightest particle of proof. The unity is demonstrated: anything else is incapable of demonstration.

Next, the Unitarian contention I say Unitarian, not because we originated it by any means, but simply because we first and chiefly among religious bodies have accepted it as to the origin and nature of man as science has unfolded it to us, thus precluding the possibility of the truth of any doctrine of any fall. This is not speculation, it is not whim. It is not something picked up by the way, that a man chooses because he likes it, and because he does not like something else. This is demonstrated truth, as clearly and fully demonstrated as is the law of gravity or the fact that water will freeze at a certain temperature. Then the question of the Bible. The Unitarian position in regard to the origin, the method of composition, the authenticity and the authority of Biblical books, is a commonplace of scholarship. There is no rational question in regard to it any more. Next, the question of the origin and nature of Jesus the Christ. The naturalness of his birth, the naturalness of his death, his pure humanity, are made clearer and surer by every new step which investigation takes; and there is nothing in the nature of proof that is conceivable in regard to any other theory. If any one chooses to accept it, well; but nobody claims, or can claim, to prove it, to settle it, to demonstrate it as true. It becomes an article of faith, a question of voluntary belief; but there is no possibility of holding it in any other way. So as to the nature of salvation. It is a matter of character; a man is saved when he is right. And that he cannot be saved in any other way is demonstrable and demonstrated truth.

Now, these are the main principles which constitute the beliefs of Unitarians; and in any court of reason they are able to make good their claim against any corner. And, if there be no other motive at work except the one clear-eyed, simple desire to find the truth, there can be no two opinions concerning any of them.

Why, then, are not all thoughtful, educated people Unitarians? Well may the listener ask, in wonder, if the statements I have just been making are true. Now I propose to offer some suggestions, showing what are some of the influences at work which determine belief, and which have very little to do with the question as to whether the beliefs are capable of establishing themselves as true or not.

In the first place, let us raise the question as to what is generally meant by education. We assume that all educated people ought to agree on all great questions; and they ought, note now what I am saying, they ought, if they are really and truly educated, and if with a clear and single eye they are seeking simply the truth. But, in order to understand the situation, we need to note a good many other things that enter into this matter of determining the religious path in which people will walk. Now what do we mean by education? Popularly, if a man has been to school, particularly if he is a college graduate, if he can read a little Latin and speak French, and knows something of music, if he has graduated anywhere, he is spoken of as educated. But is that a correct use of language? Are we sure that a man is educated merely because he knows a lot of things or has been through a particular course of study? What does a human education mean? Does it not mean the unfolding, the development of our faculties in such a way that in the intellectual sphere we can come into contact with and possession of the reality of things, the truth? Intellectually, is there any other object of education than to fit a man to find the truth? And yet let me give you a case. Here is a man, I take it as an illustration simply, not because I have anything particular against the Catholic Church any more than against any other body of believers, who has been through a Catholic college, has made himself master of Catholic doctrine, become familiar with theological and ecclesiastical literature; suppose he knows all the languages, or a dozen of them, having them at his fingers' ends. Do you not see that as a truth-seeker in a free world he may not be educated at all? He may be educated, as we say, or trained is the better word, into acceptance of a certain system of traditional thought, that can give no good reason for itself; for his prejudices, his loves and hates may be called into play. He may be trained into the earnest conviction that it is his highest duty to be loyal to a particular set of ideas.

Take the way I was educated. I grew up reading the denominational reviews, and the denominational newspapers. I was taught that it was dangerous and wicked to doubt. I must not think freely: that was the one thing I was not permitted to do. I went to a theological school, and had drilled into me year after year that such beliefs, about God and man and Jesus and the Bible and the future world, were unquestionably true, and that I must not look at anything that would throw a doubt upon them. And I was sent out into the world graduated, not as a truth-seeker, but to fight for my system, as a West Point graduate is taught that he must fight for his country without asking any questions.

Do you not see that this, which goes under the name of education, instead of fitting a man to find the truth, may distinctly and definitely unfit him, make it harder for him to find any truth except that which is contained in the system which has been drilled into him from his childhood up and year after year? Education, in order to fit a man to be a truth-seeker, must be something different from this merely teaching a man a certain system, a certain set of ideas, and drilling him into the belief that he must defend these ideas against all corners.

A good many people, then, who are called educated, are not educated at all. I have had this question asked me repeatedly: If your position is true, here is a college graduate, and here is another; and here is a minister of such a denomination, or a priest of the Catholic Church; why do they not accept your ideas? Do you not see, however, that this so-called education may stand squarely in the way?

Now, in the second place, I want to dwell a little on the difficulty of people's getting rid of a theory which possesses their minds, and substituting for it another theory. And I wish you to note that it is not a religious difficulty nor a theological difficulty nor a Baptist difficulty nor a Presbyterian difficulty: it is a human difficulty. There is no body of people on the face of the earth that is large enough to contain all the world's bigotry. It overflows all fences and gets into all enclosures. Discussing the subject a little while ago, by correspondence with a prominent scientific man in New England, I got from him the illustrations which I hold in my hand, tending to set forth how difficult it is for scientific men themselves to get rid of a theory which they have been working for and trying to prove, and substitute for it another theory. I imagine that there may be a physiological basis for the difficulty. I suggest it, at any rate. We say that the mind tends to run in grooves of thought. That means, I suppose, that there is something in the molecular movements of the brain that comes to correspond to a well-trodden pathway. It is easy to walk that path, and it is not easy to get out of it. Let it rain on the top of a hill; and, if you watch the water, you will see that it seeks little grooves that have been worn there by the falling of past rains, and that the little streams obey the scientific law and follow the lines of least resistance. There comes a big shower, a heavy downfall; and perhaps it will wash away the surface and change the beds of these old watercourses, create new ones. So, then, when there comes a deluge of new truth, it washes away the ruts along which people have been accustomed to think; and they are able to reconstruct their theories. Now let me give you some of these scientific illustrations. First, that heat is a mode of motion was proved by Sir Humphry Davy and Count Rumford before 1820. In 1842 Joule, of Manchester, England, proved the quantitative relation between mechanical energy and heat. In 1863 note the dates Tyndall gave a course of lectures on heat as a mode of motion, and was even then sneered at by some scientific men for his temerity. Tait, of Glasgow, was particularly obstreperous. To-day nobody questions it; and we go back to Sir Humphry Davy and Count Rumford for our proofs, too. It was proved scientifically proved then; but it took the world all these years, even the scientific world, to get rid of its prejudices in favor of some other theory, and see the force of the proof.

Now, in the second place, it was held originally that light was a series of corpuscles that flew off from a heated surface; but Thomas Young, about the year 1804, demonstrated the present accepted theory of light. But it was fought for years. Only after a long time did the scientific world give up its prejudice in favor of the theory that was propounded by Newton. But to-day we go back to Young, and see that he demonstrated it beyond question.

In the third place, take another fact. Between 1830 and 1845 Faraday worked out a theory of electrical and magnetic phenomena. It was proved to be correct. Maxwell, a famous chemist in London, looked over the matter, and persuaded himself that Faraday was right; but nobody paid much attention to either of them; until after a while the scientific world, through the work of its younger men, those least wedded to the old-time beliefs, conceded that it must be true.

The Nebular Theory was proved and worked out by Kant more than a hundred and thirty years ago. In 1799 Laplace worked it out again; but it was a long time before it was accepted. And now we go back to Kant and Laplace for our demonstration.

Darwin's "Origin of Species" was published in 1859. But it was attacked by scientists as well as theologians on every hand. Huxley even looked at it with a good deal of hesitancy before he accepted it. To-day, however, everybody goes back to the "Origin of Species," and finds the whole thing there, demonstration and all.

Lyell published a book on the antiquity of man in 1863. It was twenty- five years before all the scientific men of the world were ready to give up the idea that man had been on the earth more than six or eight thousand years.

So we find that it is not theologians only; it is scientists, too, that find it difficult to accept new ideas. I know scientific men among my personal friends who are simply incapable of being hospitable to an idea that would compel them to reconstruct a theory that they have already accepted. Why are not all educated men Unitarians? Why do not scientific men accept demonstrated truth when it is first demonstrated as truth? It puts them to too much trouble. It touches their pride. They do not like to feel that they have thrown away half their lives following an hypothesis that is not capable of being substantiated.

Then, in the third place, there are men, and educated men as the world goes, who deliberately decline to study new truth; and they are men in the scientific field and in the religious field. They purposely refuse to look at anything which would tend to disturb their present accepted belief. In my boyhood I used to hear Dr. John O. Fiske, a famous preacher in Maine. He told a friend of mine, in his old age, that he simply refused to read any book that would tend to disturb his beliefs. Professor William G. T. Shedd, one of the most distinguished theologians of this country, a leading Presbyterian divine, published so I am not slandering him by saying it a statement that he did not consider any book written since the seventeenth century worth his reading. And yet we have a new world since the seventeenth century, a new revelation of God and of man. To follow the teaching of the seventeenth century would be to go wrong in almost every conceivable direction. What is the use of paying any attention to the theological or religious opinions of a man who avows an attitude like that?

Faraday, to come now to a scientific illustration, so that you will not think I am too hard on theologians, Faraday belonged to one of the most orthodox sects in England; and he used to say deliberately that he kept his religion and his science apart. He says, "When I go into my closet, I lock the door of my laboratory; and, when I go into my laboratory, I lock the door of my closet." He did very wisely to keep them apart; for, if they had got together, there would certainly have been an explosion.

Another scientific illustration is Agassiz. Agassiz unconsciously wrought out and developed some of the most wondrous and beautiful proofs of evolution that the world has ever known; and yet he fought evolution to the last day of his life, simply because he had accepted the other theory. And he got it into his head that there was something about evolution that tended to injure religion and degrade man, not a rational objection, not a scientific objection, but a feeling, a prejudice.

There is another class of people that I must refer to. Institutions and organizations come into being, created, in the first place, as the embodiment and expression of new and grand truths; and after a Arile their momentum becomes such that the persons who are connected with them cannot control their movements, and these persons become victims of the organizations and institutions to which they belong. So, when a new truth appears, the old organization rolls on like a Juggernaut car, and crushes the life, so far as it is possible, out of everything in its way. Take, for example, and note what a power it is and what an unconscious bribe it is to those who belong to it, the great Anglican Church. A man's ambitions, if he has learning, power, ability, tell him that there is the Archbishopric of Canterbury ahead of him as a possibility. His hopes, the chances of promotion and power, are with the institution. And, then, it is such a tremendous social influence. It is no wonder, then, that men who are not over-strong, who have not the stuff in them out of which heroes are made, should cling to the institution and remain loyal to it, even while they are false to the truth that used to animate it and for which alone any institution ought to exist.

Let me give you another illustration. Edward Temple, late Bishop of London, and who is now the Archbishop of Canterbury, had a priest of the established Church come to him and make a confession of holding certain beliefs which he knew were heretical. The archbishop said to him frankly: As Edward Temple, I believe them, I am in sympathy with your views. As the head of the English Church, I must be opposed to them; and the opinions which you hold cannot be tolerated. That is what the influence of a great organization may come to.

Let me give you another concrete illustration. Here is our American Bible Society, which publishes and circulates millions of Bibles all over the world. It is obliged, as at present organized, to print and distribute the King James version of the Bible; but there is not a scholar or a minister connected with the organization anywhere who does not know at least, since the revision at any rate that in many important respects the King James version is not an accurate translation of the original, even if that is conceded to be infallible. So that this organization stands to-day in the position of being obliged to circulate all over the world for God's truth any number of teachings that are simply blunders of the translator, of the copyist, or interpolated passages that have come down from the past.

So men in every direction become persuaded that they must be loyal to the organization. I know cases where a minister in conversation with a friend has said: So long as I remain a member of this Church, I have got a great institution back of me, and I can accomplish so much socially and in every way on account of it. I know I do not believe half of the creed, but any number of other ministers are in the same box. And so they stay true to the organization, while truth to the truth is sacrificed.

One other influence that keeps so many of these old ideas alive or prolongs their existence beyond the natural term is right in here. Any number of men, educated, strong, prominent men, give their countenance and influence to the support of old-time religious organizations because they believe that somehow or other they are serviceable as a police force in the world, they keep people quiet, they help preserve social order. I have had people over and over again say that they believed it would be a great calamity to disturb the Roman Catholic Church, because it keeps so many people quiet. Do you know, friends, I regard this as the worst infidelity that I know of on the face of the earth. It is doubt of God, his ability to lead and manage his world without cheating it. It is doubt of truth, as to whether it is safe for anybody except very wise people, like a few of us! It is doubt of humanity, its capacity to find the truth, and believe in it and live on it. Do you believe that God has made this universe so that it is healthier for the masses to live on a lie than it is for them to live on the truth? Is that your confidence in God? Is that the kind of God you worship? It is not the kind I worship. There is no danger of the ignorant masses of the world getting wise too fast, judging by the experience of the past up to the present time. There is only one thing that is safe; and that is truth. Do you know what the trouble was at the time of the French Revolution? It was not that the people began to reason and think, and lost their faith, as so frequently said by superficial historians: it was that they waked up at last to the idea that the aristocracy and the priesthood had not only been fleecing them financially and keeping them down socially, but had been fooling them religiously, until at last they broke away, having no confidence left in God or priest or educated people or nobility or anything. No wonder they made havoc. If you want to make a river dangerous, dam it up, keep the waters back, until by and by the pressure from the hills and the mountains becomes so great that it can be restricted no longer; and it not only breaks through the dam, but bursts all barriers, floods the country, sweeps away homes, farms, cattle, human beings, towns, cities, leaving ruin in its path. Let rivers flow as God meant them to; and they will be safe.

So let the world learn,— learn gradually, and adapt itself to new truth as it learns, and there will be an even and orderly march of human progress. The danger is in our setting ourselves up as being wiser than God, wiser than the universe, and doling out to the multitude the little fragments of truth that we think are fitted for their digestion. The impertinence of it, and the impiety of it!

I must not stop to deal with other reasons which lie in my mind this morning. You can think along other channels for yourselves. I have simply wished to suggest that, in the kind of world we are living in, you may not be sure, at any particular age in history, that a set of ideas is going to be accepted by the multitude merely because they are true; and, because they are not accepted at once, you are not, therefore, to come to the conclusion that they are not true. There never has been a time in the history of the world when the truth was not in the minority. Go back to the time of Jesus: do you not remember how the people asked whether any of the scribes or the Pharisees believed on him? They were ready to accept him if they could go with the crowd; but it never occurred to them to raise the question as to whether it was their duty to go with him while he was alone, as to whether two or three might not represent some higher conception of God, some forward step on the part of humanity. Consider for just a moment, let it be in literature, in art, in government, in ethics, anywhere, find out where the crowd is, and you will find where the truth is not. Disraeli made a very profound remark when he said that a popular opinion was always the opinion which was about to pass away. By the time a notion gets accepted by the crowd, the deeper students are seeing some higher and finer truth towards which they are reaching.

The pioneers are always in the minority. The vanguard of an army is never so large as the main body that comes along behind after the way has been laid out for it.

"Then to side with Truth is noble when we share her wretched crust."

That is Lowell's suggestion, in that famous poem of his. If we care for truth, we shall not wait until it becomes popular. The truth in any direction to-day, if we had the judgment of the world, would be voted down. Christianity would be voted down among the religions; Protestantism would be voted down in Christianity; and the highest and finest thinkers in the Protestant churches would be voted down by the majority of the members.

Do not be disturbed, then, or troubled, because you have not the crowd and the shouting accompanying you on your onward march; and remember that there must be something of heroism in this consecration to truth. I wish to quote to you, as bearing on this truth, a wonderfully fine word which I have just come across in a recent number of the Cosmopolitan Magazine, the word of the Hon. Thomas B. Reed, the Speaker of the House of Representatives. He says, "One with God may be a majority; but crucifixion and the fagot may antedate the counting of the votes." But, if it means crucifixion and the fagot, and we claim to be followers of the Nazarene and worthy of him, even for that we shall not shrink. It is our business simply to raise the question, and try to answer it or ourselves, Which way must I go to follow the truth? And that way I must tread, whether it means life or death, whatever the consequences; for the truth-seeker is the only God-seeker.

WHERE IS THE EVANGELICAL CHURCH?

As you are aware, there are certain churches that have taken the name of Evangelical, thereby, of course, putting forth the claim that in some special or peculiar way they have the gospel in keeping. For "Evangel" is the word translated "gospel," "Evangelist" is a "preacher of the gospel," "Evangelical" is the appropriate name for the church whose ministers preach the gospel. And the word "gospel," as you know, translated, means good news. It is the proclamation of hope, of something that the world has been groping in darkness for, a message that should lift the burden off the human heart, make men stronger to endure, fill them with cheer in the midst of life's difficulties and dangers, and give them a trust with which to walk out into the darkness that lies at the end.

A certain section, I say, of the Christian Church has appropriated this name; and by common consent it has been conceded to it. And as usage makes language, and the dictionaries only record the results of popular usage, why, of course, we must confess that this use of words is right. Right in that sense, I say. But I wish to go back of this popular usage this morning, and raise the question as to whether these churches that claim the title are the ones to whom it peculiarly or exclusively belongs. I wish to put forward the claim that we, though the idea is entirely against popular thought, are really the ones who are preaching the gospel of God, and that the liberals of the world come nearer today to proclaiming the actual original gospel of Jesus the Christ than do any other body of Christians in the world. I wish to do this, not in any spirit of antagonism, but simply by way of clear definition, and that we may understand where we are, and may unfalteringly and trustingly and loyally and hopefully go on to do the highest work that was ever committed to human hands.

At the outset, though it will necessitate my saying certain things which I have said to you before, I must outline briefly that body of doctrine which goes by the name of "Evangelical." I will not go back two or three hundred years to include in it such dogmas as Foreordination, Election, the Damnation of non-Elect or non-Baptized Infants, though these doctrines still remain in the creeds. I will take what must be considered the simpler and fairer course of confining myself to setting forth those beliefs which are generally accepted, and which are made a part of the creed of the so-called "Evangelical Alliance" that is, an organization including representatives of all the great so-called Evangelical Churches. These beliefs, in brief, are that God created the world perfect in the first place, but that in a very short time it was invaded by the evil powers, and mankind rebelled against the Creator, and became the subjects of the devil as the god of this world. Then man, by thus rebelling against God, lost his intellectual power to discern truth, became mentally unable to discover spiritual truth, to find the divine way in which he ought to walk; and that he became morally incapable, so that, even when the truth was presented to him, he felt an aversion towards it, and was disinclined to accept it. The next point is this being the condition of things that God began to reveal himself to the world, first, by angel messengers, by prophets, by inspired men, and that then at last, through certain chosen mediums, he wrote a book telling men the truth about their condition, about his feeling towards them, about what they ought to do, and the destiny involved in the kind of life they should live here. After the world had been in existence about four thousand years, according to this teaching, and very little headway had been made even among the chosen people, the few that had been selected from the great outside and wandering nations, God himself comes down to earth, by means of a woman specially prepared to be his mother he is born without a human father. He lives, he suffers, he dies. This, after one theory or another, I need not go into them, to make it possible for God to forgive, and to enable him to save those who should accept the terms which he should offer.

Then, after his withdrawal from the earth, his Church is organized under the special guidance of the Holy Spirit. Its mission is to proclaim the gospel among all nations. That proclamation has gone on; but after two thousand years not a third of the world has heard the gospel, not a third of the people who walk the planet knows anything about the book that has been written. But they still stumble along in darkness, worshipping anything except the one only and true God. So that this effort up to the present time would strike us, if we judged it as a human device, as being a sad and lamentable failure.

The upshot of this, according to the Evangelical creed, is that the great majority of the world is to be permanently lost. Only a few, those who are converted or those becoming members of the true Church, connected with it sacramentally or in some way, only the few are to be saved, and the great majority outcast forever.

This, in substance, makes up what has been called the gospel; and those who claim that they are preaching the gospel are preaching these things as true. I am well aware and I would not have anybody suppose that I overlooked it that this creed is undergoing very striking and marked changes, and that a great many of those things which some of us look upon as more objectionable are being left out of sight, and not preached, as they used to be, though they still remain in the creeds.

I am aware, for example, that what it is to be orthodox or evangelical has been reduced to very low terms as compared with those which I have just set forth; that is to say, reduced to very low terms in certain quarters. For instance, Dr. Lyman Abbott, of Brooklyn, tells us that we need not believe in the infallibility of the Bible any more; that we need not believe in the old-time Trinity; that we need not believe that Jesus was essentially different from a man; we need not believe in the virgin birth, unless we find it easy to accept it. But the two things which he tells us we must believe in order to be orthodox, or evangelical, are that in some way, though he does not define how, the Bible contains a special message from God to the world, and that in some way Jesus particularly and specially represents God, and that he reveals him to men, so that, when he speaks, he speaks with authority, as representing divine truth. Everlasting Damnation eliminated, Foreordination not referred to, the Trinity transformed, Infallibility no longer insisted on, the humanity of Jesus granted, to be orthodox, according to Dr. Abbott, has become a comparatively simple thing.

In my conversations with clergymen of other churches during the past winter I have discovered that there, too, among certain men, the conditions of being orthodox are a great deal simpler than they were a hundred years ago. An Episcopalian tells me it is only necessary to accept the Nicene and the Apostles' Creeds, and that even then one is at liberty to interpret them as he pleases; that this is what constitutes Orthodoxy and makes one evangelical.

But this process of eliminating the hard doctrines has not gone on in any authoritative way on the part of the Church itself. There has been no proclamation of any such liberty allowed; and I am not aware that the most of these men have made any public statement in their own churches of these positions. It may be known through personal conversations that they hold these views; and, if they are rendering good service, they may not be disturbed by the church authorities in their positions.

So much, then, for a statement as to what constitutes the Evangelical Church, as to what must be the message of the minister who is to preach "the gospel of Christ."

Now I wish to call your attention for a moment to another way of looking at these doctrines. I am not to question their truth. I simply wish to ask you to note as to whether, considering them true, we should be inclined to speak of them as good news. Are they a gospel? Can we with gladness proclaim them to men? For example, suppose God, after creating the world, loses control of it, an evil power comes in, his enemy, takes possession of his fair earth, alienates from him the hearts of the only two of his children who are in existence here, and who are to be the parents of a countless race. Suppose that is true. Is it something we would like to believe? Is it good news? Can we call it an integral part of a gospel?

Suppose, again, that God writes a book, an infallible book, and gives it to whom? To a few people, to the little company of Jews who lived on that little narrow strip of land on the eastern shore of the Mediterranean.

He does not give it to anybody else. He has given, indeed, according to this theory, the Old Testament and the New to Christendom since that day. But think a moment.

According to what we know to be true now, man was on this planet for two or three hundred thousand years before God revealed himself at all; and the race went stumbling on and falling in darkness, no light, no hand stretched out to help, no voice speaking out of the silent heavens, the world, apparently, absolutely forgotten, so far as God's truth was concerned. Suppose that, after two or three hundred thousand years, God did give an infallible book to the world. As I had occasion to say a moment ago, comparatively a very small part of his children have heard anything about it. And, then, what is very striking, the proofs of its having come from him are so weak that most of the wisest, the best, the noblest of the world, cannot accept any such claim on its behalf. Is this, if it be true, good news? Would we speak of it as a gospel, something of which to be glad, something to proclaim to mankind as a cheer, a message from on high?

Once more, suppose, after the world had been in existence for two or three hundred thousand years, God comes down, incarnates himself, wears a human body, and does what he can to save men. If it is true, in the economy of the divine government, that human souls could be saved in no other way, is that good news? Would we think of it as a gospel to proclaim to mankind, that God himself must suffer, must be outcast, be spit upon, be reviled, be put to death, and that only so could he forgive one of his wandering children, and bring him back to himself?

Then, once more, suppose all this to be true, and suppose that, as the outcome of it all, the countless millions of men and women and children that have walked the earth during the last three hundred thousand years, until the Jews received their first light from heaven, suppose that they have been lost: that is a part of this gospel. Suppose that since that time all the nations outside of Christendom have been lost: that is a part of this gospel. Suppose that not only this be true, but that all people in Christendom who have not been members of churches have been lost. Suppose even, as I used to hear it preached when I was a boy, that large numbers of those who were church members were not really children of God, and would be lost. Suppose this most horrible doctrine be true. Is it good news? Could we proclaim it with any heart of courage as a part of the gospel of God?

It seems to me, then, that I am bringing no railing accusation when I say that those Churches that claim to be Evangelical are not proclaiming a gospel to the world. But, though this be literally true, they may claim that they are delivering the message of Jesus the Christ, and that, from their point of view, this is relatively a piece of good news, good news, at any rate, to the few who are going to be saved. So I ask you now to turn, while I examine with you for a few moments the essence of the gospel which Jesus proclaimed. Note its terms. Jesus came into Galilee, preaching the gospel of the kingdom of God, and saying: "The time is fulfilled, and the kingdom of God is at hand: repent ye, and believe the gospel;" that is, this proclamation of good news, the coming of God's kingdom. Was this the essential thing in the gospel of Christ?

Let me ask you now to look with me for a few moments. You are perfectly well aware of the fact that the Jews cherished a belief in the coming of a Messiah and the establishment of God's kingdom here on earth and among men. You are not so well aware, perhaps, unless you have made a study of it, that a belief like this has not been confined to the Jews. In many other nations a similar expectation has been cherished. We find it, for example, among some of the tribes of our North American Indians. It is world-wide, in other words, in its range. It is no peculiarity of the Jews. But let us confine ourselves a moment to their particular hope. It is a perfectly natural belief. It required no revelation in order for it to grow up. They believed that the God of the world, of the universe, was their God; that they were his chosen people. Do you not see what a necessary corollary would be a belief in their ultimate prosperity and triumph? God would certainly bless and give the kingdom to that people which he had specially selected for his own. And so, as the coming of the kingdom was postponed, they believed that it was because they had not complied with the divine conditions, they had not kept the law or they had not been good, they had not obeyed him. Somehow, they had done wrong; and that was the reason the kingdom so long delayed.

Remember another thing. We have come, in this modern time, to place the kingdom away off in another world after the close of this life. The Jews had no such belief about it. They expected it to come right here on this poor little planet of ours; and they expected that a kingdom was to be set up which was not only to place them at the head of humanity, but through them was to bless all mankind. Different thinkers among them held different views, but this in substance was the belief; and they were constantly looking for signs of this imminent revolution which was to make the kingdoms of this world the kingdoms of our God and of his Christ, that is, his Anointed One.

John the Baptist preached that this kingdom was coming. But he was imprisoned and beheaded, having come into conflict with the civil authority. Jesus, then, having come from Nazareth, where he had studied and thought and brooded over the divine will, takes up this broken work of John, and begins a proclamation of the gospel; and the one thing which constituted that gospel was: The kingdom of God is at hand, repent and believe; accept this statement. And note that "repent" on the lips of Jesus did not mean what we have been accustomed to associate with it. The New Testament word translated "repent" means change your purpose, change your method of life. You have not been in accord with the truth, you have not been obedient to God; turn about, come into accord with the divine law, become obedient to the divine message.

Jesus taught no kingdom in any other world. He believed that the kingdom was to be here. For, even after he had disappeared from the sight of men, and this reflects in the clearest possible way the burden of his message, his disciples expected, not that they were to be transferred to some other planet or into an invisible world to find the kingdom, but that Jesus was to come back, to return in the clouds of heaven, and establish the kingdom here.

The kingdom, then, that Jesus preached was a kingdom of righteousness here on this earth, among just the kind of people that we are. And, note, he said, This kingdom of God does not come by observation. You are not to say, Lo here, Lo there, look for wonders. He says, The kingdom of God is within you, or among you. It is translated both ways; and, I suppose, nobody knows which way it ought to be. I believe both. The kingdom of God that Jesus preached is essentially in us. It is also, after it is in a few of us, among us, right here already, so far as it extends, and reaching out its limits and growing as rapidly as men discern it and become obedient to its laws.

Now I have been asked a great many times how I can be sure, or practically sure, as to what sayings in the Gospels are really those of Jesus and what are traditional in their authority, what are doubtfully his. I cannot go into a long explanation this morning; but I want to suggest one line of thought. And I do this because I wish it to be the basis of a statement that Jesus has not made any of these things that are to-day labelled "Evangelical" any essential part of his gospel at all. Jesus, for example, does not preach any Garden of Eden or any Fall of Man. Jesus says nothing about any infallible book. Jesus says not a word about any Trinity. He nowhere makes any claim to be God. His doctrine concerning the future is doubtful. But one thing which I wish to insist upon is perfectly clear: the conditions of citizenship in the kingdom of God are the simplest conceivable. He says, Not those that say, Lord, Lord, not those that multiply their services and ceremonies, but those that do the will of my Father shall enter the kingdom. The only condition that Jesus ever established for membership in the kingdom of heaven is simple human goodness, never anything else.

I am perfectly well aware that somebody may quote to me, "He that believeth and is baptized shall be saved; and he that believeth not shall be damned." But the reply to that would be, The acknowledged statement to-day on the part of all competent scholars is that Jesus never uttered those words. They are left out of the Revised Version of the New Testament: they are no authentic part of the story of his life or his teaching.

How can we find his words? In the first place there are the great central, luminous truths which Jesus uttered, the fatherhood of God, the brotherhood of men, goodness as the condition of acceptance on the part of God. And, on the theory that he did not contradict himself, we are at liberty to waive one side those statements which grew up under the influence of later tradition, popish or ecclesiastical, and which plainly contradict these. But the main point I have in mind is one which scholars have wrought out under the name of the Triple Tradition. It takes for its central thought, "In the mouth of two or three witnesses every word shall be established." We know that the Gospels grew up through a long process of accretion after a good many years. They were not written or planned by any one person; and, so far as we know, they may not have been written by anybody whose name is traditionally connected with them to-day. If, however, we find that three of the four witnesses agree in reporting that he said or did a certain thing, we feel surer about it than when only one witness reports it. And if two report, why, even then we feel a little more certain than we do when the report is from only one. And yet, of course, the three may have omitted that which only one has recorded, and which is true. But scholars have wrought out along this line what is called the Triple Tradition; that is, they have constructed a complete story of the life and the teaching and the death of Jesus out of the words which are common to three of the gospel writers. All of them tell this same story; and this story of the Triple Tradition has no miraculous conception, it has no resurrection of the body, no ascension into heaven. The miracles are reduced to the very lowest terms, becoming almost natural and easy to be accounted for. In this story Jesus teaches none of the things of which I have been speaking.

I say, then, that along the lines of the very best critical scholarship, coming as near to the teaching of Jesus as we possibly can to-day, we are warranted in saying that this which has usurped the name of the gospel of Christ is not only not good news, but it is not the news which Jesus brought and preached. As has been said a good many times, it is a gospel about Christ instead of being the gospel of Christ.

I am ready now to make the claim that we liberals of the modern world are the ones who come nearer to preaching the gospel of Christ than any other part of the so-called Christian Church. For what is it that we preach? We preach that the kingdom of God is at hand. We preach that there is not a spot on the face of the earth where we are not at the foot of a ladder like that which Jacob saw in his dream, and which leads up to the very throne of the Almighty. Jesus taught that the kingdom of God might begin anywhere and at any time in any human heart. Note what Matthew Arnold has called the secret and the method of Jesus. He says, The secret of Jesus is that he who selfishly seeks his life shall lose it: he who throws it away for good and God finds it. Do we need to go very deeply into human life to discover the profound truth of that saying? Seek all over the world for good and happiness, and forget to look within, and you do not find it. The kingdom of heaven is within. It is in the spirit, the temper of the heart, the disposition, the life. And the secret of it is in cultivating love and truth and tenderness and care, those things which bring us into intimate connection with which we mean when we say, Be unselfish, and that in doing this we find our own souls. For the man who gives out of himself love and tenderness and care, of necessity cultivates the qualities of love and tenderness and care; and those are the ones which are the essence of all soul-building. And he who looks outside for the greatest things of life misses them; while he who looks within, and cultivates the spirit, finds God and happiness and truth.

This gospel, then, that the kingdom of God is at hand, is always ready to come, is the gospel which we proclaim. And now I wish to extend that idea a little. The form in which Jesus held his dream of human good has changed in the process of the centuries. We no longer expect a miraculous revelation of a kingdom coming out of the heavens to abide on earth. The form of it is changed; but the essence of it we hold still, the same perfect condition of men here on earth and in the future which Jesus held and proclaimed.

Now let me hint to you a few of the elements that make up this hope for man which we liberals proclaim everywhere as the gospel, the good news of the coming kingdom of God.

In the first place, we proclaim the possibility of human conquest over this earth. What do I mean by that? I mean that man is able and he is showing that ability ultimately to control the forces of this planet, and make them his servants. Within the last seventy-five years this increasing conquest has changed the face of the planet. We now use water power not only, but steam, electricity, magnetism. All these secret forces that thrill from planet to planet and sun to sun we use as our household and factory drudges, our every-day servants. And it needs only a little imagination, looking along the lines of past progress, to see the day when man shall stand king of the earth. He shall make all these forces serve him. I believe that we have only just begun this conquest. Already the wonders about us eclipse the wonders of novelist and dreamer; and yet we have only begun to develop them. What follows from this? When we have completed the conquest of the earth, when we have discovered God's laws of matter and force and are able to keep them, it means the abolition of all unnecessary pain, unnecessary pain, I say; for all that pain which is not beneficent, which is not inherent in the nature of things, is remedial. And we preach the gospel, the coming of God's kingdom when pain shall be abolished, and shall pass away.

Another step: We preach the gospel of the abolition of disease. We have already, in the few civilized centres of the world, made the old epidemics simply impossible. They are easily controlled. Nearly every one of those that rise to threaten Europe and America to-day come from the religious, ignorant, wild fanaticism of Asia, beyond the range of our civilized control. The conditions of disease are discoverable; and the day will come when, barring accidents here and there, well-born people may calmly expect to live out their natural term of years. We preach this gospel, then, of the kingdom of God in which disease shall no more exist.

We preach a gospel that promises a time when war shall be no more. At present wars are now and then inevitable; but they are brutal, they are unspeakably horrible. And how any one who uses the sympathetic imagination can rejoice, not over the victory, but over the destruction of life and property which the victory entails, I cannot understand. We have reached a time when civilized man no longer thinks he must right his wrong with his fists or a club or a knife or a pistol. On the part of individuals we call this a reversion to barbarism. The time will come, and we are advancing towards it, when it will be considered just as much a reversion to barbarism on the part of families, states, nations, and when we shall substitute hearts and brains for bruises and bullets in the settlement of the world's misunderstandings. We preach, then, a gospel of the coming of the kingdom in which there shall be no more war. And then life under the fair heavens will be sweet.

There shall be no more hunger in that kingdom. To-day see what confronts us, bread riots in Spain and in Italy, thousands of people hungry for food. And yet, if we would give ourselves to the development of the resources of this planet instead of to their destruction, this fair earth could support a hundred times its present population in plenty and in peace. There shall be no more famine in that kingdom the gospel of which we preach.

Then, when men have lived out their lives, learned their lessons, and stand where the shadow grows thicker, so that we try in vain to see beyond, what then? We preach a gospel of life, of an eternal hope. We believe that death, instead of being the end, is only a transition, the beginning really of the higher and the grander life. We cannot look through the gateway of the shadow; but we catch a gleam of light beyond that means an eternal day, when the sun shall no more go down. This we believe.

And we do not partition that world off into two parts, the immense majority down where the smoke of their torment ascendeth forever, and only a few in a city gold-paved and filled with the light of peace. Rather we believe it is a human life there just as here, that we are under the law of cause and effect, that salvation is not a magical thing, that we are saved only in so far as we come into accord with the divine law and the divine life. And, if anybody says we preach an easy gospel because we eliminate an arbitrary hell, let him remember we preach a harder gospel, a more difficult salvation, not a salvation that can be purchased by a wave of emotion or by the touch of priestly fingers, a salvation that must be wrought out through co-working with God in the building of human character, a salvation that is being right.

This is our gospel; but it is a gospel of eternal and universal hope, because we believe that every single soul is under doom to be saved sometime, somewhere. We preach the inevitable results of law-breaking, are they to last one year, five, a hundred, a thousand, a million, ten millions? There is no possibility of heaven except as people are in perfect accord with the divine law and the divine life; for that is what heaven means. You can no more get heaven out of a disordered character than you can get music out of a disordered piano. This salvation which we preach is the constituent element of life. You cannot have a circle if you break the conditions of a circle. You cannot have a river if you break the conditions the very existence of which constitutes a river. So of anything in God's natural world. There are certain essential things that go to make these what they are. So heaven, righteousness, happiness, the constituent elements of these are right thinking, right feeling, right acting, obedience to the laws of God, which make them possible.

We believe that God, through pain, through suffering, down through the winding ways of darkness and ignorance, one year, a million years, must pursue the soul of any one of his children until that child learns that suffering follows wrong, and must follow it, and that God himself cannot help it, and so, learning the lesson, by and by turns, comes back, and says: Father, I have sinned against heaven and before thee, and am not worthy to be thy son: make me at least as one of thy hired servants. And then the love that has pursued all the way, that has been in the light and that has been in the dark, shall go out to meet him, and fall on his neck in loving embrace, and rejoice that he who was dead is alive again, and he who was lost is found.

This is the gospel we preach, a gospel of God's eternal, boundless love, the good news that every human being is God's child; that here on earth, co-operating with God and discovering his laws, we may begin the creation of his kingdom now; that we may broaden and enlarge it until it encloses the world; and that it reaches out into the limitless ages of the future. And this, as I said, is the gospel of the Christ, changed in its form, if you please, but one in its essence; for he came, preaching the gospel of the kingdom of God, and saying: The time is fulfilled, and the kingdom of God is at hand. Change your purpose, accept the message, and come into accord with the divine life. This is the gospel that the Christ preached: this is the gospel we preach to-day.

Do I make, then, an extraordinary claim when I say that we are the Evangelical Church, that the church which preaches the gospel is here?

Printed in Great Britain
by Amazon